Succeeding in
the Big World of Music

By Jim and Jean Young

The Woodstock Craftsman's Manual
The Woodstock Craftsman's Manual, II
Garage Sale Manual
People's Guide to Country Real Estate
When the Whale Came to Our Town
Woodstock Kid's Crafts
Kid's Money Book
Getting Rich, Buying Used

Succeeding in the Big World of Music

Jean Young and Jim Young

Little, Brown and Company   Boston   Toronto

FIRST EDITION
Third Printing

Library of Congress Cataloging in Publication Data

Young, Jean.
  Succeeding in the big world of music.

  1. Music trade.   I. Young, Jim, 1930–
joint author.   II. Title.
ML3790.Y68   338.4'7'78   77-24666
ISBN 0-316-97709-8

The authors are grateful to Macmillan Publishing Co., Inc., for permission to reprint excerpts from the book IN THEIR OWN WORDS by Bruce Pollock. Copyright © 1975 by Bruce Pollock.

Designed by Christine Benders

*Published simultaneously in Canada
by Little, Brown & Company (Canada) Limited*

PRINTED IN THE UNITED STATES OF AMERICA

MV

Contents

Introduction

THIS BOOK was written because we knew there was nothing in print that gave the person interested in the world of pop music insights into the mechanics of each of the many careers that make up that world. Only a handful of colleges offer courses that directly relate to the realities of pursuing a future in the highly commercial and competitive world of music. So we have incorporated in each chapter an analysis of the profession along with information on attitudes and techniques; together these will serve as guides. The book is designed after the nature of the business itself; all the jobs are interrelated and work together to give us that final product, music. It's only after reading about all the careers that each one becomes clear.

To a large extent we are indebted to Mike Young, who has made us most appreciative and aware of the artistry and excitement of today's pop music.

Without the help of Leeds Levy and Geof Daking it would have been much more difficult. And thanks to all those who were generous with their time in talking about their own careers and functions: John Holbrook, Nancy Daking, Roger

INTRODUCTION

Powell, Tim Hardin, Bernard Purdie, Rob Stoner, Bob Feiden, Dick Fox, Sid Bernstein, Stu Kuby, Warren Bernhardt, Jerry Schoenbaum, Barbara Davies, Mike Lang, Eddy O'Laughlin, Maria Muldaur, Mitch Schoenbaum, Lynn Goldsmith, James Tyrell, Paul Adler, Russell Sanjek, Horace Ott, Landy McNeil, Alan Douglas, Michael Cuscuna, Richard Fusco, Bob Bruno, Bruce Morrow, Lisa Karlin, Mike Mantler, Tom Edmonds, Rob Davis, Jane Friedman, Rob Jacobson, Martha Velez, Artie Traum, Harris Goldberg, Lorraine Traum, Mary Frampton, Jean Shaw, Joe Pellegrino, Happy Traum, Jane Traum, Barry Schultz, Chet Gerlack, John Betaudier, Barbara Matera, Bob Tullipan, Cathy Chamberlain, Michael Sukin, Joel Dorn, Alan Abrahams, Jack Weisberg, Peppy Thielhelm, Danny at Manny's, Charlie Bermant. Our special thanks to Art Klebanoff and Mort Janklow, Dick McDonough, Peter Hughes, and Betsy Pitha.

Succeeding in
the Big World of Music

1

Getting a Record Contract
(Practical and Legal Aspects)

AT ONE TIME or another, most artists have had to take on all the functions and business responsibilities outlined in this book long before they were earning enough to take on some professional help. There is no one way of going about anything in the music business, especially when it comes to getting a record contract. Those drives to communicate, to express oneself, and to make money motivate an artist to do everything possible to put his career in gear. Arista Records' Bob Feiden told *The New York Times:* "If artists are not willing to kill themselves selling themselves, why sign them? It's not worth it." So by the time artists have earned some credibility among their peers, they have more than likely been all things: booking agents, managers, road managers, song pluggers, producers, arrangers, and financiers of their own careers.

To discharge all these responsibilities seems a lot to ask of the person who, in addition, must develop a talent, perfect an act, perform, produce a selling product, and carry the ball artistically and financially for everyone in an entourage. Because a future in music is based on expensive speculation, it's going to be very helpful if other people along the way give one some financial help and encouragement.

Michael Sukin, a lawyer active in the entertainment and music field, told us, "It's very unlikely that an artist is going to come out of nowhere, with no management, no representation of any kind, and be signed by a record company [see Chapter 21]. It almost never happens. *Discovery* is a funny word. Usually, somebody comes to somebody else's knowledge through somebody else's suggestion. Usually, an artist who's not connected with a producer comes to a record company through some sort of agent or manager, or an attorney — or a businessman represents him. It's not that often that a record company signs an artist directly. It's possible that a record company may hear of some guy performing in Lovett, Texas, and go down and see him. But probably even in Lovett, Texas, that artist has a manager or somebody that's looking after his interests. So while the record company goes there on their own steam, or maybe because the local promotion man from the record company called up the home office and said, 'You have to see this act. Send somebody down,' the artist is *usually* represented. It's almost never that the artist isn't represented."

It's not without significance that the new artists who rose in the Sixties appeared within the matrix called "the group." Dealing from a position of strength, exuding mutual support in their self-contained acts and their life-styles, they made themselves felt. Sometimes one of the members actually supported the group financially, as The Blues Magoos' lead guitarist did, with income from inherited stocks, for a year before the band earned gold records. Just plain "lucking out" was easier in the expanding Sixties. Many acts found the events leading to a recording contract so smooth that trouble only began later, when they found out the legalities of what went down. In respect to getting a record contract, *the group* today in the mid-Seventies still has an advantage over the artist-writer who is alone.

4

In some groups, everyone has a hand in the songwriting, *or* all share in the profits made by the group's songwriter (or songwriters), in an effort to try to settle discontent that stems from unequal income. As it gets its act together, and its sound and songs worked out, a group can make a living working clubs. Then it can book dates in better clubs and, hopefully, create local enthusiasm. Slowly, word of a group's popularity finds its way to an Artist and Repertoire (A & R) representative. Because of the following the group has established, the record company knows that it is not going to be dealing with too many unknown quantities. There's the band; there's the leader; there are the songs. There's proof in what they've achieved, knowledge of their ability to perform live and draw an audience.

Solo artist-writers, of which there are more today than in the Sixties, have a hard time reaching the record companies' attention if they are unknown, or have never appeared in a well-known group. On the other hand, single artists have some distinct advantages over groups. They can achieve a personal sound more easily than can a group. Solo artists make independent decisions about following musical directions; they don't have to compromise their taste. Unevenness in artistic sensibility is avoided. There are no group decisions, no one to fight with, no worries about another member splitting. No one is singled out for blame when things aren't happening. What's more, when solo artist-writers do make records, all the songs can be their own, with all the income from the songs and advances going into one bank account.

The mid-Seventies have been a tough period for a new artist to break out in. No one wants to take risks. Formulas have been established, so that the music business is more of a business than it ever was. It isn't competition among talents, as people would have you believe, that makes it tough to break into the business. It is just that record companies have so many other options open to them — guaranteed sales from pretested people they can't lose on, people making comebacks, people regrouping, and from artists they've label-raided (see Chapter 7). They have slimmed down their rosters, and prefer to spend the money building up established artists, hoping the "new" release will become a success or even possibly a monster.

Geoffrey Stokes, in his book *Star-Making Machinery,* says, "FM had become so important to the success of an album that, as Stan Cornyn [Warner's senior vice president] sadly told a music-industry convention in the spring of 1975, 'Warner Brothers Records won't put out an album unless we think it'll get airplay.'" Record company executives like to say, with wheeler-dealer smugness, "I never speculate!" How, then, can you, a new artist — who doesn't have a following, doesn't have a powerful spokesman with lots of contacts in the business, doesn't have a financier to act as sponsor — expect to convince anyone that your "product" is going to make money? How can you present your "product" (the tape) in a way that will get record companies, producers, or whoever excited, and make them feel that your bandwagon is going to be part of the big parade? Well, that's the task you face. But overcoming it isn't impossible. No matter what vibes you get from the business heads or other established musicians you come in contact with, the industry *does* need new blood. But don't, however, believe for a minute that your material is going to speak for itself to everyone — or perhaps to anyone.

When you know you can cut it, when you know you have something to offer the industry it can use, that your material matches or is better than material recorded on albums and/or getting radio play, that your voice is a "today sounding voice," it's up to *you* to make everyone you know realize it, too. Make every effort you can to get the right people to listen and to consider your capabilities. That's when you do the things a manager should do, or a song plugger, when you take on these responsibilities and shift into high gear. To build enough momentum to attract managers, agents, publishers, A & R people, you will have to do everything yourself — even invest the money needed to make demos, and then hustle your own tapes.

A demonstration record (demo) is your basic means of taking the first step. Making a demo, as we point out in this book, comes down to dollars and cents. Try for the kind of demo you think best sets off and represents what you've got. It could be a simple reel-to-reel recording, or a 4-track recording, or it could involve using a 16-track studio. The pros often make a master quality recording, then try to get a bidding situation going. Despite the heavy investment this approach requires, Michael Sukin suggests it: "Assuming that an artist's goal is to have a record in the charts, there are lots of ways to do that. The most mundane is that he can record it himself and sell it. I mean, literally go out and sell it to distributors. It's very difficult to do, and it's expensive. He can get signed directly by a record company." We asked if that's the best way, assuming you can afford it. "No, it's *a* way," he answered. "It depends."

Another way to land a contract with a record company is to go through publishers. Publishers often invest less than record companies in their commitments; they can help get record contracts; and good songs *are* in demand. (Read the chapters on publishers and the professional manager.)

And it's true, some people have been "around" *in* the business for years in minor roles before they make it big. There is no one way to break into the business. Some people are just lately making it on the first albums, as we write about in the A & R section, such as the group Boston, whose guitar player had a 16-track console in his basement, and worked as a Polaroid researcher in the daytime. He'd send drum tracks to Lenny Petze at Epic, with a note saying the rest was coming. This had been going on steadily for about a year, and Petze was getting really interested. Finally he asked for an audition and Epic signed the group. The hit single from the album was written five years earlier. From a small Canadian record company came Heart's first album, which has gone platinum with an AM hit. And then, even though he has made records, no one yet understands the recent success of Peter Frampton, the only superstar to emerge in 1976.

We are all familiar with at least a few of the big stars of today and how they made it in the past. There are countless histories about pedestal personages such as Elton John, The Who, certainly The Beatles. But that was yesterday. Even the more recent pop pasteurizers like Olivia Newton-John and revival artists like Sedaka have been subjects for many stories in the trades, fan magazines, and the general press.

That's why it is interesting to have *current* insight into getting a record contract. Mike Young, an unrecorded musician who as we are writing this is operating pretty much all by himself trying to get people in the industry to listen to his tapes, hasn't yet landed a contract. At a time when he was too young to become part of the Sixties' expansion of the music industry — nine years ago when he was fourteen — he started learning lead guitar. Today he has worked up a whole gamut of abilities: songwriting, lead singing, arranging, and producing. At the top of his list of advice to give people in the same position is: "Make sure you are good, that you're as good as people you hear on the radio or see in live performances. Work for that first. You have to have confidence and believe in what you can do, or you won't be able to take the rejections almost everyone gets at first. You have to believe in yourself 100 percent. After that," Mike continues, "you've got to build yourself a track record of people knowing you. And even though they've said 'No' to you, you still have that stash of people who you can keep on sending your stuff to.

"You're building your credibility at the same time," Mike goes on. "Go to other musicians, or anyone you know in the business for names of people they know, so you can use their names as introductions. If a manager or producer is interested, perhaps he will let you use his name to expedite making an initial impression on someone else. If you call a record company cold, the receptionist will probably tell you, 'We aren't listening to any new tapes.' If you come recommended, they may say that too. But chances are you'll make contact. If you know no one, get all the *Billboard* magazines, the *Record World* magazines, *Variety,* and *Cashbox.* There you'll find a lot of names of people in the business. Learn what they do, and what they are doing now. Track down addresses and telephone numbers, and write letters personally to them. Those people read their mail. Make your letter simple but interesting, and send your tape. If you are in one of the music centers, try to take your tape around personally . . . that takes pushing to get appointments. Sometimes it will work!

"Use your imagination to feel what's going on within the business and with the people you've contacted. After they've heard your tape, call them and try to get a suggestion from them."

It taxes the imagination to learn that a group called Mason, Florida-based, sent their tapes for *five* years to Eddie Offard, the English producer of Yes and other heavy rock and roll groups. Offard kept sending the tapes back, saying he didn't hear a "sound." One day, after hearing their latest tape, he called them up and said he wanted to produce them. "Each time you send in a tape, try to top your last efforts," Mike Young says. "Make sure your voice is good and the songs are right, and the form of your song is arranged tightly. A succession of tapes will help familiarize the listener with your style or sound.

"Not everyone is going to be looking for what you have to offer. Consequently, you might have to run through a lot of people before you hit on someone who's right and *ready* for you. If you really research well, you could save time by knocking on the doors of people who will be the best bet for what you have to offer, be it a manager, producer, or record company.

"It's hard at first to deal with the music business's exclusive concern about people's reputations, rather than their music, and also their interest in making money. This exists on many levels . . . and some people, you can tell, want to take advantage of you. You can be shy or whatever, say, 'Give me an offer. What do you have?' And then, when they do, as happened to me when a producer gave me a contract to sign, the lawyer tells me, 'Ugh! I won't represent you if you sign this!' So, you go to someone else, and you try and feel out what they are all about, and you have to stay on the case until you lock into someone who responds to your music and will be good for you, and perhaps try and help you out. And there are those people around.

"Every time something positive happens to you, you have to go back. Because things work slowly; it only gets a little bit tighter. No one might say anything concrete really. You go to a manager and he says, 'I like you, but what have you got going for you?' Then you go to a publisher, and he says the same thing. And you tell the publisher, 'Well, I have a manager who likes me and is interested.' And then they call up each other. You get them together, and you hype up each one of them. You don't lie. But you have to tell each one what the other said, and you put a little bit of energy in there. They like energy. You try to look good, and you do all those things that other people would do for you, if you were in a position to have help. Although lawyers do run the business, and do help people get recording contracts, as do publishers, they too have to be convinced. They might also say, 'Yeah, I'll help you. I'll make sure they don't rip you off. But come back to me *when* you have the contract.' So it may happen that you will have the same problem record company promotion men have in order to get records played on the radio: the program managers won't give the record airplay until there is some proof it's selling well in the local stores. And the record stores won't order the record unless it's getting radio play. So these guys will play off one another with little hypes."

Using imaginative strategy is another method, which in one case worked in getting the attention of Freddie Ruppert while we were at Buddah Records. He showed us a tape a group had sent him in a beautiful hand-tooled western-type leather case. He loved the case; wanted to keep it; pondered whether he really had to send it back if he rejected the group's tape. It was just what *he* wanted to carry *his* tapes around. He immediately played the tape, even though he had many stacked up he hadn't heard yet . . . and listened with a favorable ear. We asked if tapes come in pretty packages very often. He said, "No, almost never has it happened."

Imagination is *one* way of getting the attention of the business world. It can also be *so* out of the norm you'll run into snags. When Mike did an audition for Polydor, he wanted to be imaginative in his presentation. He played lead guitar and sang the vocals live, while a tape played the rest of the band with dubbed-in audience applause. The stage was set with Styrofoam musicians eight feet tall, and Mike had foot pedals to control the lights which he could dim at the end of a song, and switched on a strobe light at the end as he kicked the figures apart and up in the air. Afterward, the people from Polydor appreciated the uniqueness of this audition, but at the same time couldn't make a decision because they still had to hear the live band.

The reason that we can't be totally upbeat is that it's best to know the reality, and not to zero in on fanciful expectations and delusions. Being realistic creates the best possibility of winning in the long run. Speaking from a long background in the business, production company head Jerry Schoenbaum said, "You have to deal with what exists, and find your way through the maze and tricks and the mirrors and the half-truths, the lies and the people who are mediocre. You just deal with it, and you have to learn how to maneuver and work with them and within the framework."

When it comes to working on a contract, Michael Sukin told us, "Most people who are starting out are not in a position to understand what they want, and what they want may not be really important." Sukin said that one doesn't have to be an attorney to give advice to artists. There are no courses in law school that will give you the wisdom of experience — understanding contractual dealings in the sense of having some knowledge of the business. "The person giving advice could be a manager — or the artist's mother — if they're knowledgeable," Sukin says. "But no business," he continues, "can take place without a lawyer being an integral part of it. What is business? It's trading one thing for another, really. There's no way that you can trade in music except by exchanging rights. Rights don't exist per se; they have to be identified and described; and the people who do that are lawyers."

He further told us that he doesn't like working with artists who don't want to know anything about the kinds of situations they are getting into. It's those people who will be the first to blame the lawyer for anything that goes wrong with their careers and who also will get themselves into situations that can be troublesome. Burt Padell, who was the business manager for Peter Frampton, said that Peter was "the best" in keeping himself informed and asking questions. Mary Frampton, his wife, agreed, and said that he always read everything that was sent to him to be read.

When someone is interested enough to make a verbal proposal to you, it's up to you to counterpropose — to tell them what *you* want (unless you want to say nothing, which might be best). Just consider that the people you're dealing with have obligations to themselves or to *the company* to make the best deal they can. So try to feel the same way about yourself. Old salts in the business, those with integrity, can give a newcomer clues. "You don't have to agree with this," a manager might say. "Think about what you want and tell me." Or: "You know it's my job to rip you off." Most people, if they are interested, will make concessions, will negotiate on the terms. But you and your lawyer have to present your side *first!*

Advice that Mike Young has to give, at this point, is: "Be cool. Continue to keep your basic tool in good shape: an address and phone book! Nothing happens until you sign contracts. What you may run into are promises, promises, promises. Someone may really like your tapes, and then the next week they won't answer your calls. A lawyer may say, 'Let's send it to this producer and that producer,' and be really excited. And nothing comes of it." Like a book publisher who rejects a book, after initially liking it personally, because a hired reader has negative feelings about it, so people in the music business will, for no apparent reason, drop active interest in a musician. Most people take the easiest way out (it's always easier to say no). And many big wheels in the business are easily intimidated: *they* can't cope with having *one* rejection connected with their reputation, so projects can be dropped because of a single negative response. Most songs and most artists make it after many rejections. It's up to the artists to keep plugging. One rule: try to deal from a position of strength, giving the impression you are not up for grabs. If you give the impression that you are a pushover, poor terms may be offered, and if not accepted, the offer may be withdrawn.

Michael Sukin told us, "Record companies are very wary about signing an artist who's not represented by anyone, and they'll send him to a lawyer. Because they're open to an attack of duress, unconscionability."

By the time you get to a lawyer, you might also have acquired a manager, or a publisher, or some experienced person who is interested in you. It's also possible that you may not. "And that's just within the dynamics of a deal," says Sukin. "I mean, if an artist is really starving to death, or struggling or determined to get a record out, and the offer he has is his only route to do that, then the deal may stink. And the contract may be terribly onerous. But he has to make a basic business-like decision: OK, am I going to take this step? In order to run, you have to walk a little bit. And in order to walk, you have to take your first step. Is this going to be my first step? Shall I take the plunge? The dynamics change. A new artist starting out is one thing. Grand Funk Railroad is another.

13

And in between is an enormous spectrum of who has the power, who has the control, who's offering and who's buying, how strong is the competition. A new artist out of nowhere, whom no one has ever heard of, that *four* record companies are bidding on, is going to wind up with a much better deal than a new artist no one's heard of and *one* person is interested in. It's all a question of dynamics." And this is why (although it is sometimes not necessary), as long as you're out there hustling for a record contract, keep in mind the advantage of a bidding situation. It might mean everything to your eventual success, since contracts last a few years, to say the least.

Attorney Sukin gives a long list of concrete legal aspects most important to an artist: "The areas you are looking for," he advises new artists, "are: is your performance going to be recorded? Are you going to have any kind of artistic input? If it is recorded, will you be able to approve the quality of the recording? If it's a finished recording, what's going to happen to it? Is this independent producer going to put it out himself? Is he going to sell it to a record company? If that's his undertaking, when does he have to sell it by? How much of the sale price do you get as an artist? What are your obligations, once the sale has been made? What happens if he doesn't make the sale? Is the contract over? Do you get the record back? Can you record it for someone else? After he makes the sale, are there more records to be made? Do you make money? Do you get an advance? Is it ten percent or more of the money spent? What's your royalty going to be? What's it computed upon? When is it paid? By whom? What's deducted from it? What's the split between you and the record producer? Is the sale of the record just for the United States, or is it for the world? How long does the record company, or the independent producer, have the rights to your record? How long is the contract? Does the record company have the obligation to release that record, once it buys it? What happens if it doesn't get released? Do they have the unlimited right to use your name and likeness in publicity? Do you have any approval over that? Or over the artwork they use for the album? What are all the miscellaneous rights? What warranties do you have? What are you guaranteed? Are you guaranteed that no one else can use your name, let's say, if you're a group? Do you know that you have the right to record the song you've just recorded for someone else? Has a publisher granted you the mechanical license you need, if it's never been recorded before? *We can go on forever!"*

When you think on these questions, you also need advice and answers from a lawyer. Artists need help more than managers, record companies, or publishers, because they are generally the most inexperienced. They may make two or three basic deals in their productive years, while the managers, record company executives, and publishers make many more deals with many more people, and gain that experience. A lot of executives and managers are also lawyers, as are Clive Davis and his A & R man, Bob Feiden. Few artists, in contrast, ever are also lawyers. Sukin says, "The best thing that a lawyer can do is point out to the artist what he's getting himself into, and then the artist has to decide. At least, he's making a knowledgeable decision. 'OK, this is what I'm getting into, this is what I have to *pay,* or *give up,* in order to step further along the line, so I will.' Hopefully, he will have at least the minimal amount of protections to insure that if he is successful, he will get remunerated. Maybe he won't get *all* of what he should, or even fifty percent of what he should. But you know there'll be something."

Michael Sukin tried to avoid giving legal opinions, but he did point out that anyone about to sign a contract should be aware that although most contracts say very clearly in the beginning that the artist's obligation is to do a minimum of two albums, at the back of the contract, hidden away, is the so-called play and pay clause. It says that if the record company fails to put out or do the two albums the only commitment it has is to pay scale. And he stressed stipulating that you get paid (as does Johannan Vigoda, Stevie Wonder's lawyer, who negotiated the thirteen-million-dollar Motown contract for Wonder) directly by the record company. "It just cuts out any chance for a slippage," Sukin says, "and it also means you get your money faster." In addition, he pointed out that monies should be provided in the event of touring. "I've seen in a couple of contracts that record companies have these little provisions that say, 'If the artist doesn't tour actively for X amount of time, the record company has the right to terminate the agreement'! It's that crucial for certain kinds of acts. I try to get that clause taken out, because it's very difficult to tour, when you're a new artist. Nobody wants to go see you. The problem record companies have is that they may have an artist in whom they have a substantial investment and continuing obligation to invest, who refuses to tour and, therefore, they can't promote his records as effectively as they would like to, et cetera. Well, OK, that's their problem. Some artists aren't made for touring. Sly Stone and The Beatles are examples of people who didn't tour for years. I think that's a very harsh condition."

Another provision that might come as a shock to a newcomer and someone without too much negotiating power is that record companies like to sign people to five years — and at their option for renewal! It used to be seven. Still, Sukin says, an independent producer, or independent company, will sign you for seven years, "or at least have rights for seven years, on the theory that they've made a five-year record contract for you, they've won an edge into the next deal, so they can negotiate that, too." In the United States the standard is five years. "Hopefully, you'll make the sort of deal that requires that if they do pick up an option, they have to do something, or guarantee something in addition. I mean, there's a line of thinking in Britain now that says that any record contract in excess of three years is unconscionable."

If you come recommended to a lawyer, he may be more considerate, play your tape, charge you a minimal amount or

16

nothing at all. See if he will send you to someone he knows. Lawyers are in the middle of everything and, therefore, have great referral power. There is also VLA, or Volunteer Lawyers for the Arts, in New York City, which is a legal clinic. But finding an active music lawyer who takes an interest in you is naturally the best. "Almost all lawyers, in certain circumstances, will work on a percentage," a music lawyer told us. (We assume that arrangement is particularly possible for a hot client.) "Often you have a circumstance where a client can't pay — that sort of thing. Fees range like any other lawyers'. It's almost nonexistent to find a lawyer who'll work for less than forty dollars an hour. But the fees go up. Any lawyer with any experience is charging more than that." Jerry Schoenbaum says paying the fee, $500 or whatever, is cheaper sometimes than when the lawyer takes a percentage, which could be many thousands.

"Speaking for myself," said Michael Sukin, "I can't be generous with my time. All I have to sell is my time. If you're a songwriter, and you write a song and that song is a hit, you may collect for thirty years. If I give you a piece of advice today, the five minutes that it took for me to give you that advice is all I'll ever get for that. But that, on the other hand, is narrow. In other words, if I'm willing to take the gamble to participate in somebody's career and not get paid for it, I want some kind of a contingent interest . . . a percentage . . . a percentage of their gross income. But it would depend. If it's a question of making a record deal, then a percentage of the record deal. If it's a question of making a publishing deal, a percentage of what they did with the song. If it's a question of giving them overall advice for their career, then a percentage of that. Questions of percentages requiring an agreement with the client become a little awkward. But it depends on the circumstances. I have X amount of hours in the day to use. I'd rather be paid by the hour. But if four people come in here, none of them able to pay fees, or asking me things for which I don't want to be just paid a fee, I have to make some choices. Because I'm gambling, right? — like a manager, or an agent, or a record company. If I take you on a percentage, I'm not going to get paid. I'm going to spend hours and hours and hours on your matters, and I'm going to gamble. But I would like to go with a gamble I believe in. So, I'm not going to take on everybody. I'm going to take on people I think I really have a chance to be productive for, and produce income for myself. Other than that, I think most of the lawyers' fees range sixty to two hundred dollars an hour."

When it looks as if gaining a contract is getting close, start reading *This Business of Music*, Volumes 1 and 2. It will familiarize you with all aspects of making contracts, and help you get into the questions Michael Sukin brought up.

2

Producer

THE TOTAL EFFECT an album has on us isn't exclusively the work of the songwriter and recording artist. The next person who can lay claim to creating it (theoretically anyway) is the producer. He controls it, he organizes it, which in itself is no small contribution to the creation of the product, and to the degree that he involves himself, he makes his own personal imprint on the recording.

This degree of involvement can vary enormously. Some producers have a hand in almost everything, even in the performance, while others are at the recording sessions in name only. In that case, the artist or group actually produces itself, possibly with the help of a good arranger and engineer.

Most individual artists, though, don't relish taking on all the responsibility and command of their in-studio performance. Just as a writer needs a director to adapt a story to the stage, recording artists need the producer to help them commit their talent to vinyl, so to speak.

Successful producers are often solicited as if they were superstars themselves — by record companies, individual artists, managers, or anyone working in the interest of the act.

Some producers, on the other hand, may get jobs by just hanging around, while still others will really have to hustle, soliciting the artists, managers, and record companies. The usual and easiest way to an assignment, for a producer without clout, is to approach the artist. Artists usually have some say in choosing a producer, because personal relationship and "chemistry" are so important in this business.

The hit record typically makes the recording star a star. Until that time, for those artists who have not yet struck gold, their producers may be "top dog." Some producers are "stars" in the same sense that today's movie directors are considered more important than the actors and actresses in their films. Although the parallels between movies and the music industry don't entirely hold, the auteur theory of films (so named by *Village Voice* writer Andrew Sarris), where the director leads and creates the performance, has its counterpart in the music business with today's producers.

Not only are producers becoming famous and rich — and the chance to make big bucks from producing is greater than ever before — they are increasingly crucial to the creation of an album, and the specific function of producing a record is one that is expanding in the industry. Today everyone at all familiar with the system, even the artists themselves, wants to produce. Many who are not all that artistically creative, such as business heads, financiers, managers, and agents, also want to work their way into producing. Musicians, all the way from those who have never recorded to the fairly famous ones such as Robbie Robertson of The Band, are producing. Robertson produces people you've never heard of, such as Hirth Martinez, in addition to people you have, such as Neil Diamond.

Among producers, there are some who have a belief in the power of the "street," the grass roots, who enjoy its sense of immediacy and the social involvement with lots of musicians, performers, engineers, and writers. Some of them have made it, some haven't. They may make many judgments and decisions closer to the beat of the time than, say, a record company executive who never goes to clubs, is never out there hustling to get a production together. Ideas happen on the street way before they make it big on a commercial level, for the street people, and musicians, are often the real taste-makers and pacesetters. The veteran producer with a string of successes will find himself so busily entwined in the gears of the business that he will already be part of the establishment and won't know it. However, Jerry Schoenbaum, a past president of Polydor, now running his own production company, essentially doesn't feel that there is much difference in "where" one is from, because whenever there is a new sound out there with enough public response, there will always be some astute producer who is going to bring that sound from the underground to wider acceptance. The possibility is there on the street level, however, for someone to work out a production arrangement before it comes to the attention of an established producer or record company executive.

While it may seem contradictory, there is a common occurrence in the hip community that does inhibit fresh insights. Sometimes hip people are so much into their own group scene that when they are exposed to new, interesting talent that is not endorsed by their peers, they just don't pick up on it. That's when a producer who is removed from the scene may have a clearer, less biased approach, with more insight into new talent, *if* he has occasion to be exposed to it. One of the few rules we've learned in our research is that there's no *one* way anything happens in the music field.

Every drama must have its beginning, and the producer with ears to the ground, through active involvement in music on the small date level, will have a chance to find an act he can believe in.

It's not easy to define what the qualifications are for a producer. They are as flexible as everything else in the business. You might think that a fairly thorough background in the rudiments of music is a must for a producer, but this is conventional thinking; when it comes to creative work, the unconventional usually writes, if not the norm, certainly the legend. For instance, Joel Dorn, an independent producer, is deaf in one ear: he hears in mono though he produces in stereo. He doesn't even read music, and plenty of other producers don't either, such as Jerry Wexler of Atlantic Records. Some producers will tell you that one should at least know when an instrument is in tune or not, but others say that it's not important, because there is always someone around who knows. Chet Atkins says that kind of thing is not really important, so don't worry about it. Musicology can easily be overemphasized. People with fabulous backgrounds in music theory and harmony have their own problems. They must make sure there is a balance, and that their training doesn't get in the way of the artistic statement or the commercial acceptance. One producer who successfully blends musical learning with popular taste is George Martin, producer of The Beatles. The late Brian Epstein, The Beatles' original manager, said of Martin in his book *Cellarful of Noise* that besides having a classical background, "he had an innate sense of the public mood, was easy to work with, worked well with the material presented, was there for analytical sessions in which all aspects of the tune were discussed." Epstein stressed that Martin was a great collaborator and had a respect for the public taste, implying openness not only to contemporary sound but to those sounds that would become accepted as contemporary in the future. So there is no hard and fast rule about having or not having musical training. It could get in your way, or it could help you. An important element in producing isn't what to put in, but what to keep out.

It seems that just about all the people in the music industry, including producers, lay claim to one qualification that they think earns them a carte blanche — that is, having been fans of music since the age of three. They all have some kind of umbilical association with music, an emotional qualification, which everyone feels is the strongest and most motivating. So if you have that . . .

Joel Dorn told us, "For as long as I can remember I wanted to be a record producer. I heard a Ray Charles record when I was thirteen, and I just wanted to make records with people. When I was a kid, I heard records from a certain company, Atlantic, and I saw that they treated them in a certain way, and I couldn't believe that one company could have so many artists that I loved so much, the work, the quality of the work. And there was Chess in Chicago." When our son was around eight years old, we showed him a picture of a huge orchestra and asked him what instrument he wanted to play. He pointed to the conductor! He has been making overdubbed recordings on his Revox since he was thirteen, playing drums, guitar, autoharp, and simple horn, singing, writing the songs, producing and arranging it all. He wanted to be every part of the music, just as Joel wanted to associate himself with special kinds of music and singers at an early age.

There are no set qualifications, no prescribed courses, and nobody graduates from Berkeley with a Ph.D. in record producing. Probably those people who have been inspired so early and then go on to develop professionally will have the kind of motivation and emotional relationship with their objective eventually to work themselves into producing. But just because you weren't particularly ablaze with musical fervor in your preteens, you shouldn't regard yourself as necessarily missing anything. Everything has its season, and there are equally valid, self-sustaining ways to approach the role of producer. Experiencing your own ability really to hear a record, and watching that ability get stronger, may be all you need to give you confidence and faith in pursuing a producing career.

"Lots of producers are insecure," says producer Alan Abrahams. "The fact is that a lot of people don't really know what producing is. It's such an abstract, the music — 'Hey, I like it.' 'I don't like it!' Most producers are so insecure, they don't know what they're doing. They've either fallen into it (the prevalent way of getting into the record business), or they've watched. So they've got a hit engineer and a clever arranger, and they just sort of let the guys run with it." Even if a talented producer has been lucky enough to have fallen into it and intelligent enough to take advantage of what's around him, he may be running scared for a while, until he has a few jolts under his belt and realizes what he can and can't do. But it's better not bluffing too long, though, because it won't help your career in the long run.

For people with strong artistic sensitivities, it may be difficult to come to terms with what makes a record a commercial success. Most producers are hired to make the record sound commercial. The kind of artistry in the music you really love might not be the same kind that goes into the making of a hit record. The result of this discovery for Chet Atkins was that he got to be rather cynical, knowing as he did that great records weren't always hits, and he found it hard to be enthusiastic in the studio.

But too much enthusiasm from a producer, by the way, can have a dampening effect on those around him. Some people tend to be smothered by an overly enthusiastic personality, so it's good to remember that such spirit, to be effective, should be contagious. One should know when to pass the ball to get the maximum from a performance.

The special talent the producer beings to a recording, most people we've talked to agree, is an ability to work with people, to get into the artist's vision of the record, and to help him or her bring it out in the best possible way.

The producer of pop music might be described as a diplomatic aesthetician with a prophet's vision of monetary success.

Types of Producers

There are different kinds of producers, but any detailed description of their functions is likely to give the false impression that producers are locked into special and specific ways of working. The truth is that there is no one way.

The "indie" (independent) producer, a term not used as much as it used to be, is a person who wants to call his own shots and make his own deals, and floats from assignment to assignment at will, with perhaps a minimum of restraints and long-range obligations. Some are booked solid, while others are not booked at all.

It can work many different ways for the indie. He might have a deal with a record company (if he's lucky) that allows him to produce a certain number of albums a year, the particular artist to be either his choice, the record company's choice, or a mutual one. He can also function fully independently, producing anyone he chooses to work with. He might make a deal with an artist-writer-singer for publishing rights, then produce a demo and take it door-to-door, making his own deal with a record company for it to buy the forty-five or the album and let him produce the master.

For someone with a reputation or track record, or simply someone "hot" who has produced a hit record (even if it's a first), funding problems are at a minimum. He can get upfront money to produce a demo from a record company, or if the writer-singer himself has a track record, the producer might get an advance from a performing rights agency. But for the newcomer, getting the money is always the biggest burden. Funding may have to come out of the producer's own pocket, so he winds up taking financial risks. If a producer manages to interest an artist with a reputation in working with him, naturally that artist's name alone will open necessary doors. Talented producers new to the field have gotten started this way. Many aren't talented at all, yet somehow manage to produce records. About these Alan Abrahams says: "You can have a shoe salesman, or be in the garment business, say, put out a first record, and if it's a hit, suddenly this guy's a maven!"

How do would-be producers hook up with artists to produce? Sometimes it happens this way: many artists have non-creative periods when they are stagnating. An artist with a track record, but no current success, is often forgotten by people in the industry until someone, often a relative newcomer, convinces or hounds the artist into getting back to work and letting him manage or produce him or her.

Many indie producers were formerly or are still musicians, who have been called on by a friend who believes in their abilities to produce. Such producers tend to have a genuine sensitivity to music and, like Robbie Robertson, are often the ones who make it possible for new talent to be heard.

An indie is usually more approachable for an artist than in-house producers or big production company producers or anyone in the A & R departments today. Material and talent don't reach the producer the same way each time, and the kinds of financial arrangements one makes are different every time. But the relative openness makes the indie the hope for tomorrow's music.

During the Forties and Fifties, almost all producing of major acts was on an in-house basis. That means the in-house producer was working full-time on salary for a record company. For instance, Chet Atkins became a record producer in RCA's Nashville operations, and the term "Nashville Sound" is in part attributed to Atkins' work in the RCA operations there.

When individuals and groups began to arrange their own material in the mid-Sixties, the process of self-producing became natural. Since someone must have the total picture in mind, who knows better than the musicians themselves where they're coming from and where they're going? A group that plays club dates can measure audience response to their new arrangements, and the songs evolve as they test them out live. They may increase the tempo, change the vocals around, stress different words, shorten the bridge, increase the number of choruses, or emphasize instruments other than those they were originally counting on. All this comes under the heading of producing.

Such an apprenticeship might carry the group through its

first studio sessions with only the help of an engineer, who will just sit there and record. An outside producer may be brought in to carry out only minimal duties when working with a group who have learned to be all-around artists, rather than mere performers. If a self-contained group should happen to require a producer, such early experience as we've described should at least enable them to make knowledgeable judgments about a producer's effectiveness.

Obviously, it's the group that cares the most about its successes and failures, and many a group and many a singer have been reported to have been dissatisfied with a producer because of his lack of concern . . . when he isn't concentrating enough really to make a contribution. Tim Hardin was a friend and neighbor when he introduced us to a guy who looked and acted totally out of place during an entire recording session. He was the producer and Tim explained that he was a friend of the management. Tim proceeded to do exactly what he wanted, producing himself.

During the late Sixties, record companies experienced a general inability to keep artists and their producers within the budget for recording sessions. Costs got out of hand. In 1967, for example, a record company might have allocated a new album $30,000, a top production figure in those days. But things were loose, and quite often no one was keeping a very accurate watch over the budget. We can imagine how it might go: one day the administration A & R person comes running to the head office to announce that the album has gone over $50,000, and not even half the LP has been cut!

That's when the record companies began to contract studio production out to independent producers or production companies for a definite amount. Any surplus not spent in the studio belonged to the producer, or there was a split between the producer and artist. The product began to get produced with the most efficiency. (The "product" is vernacular for "the record," forever reminding one that the destiny of every record is the marketplace.)

Although it varies with his reputation for hits, the in-house producer doesn't make as much money as some independent producers, who may be making several hundred thousand a year and more. After all, it would mean that the in-house producer would be paid a salary higher than that of the company's president! Yet today there are record companies that are reverting to the practice of producing in-house because, among other reasons, they feel that the tougher and tougher deals with outside producers have begun to cost too much. In fact, even large publishers who often arrange for the production of a song are just beginning to think about the necessity of hiring an in-house producer since "sound" is an important selling feature today.

One good thing about working on the staff of a record company is that you get some knowledge of all the departments that fuse to make a record sell. You learn about the pressures within the organization, and you get to meet more people who are involved in the facts and figures of the business. And through that exposure, you will better understand what makes the record spin. Contacts and friends are made; the conventions, parties, and banquets, the interaction among various record companies, all go a long way toward forming the foundation for a long career.

Some production companies occupy as much Big Apple office space as a record company does, and have a staff of producers. Some do everything a record company does but press the records, distribute, and collect for them (see Chapter 3, Production Company).

Discovering Talent

People generally think of the producer in terms of only two of his functions, both of which exist as more the exception than the rule: producing the hit song and discovering new talent. Of the two, the latter is the rarer.

Many industry-famous producers, such as Jerry Wexler, take much pride in reminiscing about their discoveries of individuals. Others, and these are fewer, can take pride in the exhilaration of being acknowledged for the discovery of a new sound, as does the founder of early Sun Records, Sam Phillips, who saw in Elvis Presley "the white R & B vocalist" he was looking for. Individuals take the most pride when they discover a whole new movement, an authentic one that is an expression of the feeling of the people, regardless of musical source, whether it's the protest of the early Sixties, blues, late rock and roll, or the psychedelic sounds that sprang directly from the youth movement.

It takes one to know one, it is said; and, indeed, most new movements in music have been hailed by musicians and artists first. This is why industry executives rely heavily on musicians as guides to turn them on to new talent. But since history has a way of turning itself around (not repeating), one can't always count on an altruistic receptiveness from seasoned musicians, because of the insecurity of their own positions in today's competitive market. Musicians are probably more insecure than producers, because they're farther removed from the security of corporate headquarters.

One may not always be able to count on congested little cultural movements making waves. Most people feel that there is no true underground movement today. But whenever a cultural saturation point is reached, an antidote is always needed; and when the antidote becomes available the public may take to it. Peter Frampton's coming alive, especially to the extent that he has come alive, producing the now all-time best-selling album ever, was an antidote to the overproduced top forty (he produced himself in a live album) and to the dominant trend of MOR (middle of the road) tunes. People in the business, critics included, at the moment still cannot understand it.

Artie Traum, musician, singer-writer, and sometimes producer, remembers when today's stars were long shots, before they were actually discovered by a record company and/or producer. They had the advantage of the support and reinforcement from a whole movement, however. "They were around, all those people in the early Sixties in New York's Greenwich Village, sharing rooms, performing for next to nothing in coffeehouses. They all knew each other, Dylan, Hammond, Hardin, Sebastian, and many, many others, and were known within a larger circle. But then another sound was featured on the radio, and on the powerful 'Ed Sullivan Show,' which some people refer to as the show of discovery, but in reality it was featuring those acts which were getting lots of attention already."

The peer-group support of an artist sustains those artists whose music places them outside of major contemporary movements. Cathy Chamberlain, creator and singer of the "Rag 'n' Roll," has a style that tastemakers at the moment find hip. Although Cathy doesn't know how long her act will be able to hold onto this enthusiasm from her peers, it's been sufficient to keep her from giving up and getting into something a little more commercial. "No one knows what's going to take rock and roll's place — it's going down fast," she says. "The industry always falls back on MOR when they don't know what's going to happen: 'Let's go with the surefire that's not taking any risks.' In the music business there's nothing creative happening when you are that way."

Today's new talent tends to be composed of previously successful but presently unsigned artists who are ready for comebacks, some regroupings of musicians from two or more famous groups, or some artist from a known group who is isolated and now featured alone. Recycled talent has been the "new" talent of the mid-Seventies — although perhaps one can agree with Cathy that it doesn't take talent-scouting ability to pick the right people from any pretested lineup.

When the trends are *not* very revolutionary the producer needs to be more of a maverick in his selection of talent. That's assuming, of course, that one wants to come away with the greatest of coups, the discovery and production of some real, authentic new talent.

As we've said before, Epic's Boston has won a special place today as a truly "new," never-before recorded group, who with a single from their first album made it to the very top of the top ten. There are other indications that this kind of action could become a trend.

Certainly there are many places where talent is to be found. Often it will be right in your own backyard — wherever that may be: at the William Morris Agency, down in the bayous, or in Omaha, Nebraska. Certain areas, however, are more fertile for talent than others; but even in those places like New York City, where you might think a lot of people are grabbing up talent right and left, remember, "insights are nobody's private monopoly."

There is truth in what Picasso told Gertrude Stein, that it is impossible for people to be continually accurate in discovering talent for an extended period of time. It has something to do with being tuned in to the Now, of feeling the timeliness of the thing, the nuance that makes Now different from Yesterday. So the need for *new talent seekers* is as great as the need for new talent, to revitalize pop music — the largest cultural system of all.

Lots of times, ethnic or other demographic groups discover talent before the industry chieftains get attracted. Bette Midler was talked about plenty in the Big Apple, and Doc Thomas, a songwriter, carried word of her around among producers, then Joel Dorn produced her. The trouble is, producers tend to look in the same well and come up with the same buckets.

The truth is, everyone is "looking" for something new. It is a matter of willingly giving someone a chance, of being ready to convince others, of helping to support the talent until some level of success is reached. Porter Wagoner gave Dolly Parton her big chance. When interviewed for a *New York Times Magazine* article Dolly said that when Wagoner took her to

RCA and told Chet Atkins that he wanted her signed to a recording contract, Atkins said, "Porter, I'm sorry, but that girl just cain't sing." Porter then told him, "Well, I tell you what, you take out of my royalties what she loses RCA, because I know she can sing."

Jerry Schoenbaum put it to us this way: "The music business has become the tail that wags the entertainment-business dog. If you look today, you'll find Sonny and Cher, Mac Davis, and a multitude of artists doing variety shows. Before, these shows were done by variety-type artists, comedians, et cetera, rather than hit-record acts. The movie business is loaded with people who were former singers who have made it."

The bottom line is that producers are caught in the middle. They are concerned with two sometimes contradictory things — commerce and art. There are periods when the two coexist better than they do in others.

Selecting Material

Making the right selection of material is the single most important function in presenting an artist. There are heaps of good voices, bunches of beautiful people, tons of good musicians, but good material, in the right hands, is scarce. Just as coming up with a title is half the battle in writing songs, so choosing the right songs for a performer to record is half the battle in producing.

When it comes to selecting material, an artist may be unaware that he or she lacks the skill and objectivity to choose appropriate material and really needs help. Whoever offers it — producer, manager, A & R man, or a friend — he or she has to be diplomatic. When acts keep making flops over and over again, and the only acts that can afford continual failures are the ones lucky enough to have bulldog management that keeps the contracts coming, chances are the *material* counts for more than half the problem. A good producer will get to the bottom of it. He will want to go through everything the act has to offer, help pick and choose from the act's own material, or suggest outside material.

To make selections takes real conviction and confidence. If a producer has a fine ear for commercially successful songs, as George Martin (The Beatles' producer) did, he can take good tunes and help them become exceptionally successful ones. When working toward the hit single, one must have confidence in the timeliness of the basic melodic line, the lyrics, and especially, the sound. (Even the quality of a singer's voice, the phrasing, and the way he or she pronounces the words have an exact timeliness.) For instance, in 1976 some tunes with a classical strain incorporated into them became a trend. In Eric Carmen's "All By Myself," the hook line (which is also the title) was repeated over and over again; the only relief — one that added a serious intention to the hook — was a classical Rachmaninoff-like piano passage. Perhaps that trend explains why Beethoven's Fifth Symphony was successfully turned into a disco number.

Joel Dorn, producer of Roberta Flack, told us, "Roberta is an interpreter rather than a writer. So she and I try and find material for her." Both the artist and Dorn have to know what kind of music, thought, mood, she expresses best. All singers, of course, are interpreters, even if it's their own music. Some vocalists with restless souls can deliver the lines differently at almost every performance, putting their current personal feelings into a song.

Material may include songs written by the musician being produced, and tunes sent by song pluggers from publishers or record companies. Independent writers who have heard that So-and-so is looking for songs for a new album will also present their tunes. Plenty of producers are eager to get some of their own songs recorded. A song that has already been recorded has a very good chance of getting covered (meaning, performed or recorded again) when either management or the record company puts in pretty insistent plugs for tunes written by other artist-writers in their stables. And of course if the management and/or producer owns a piece of a tune, he's going to work hard to adapt it to the singer and convince him or her to cover it. Songs become "standards" only if other singers record them. Producers who are looking for *new* material get deluged by standards some music publishers keep on plugging. One had a fierce argument with a publisher about the amount of standards it sent him over the new material it presented.

If the selection is for a major recording artist, the producer is first going to listen to things coming from sources whose taste he trusts, often from friends who have brought in some material. And perhaps the clincher is when friends are close enough that the producer knows he will be getting a piece of the publishing income.

Then there are thousands of albums and singles to choose from, new ones as well as the oldies that are ripe for modernization or revival. And ideas can come from any place and anywhere. Alice Cooper reportedly told Todd Rundgren in a New York restaurant that "Locomotion" could be a hit. He took it to Grand Funk, whom he was producing at the time, and it did become a hit. Maybe too, a producer will find a tune that was ahead of its time that never made it when it first came out.

An artist might be categorized as, say, a singer of nostalgia, which was the case with the early Bette Midler. She would get deluged with songs from all sources that evoked nostalgia. Sometimes the aim is to get the artist out of a category, so one looks for entirely different material.

Music publishers who have seventy or eighty thousand songs in a constantly growing catalog are the biggest source. Here a producer has to watch out for jaded tastes, being aware that older publishers may be too conventional. An active writer, working and living during the era in which the song is recorded, is more likely to be an interesting, vital source for material than one of those old-line Broadway publishers who are constantly milking catalogs of, say, ragtime tunes or Thirties' cabaret torch songs. It may seem contradictory — those old songs sometimes do become hits again. But they cannot be as "interesting" as new tunes. The production of Bowie's "Golden Years" may have been intellectually contrived, but it remained new sounding and therefore interesting for a longer time than one might expect.

In many cases, success comes down to a matter of your direction as a producer, what you like, what kind of taste and judgment you have, what "interesting material" means to you, and what kind of commercial goals you have.

People tend to have one ear *open* to new material and one *closed*. Dorn claims a preference for music "to make love by." Johnny Cash wants to "tell a story." Almost everyone we've observed going through a process of song selection, however, does one thing the same, signifying to us that at least one element is a constant: they will start the tape, listen to about three seconds of it, press the fast-forward button, stop, listen to three more seconds, and come to a decision. Or else they'll talk while the tape is on. This is not at all consistent with what most of them claim: an ability to hear a song in the rough, with just voice and piano. While it's possible for the wrong three seconds to turn someone off, what else can one actually hear well in three seconds but the type of song it is, the quality of the production, and maybe catch an idea of voice quality?

The reality is that most producers are like everybody else in the business: unless a rough tune comes to them through a hit-maker, they are going to respond most favorably to the more finished production.

After about an hour of discussing the methods and problems of acquiring the right material with Joel Dorn, he brought in the note of reality we'd been looking for in an industry that's half hype: "I think that people who say they know a hit or even a good artist when they see one just aren't telling the truth. . . . Maybe they're embarrassed. In the course of a week, I passed on others besides Jim Croce that turned out to be hit material. I had a very bad week. Those overnight exceptions, those sensations that just fly out of the wall, they have been around for a while, have knocked on every door, and been taken to a lot of people. If you sit in a place like Al & Dick's, a music-business restaurant, you can listen to guys all night tell you about 'The big one that got away,' and about So-and-so who used to beg and plead for someone to listen to his songs."

The story of how "Joy to the World" got recorded illustrates how capricious getting the material is in the first place. Interviewed by *Songwriter Magazine,* Hoyt Axton told them he had just done a demo of his song and had it sent over to Three Dog Night, who had three guys listening all day, looking for songs for their new album. It was a screening process, and Axton's song got screened out. The singers eventually got to hear the song only because the guitarist and bassist happened to be shooting pool in Axton's house and heard the demo. Three Dog Night later sang it on the Grammy Awards Ceremony.

Writers of hits want their songs to be recorded the first time out by the best production and performer team possible because if the song succeeds on the first recording, other performers will want to cover the song too. So naturally a team with clout on the charts gets approached by the most successful writers. On the other hand the direction might be reversed and the performer and producer may want the kind of song like those by Leiber and Stoller, who keep turning out successes over the years, and approach them. In either case, success breeds success.

There are writers whose songs were hits years ago and who are still around, friends of producers and musicians and just hanging out. Bobby Charles, famed for "See You Later, Alligator, In Awhile, Crocodile," makes periodic forays into the music centers, seeing performer and producer friends, taking his songs around, with some successes here and there, then he ducks back into the bayous, where he lives. Any one of the hundreds of Tim Hardin's or Bobby Charles' tunes might be just right for a producer, but the preference is for current market success.

Sometimes not enough weight is placed on the kind of material responsible for the initial attention given the performer. Many times a relative newcomer, on his or her way up, is vulnerable to pressure from producer, management, and record companies, who may be very persuasive and irresistible about changing material. Decisions made for the artist may be right, and they may be wrong.

Artists can be charming, persuasive, and conspiring, themselves. It's up to the producer to act as a correcting force with as much diplomacy as he can. Suppose a woman is obsessed for a long time by a desire to sing like Janis Joplin but hasn't the voice to carry it off. Suppose she is another type of talent. In selecting material the producer has to be on guard always to nurture the talent, rather than cater to the self-delusion. Artie Traum, who has been produced himself many times and has worked on or audited hundreds of sessions, observed that holding on to an image fantasy is one of the biggest obstacles to be overcome, not only in life but in one's music career. He made an analogy to "the white-collar executive who has a thing about looking like a biker, but would never make it, no way." It's a tragic flaw not to know what you're meant to be. A great critic, José Ortega y Gasset, claimed that, and showed why, Germany's greatest poet, Goethe, should have followed another craft to have really fulfilled all his potential and found his true direction.

Cathy Chamberlain has been turning down offers to become a carbon copy of Bette Midler. Instead she is sticking to her personal concept of the right style for her, knowing that once she gets launched there will be a possibility of greater longevity as a performer.

The problems of a producer are enormous, and it is he

rather than the artist who most often bears the credit or the blame for selecting the right or the wrong material. And anybody's powers of prediction can be wrong. Even Jon Landau, ex–rock critic, said when he produced the MC5 album *Back in the USA* that he thought it would be a hit. It wasn't. When he produced Livingston Taylor, he didn't think it would be a hit. It was.

Joel Dorn has a pretty loose formula that he claims enables him to do what he wants: "You're on your own all the time and you have a certain amount of leeway to make decisions commercially. You can make the right decisions or the wrong decisions. Either you have the job or you don't. Over a given period of time you have a few losers and a few winners. You sit down and do the best interesting things you can. One of them will catch and one of them won't. Who cares? It's what you want to do with your life." Joel produces hits and he also keeps his hands in producing jazz records, which he loves and which aren't so commercial. He says of insecure, underconfident producers, "How are you going to make judgments if fear is your first consideration?" The answer, naturally, is that you can't. While Joel is awake to the realities of working and making decisions and has arrived at a personal solution for himself, our experience tells us that there are more people in the business who have not found a clear direction that they want to follow. Most are undecided about what they can or cannot do. This may be the emotional reason for why there is so much pretested product on the market. Word does get around in the industry, among musicians, artists, and other heads when someone completely lacks confidence. It's a matter of degree that is important, for as Joel points out, "There is a chain of insecurities that go on in any business that feeds off creative people, not in terms of your living, but in terms of your work."

You have to know what you love, what you want to do. It all depends on your aspirations. No matter what type of music you're into, you can only go so far out before you have to

38

bring it all back into the commercial field of reference. The top and bottom lines for staying in the business are the hit record, the gold. Your creativity lies in your ability both to work with the material and people you like to hook them into the elements that make for current success.

Functioning in a Studio

Unless you're producing someone who's allotted a big budget for production, you'd better not look upon the studio as a laboratory for experimentation, though you might have been able to not so long ago. At $125 to $150 an hour, plus union scale for five-plus musicians (approximately another $40 an hour each), tape at roughly $50 a session, and all the other extras and unforeseen studio expenses, such as $50 to $100 a day for meals and hotels — a month of recording will move the cost well over the $25,000 mark. Seldom today does one hear anyone bragging about how much they spent in the studio. Now the times dictate an attitude like that of Medress and Appell, California production team, who boast about how little they bring in a hit album for. In fact, producers have become more powerful because they are instrumental in keeping costs down.

Although the studio bills may have been high in the Sixties, a lot of great stuff came out of those long sessions when self-contained artists could experiment on the spot. But many of those sessions didn't come out. Some say The Beach Boys started the whole extravagance by taking four months in the studio to create the album *Good Vibrations*. The label made much publicity out of that fact. And then came the rumor that The Beatles spent six months on *Sergeant Pepper*.

The public got a lecture from the PR man that went: "It takes time to create a great work, and it's commendable that the genius behind it took all the time necessary to make a major musical statement. How could you ever criticize the

39

long-suffering work of a genius?" In short it was intimidating. A whole slew of performers started demanding all the studio time they needed and then some. Record companies went along with footing the bill for practically unlimited studio time, and not always exclusively for their big money-making acts.

At the time no one seemed to realize that art is not always long in the making. Keats wrote "Ode on a Grecian Urn" in a couple of hours one afternoon; Shakespeare's entire oeuvre went down in two decades, van Gogh's in one; Voltaire wrote *Candide* in less than a week! Sometimes by spending too much time one can lose sight of one's original intentions. Some people are suited for working long hours, while others aren't. Both styles of working can have their pitfalls. Probably the longest, most extended time spent in the studio we have personally ever heard about is that of Full-Tilt Boogie, Janis Joplin's last band. They worked for several years after her death, filling up a whole library wall with two-inch demos. To this date they have not produced an album, and the group has disbanded.

Somewhere along the line someone has to check to be sure that if union members are used in a recording session, they are being paid union scale. All the record companies insist on that, and it's part of the contract with the licensing agencies.

A producer in the studio is dependent on the engineer, more now than in years past, when the process was somewhat less complicated. Many producers claim they don't need to know the technicalities or even the full range of which sophisticated modern studio equipment is capable; but if you ever start producing, we'd suggest you try to pick up as much as you can about the equipment and how it is used. For one thing, it helps you have more immediate rapport with the engineer — and more credibility with the musicians, who are depending on your ability to communicate what they want to the engineer. We can best illustrate what we mean by the story of the modern American sculptor David Smith, who worked with welded iron. Toward the end of his life, the Italian government put an entire foundry with twenty welders at his disposal. As soon as the men saw that Smith himself knew how to work with a torch, they were 100 percent behind him. The fact that his abstract artistic vision was very different from theirs didn't seem to bother them.

In a weak moment, feeling the stress of being a step or two below the producer in the pecking order of the studio, or for whatever other reason, the engineer who can't respect a producer because he is ignorant of the technical aspects of the craft may take advantage of him and undermine his project. He can give the wrong advice, trick him into thinking something was recorded and play back a previous track instead, or deliberately fail to understand what the producer is trying to tell him. Being in the studio is like being in any foreign country: you've got to make an effort to speak the natives' language, to ensure a better chance of obtaining respect and cooperation.

The tendency for producers to talk in poetic terms is described in more detail in the engineering section. This kind of language is used sometimes as a short cut to telling the engineer what to do, and sometimes as a cop-out for the producer's inability to give specific instructions. Jerry Wexler is given credit for coining the word "sweeten" (and is criticized for excessive sweetening!). Everyone in the business knows what this means now: the adding of backup vocals, strings, and so on, to the basic performance.

You will have to be able to interpret the complaints and observations of the artist. Artie Traum tells us, "The artist might say, 'The texture is too boring, too light, make it darker'; so the producer will make suggestions to the guitarist on a different way to play the same or similar notes, like perhaps, 'Play down the neck and maybe we'll get the right sound.' "

Artie insists that the producer must have a good ear to make sure that everything is in tune; and another friend, who recorded on the *Area Code 615* album in Nashville with those famous studio musicians, verified that by saying they might take over an hour tuning up! But a perfectionist can take up a lot of studio time, which isn't always desirable from the creative point of view. Along these lines it's good to hear Chet Atkins telling *Rolling Stone* magazine that as a producer, "You're selling emotion. . . . Certain musicians will work thirty minutes finding the right chord, and that's not important, it really isn't."

When heavy, negativistic attitudes intrude, they will rarely get the best performance from the musicians. It is often a schoolmarm inclination to humiliate that makes a producer put the musicians through the drudgery of many takes. Having them repeat a passage over and over again may eventually get results, but it can kill the spirit. In the old days of early jazz recordings there was only one take (in fact, guitarist Robert Johnson once recorded in a hotel room, with a simple art-deco machine, and you can hear auto horns honking outside on the street).

Cathy Chamberlain's experience with a producer shows how rough a relationship can be. Electric Lady Studio was paying for Cathy's demo and also for a coproducer whom she thought she needed because she felt she didn't know how to communicate to the engineer. "I get into the studio and the first thing the producer says is, 'Now, we're going to find you a sound.' From there on it went downhill. I was supposed to coproduce, and every time I said anything to this guy, he smiled, and it went in one ear and out the other. He ignored it. Two minutes later Rich [Cathy's co-writer and piano player] would make the same exact comment and the lights would go on, 'Well, that's a great idea!' It was more credible to the producer because it came from a male. But when this guy wouldn't listen to me and when he wanted to go it alone and told me, 'If you want to say you're coproducing, dear, go right ahead . . . ,' " here the producer was laying his problem, chauvinism, on the artist, which will have an effect of deadening the material, no matter how good.

Some producers manage to get real, exciting energy flowing. This is their chief concern. Others act bored and read newspapers while the session is going on. That kind of producer is phasing out fast. Not too long ago a major hit singer went to record her first record and felt the sessions in the studio were failures because not only did the musicians act bored but so did the producer.

Then there is the producer who goes into a studio with a kind of alienating, imperious quality, a nothing-is-good-enough-for-me air. He puts down the studio equipment as pre-Spector (Phil Spector generally gets the credit for initiating lots of technology in production), obsolete, makes unkind remarks about the engineer, notices every possible defect, and then instructs all the musicians and vocalist to get to work. He undermines the confidence of everyone involved in the project.

If you do have to use a studio that isn't up to what you want (perhaps your budget is so low you are using an 8-track studio for $20 an hour), you can try to make the best of the situation, and maybe take heart from the answer that Edward Curtis, the photographer of North American Indians, gave back in 1917. A journalist asked Curtis, who was halfway through his amazing forty-volume oeuvre, *The North American Indian,* what kind of camera he used. His reply was that he didn't know and that all he was concerned with was its working order! For the producer who's well prepared for the session, knows the studio, has overseen the rehearsals, has charts written and the arrangements worked out, and has everything pretty cool and in the ready position, there is less inclination to blame or find fault with the peripheral elements, such as the hardware.

Robbie Robertson of The Band, who is recently emphasizing his role as a producer, says in *Crawdaddy* magazine about working with Dylan on *Planet Waves:* "We know the technique very well. We've been playing with Bob for years. There's no surprises involved. We did it, and it was over be-

43

fore we knew it." "Head" producers, those with a great faith in improvisation and more than an inkling of what the finished sound will be, tend to count rather heavily on the musicians' genius and also tend to be relatively indifferent to the material.

Instilling confidence is probably the one most valuable in-studio technique if you can call it that. A member of the group Lynyrd Skynyrd said of the producer-engineer, Tommy Dowd: "He's like magic. He gave us back our confidence, showed us how to be ourselves. You know those riffs? They're all Dowd. I'd play them and I'd think, 'That's dumb, that's too simple,' but Tommy would say 'That's OK.' It took Dowd to say leave it be."

In a relaxed show of American intimacy, The Eagles nick-named their producer, Bill Szymczyck, "coach." After a string of not so happy producer-artist relationships, one of the group said of Szymczyck in *Circus* magazine that his job was not arranging or analyzing the songs so much as, "Just to keep us up, keep us loose, make sure things didn't get too intense, but that they get intense enough." Developing an ability for coaching to win is enormously helpful, and so is having the knack of putting positive energy into the sessions. Many self-contained, well-rehearsed, and mostly self-produced groups tend to use producers for expertise in realms other than the aesthetic.

We've heard the results of one producer's method that seems to be well intended. A friend played us his new album and instead of listening with us he proceeded to point out how much money had been spent on it and rave about how the producer had a Ping-Pong table set up to keep them loose between the ordeals in the studio and how they played basketball and were wined and dined. He loved the whole thing. But what came out in this instance was an overly produced record and what could have been a good tune became merely a cut with a minimized melody. Another friend told us that when a producer he knows sees that the artists and session men are going to get real wasted before recording, he catches them just as they are coming up, a prime moment, a balance between alertness and relaxation when everything feels right, to begin recording.

Realizing that the right vibrations can make or break a session, the producer should be ready to solve any problem. Artists are temperamental people, and any performer can get edgy and feel unsure of her or himself, just as any sports person will tell you that there are peaks and there are off days. And yet the producer has to be able to alter emotional vibrations as much as possible in a positive direction. Producers like to tell you that, like psychiatrists, they're on call twenty-four hours a day. Maybe the artist, in a fit of paranoia, is convinced the engineer is sabotaging the sound or the mix. The producer has to step in to reestablish confidence and cooperation.

Michael Cuscuna, Bonnie Raitt's producer, told an interviewer from *Gig,* "Often you have to play the shrink. There are always some sort of ego problems, and you have to protect the musician from the sideman or the engineer. You have to second-guess a lot of bullshit."

Some hungry souls will relax when there is an abundance of food around, a symbol of nourishment, energy, love. Depending on the eating habits of the performers, sometimes there'll be lots of junk food in the studio, and nothing but; sometimes the group has more refined tastes, and wants to have a picnic in the studio ordered from Chasen's in Beverly Hills! Health-food-oriented performers will have nothing less than pure orange juice squeezed by hand — to wash down the vodka. Dusty Springfield brings natural orange juice to the studio. We heard of a San Francisco producer who takes the whole crew out to an expensive restaurant, keeps a flow of easy talk moving, and then brings them all into the studio like a big happy family. Atmosphere manipulating might not come naturally to you, but it can be a method that will produce the effect you want in certain cases.

There are producers who really do all the innovative work. They can make a huge sunflower out of a forget-me-not. They literally make monster hits. Some producers feel that a hit can be made out of any good song, that it's what the hitmakers do to the song along the way that counts. Joel Dorn agrees that there are some producers who really can *make* a hit record. "They understand how to make hit records, and they make them for long stretches, year in and year out." He goes on to add that "most people who do something that well have a run, and that's it." He's referring to songwriters like Jim Webb, who had ten or fifteen standards that he wrote in a space of a year or two. "I'm talking about people who grind out smash after smash. They don't last." Of course, there are plenty of exceptions, but we're offering this observation as a kind of general rule of thumb.

Some artists basically want a hit and will do anything to get one; others want only to commit what they do to a recording and worry about commercial success afterward.

You'll do best to understand the trends at the moment while at the same time keeping yourself open. It's a touchy matter just thinking that often the use of just one musical instrument — harp, oboe, bassoon, clavichord, clarinet — which a certain market can't accept can be the cause of failure. Dylan simply went electric and it worked. Of course he was merging folk with an already accepted electric sound. So whatever you do that is special must not be too far off the beaten path to get wide acceptance. Most people behave automatically, and are thoroughly influenced and conditioned without realizing it. Others think things out with varying degrees of independence. We think it's best to examine your work every so often and try to see exactly where you might be off base in hitting the market you want. Most producers will find their problem to be the fusing of what's "in" with what's "out" or what's "coming in," in order to come up with something both acceptable and fresh.

Whatever the forte of an individual artist — soul, pop,

sweet, rock and roll — the job of the producer is to retain and put forward the unique essence of that artist, the way ambergris in perfume prolongs and emphasizes any scent. "Don't typecast an artist," says Artie Traum, feeling that the one-track approach is a hack way of producing because it is always carried to extremes, and one record ends up sounding pretty much like another.

The most real hard-line aspect of producing is the budget: the amount of money allocated to the specific task of bringing in the demo, single, or album. This is the time when a producer wears his business bonnet, watching costs, on his own if he's an indie or with a production company, or keeping to the production costs if he's working for a record company. If there is some leeway in the budget, the producer will be the one who has to decide whether the product he is working on is worth an increase or not. Barbara Davies, a former A & R administrator, told us that the creative end of the companies she's worked for most always has a hard time keeping within the budget. There is usually just too much creativity going on, and A & R heads will plead for an expansion of the budget on the grounds that the artists are artists, that they can't be budgeted out of doing their best. But somewhere, decisions do have to be made.

In general the producers who really know how to work fast and efficiently are the ones who do jingles. Even in this field, where everyone makes so much money, there is no elaborate spending going on. We once watched a commercial producer work on a first album and in a single incidence save at least a thousand dollars in production costs by his intelligent handling of the musicians. They were on their fifth take on a couple of final bars, when the producer said, "It's good, we'll try it again tomorrow." They were a calculated few words: the musicians, realizing that the end of the song was in sight, insisted on staying to try the phrase once more. That was all that was needed, and the session was at an end without everyone having to come back another day.

SUCCEEDING IN THE BIG WORLD OF MUSIC
Working with Session Musicians

Ken Mansfield, an independent producer, is from maverick country: he lays claim to having produced over twenty country and western singles, and none of them has come from or gone through Nashville. He looks upon recording artists with the eyes of a manager, and he wants every studio band to be put together as though it were going on the road with the artist. In *Billboard* magazine he says, "I used to cut fairly bare tracks and then overdub for hours. . . . Then we got into cutting live, the singer and the basic band. After that we do simple overdubs if we have to. It's all more personal and it becomes a structure in an unstructured situation."

In the same article he claims a preference for younger musicians in the studio, not that it's less expensive — inexperience can be very expensive. But young people trying to get a foot in the door, trying to get that name and those credits that count for everything, will aim higher and venture more. One thing for sure, they might not have been indoctrinated yet into studio pecking and politicking; they don't know yet that the walls have no doors. All of this makes for more personal freedom.

What would you as a producer do, if the best studio bass man in the business showed up a couple of hours late and acted as if nothing was wrong? Or the sweetest of keyboard players showed up both late and with an entourage of personal guests? Every producer claims he won't tolerate arrogance from anyone but the superstar who can't be replaced, like the temperamental movie stars of the past who would keep entire production companies, costing many thousands of dollars an hour, waiting for half a day. Such prima donna jive from session people can undermine a producer badly, not to mention the artist. Some producers invent techniques to handle a difficult session man. We've heard of one producer who will make sure the supersession sideman gets home early the night before a studio date, to ensure that he will show up the next day. Another, who doesn't want to baby-sit, might just bring along a second percussionist when the drummer he really wants to have play is unreliable and might not show up for the date. If the drummer does show, the percussionist will play a minor instrument on the recording.

In the late Sixties, "family" was practically a cult word, meaning close friends. There was an emphasis on friendship: male camaraderie appeared persistently in films at the same time that a romantic dependence on it showed itself in music, with producers and artists using friends as session musicians. Friends can make for a happier and more stable working condition but one criterion from the point of view of the producer should be, don't put a friend in the studio unless you know you would fire him with the same speed as you would anyone else. Cronyism promotes a closed structure that can easily cause a sacrifice in quality. Remember Watergate? A reviewer for *Rolling Stone* recently ended a piece on another of those "So-and-so and Friends" albums with the question, "When are you going to cut a tune for the rest of us?"

Often, of course, a producer uses friends to save money. Some friends will work for nothing. You can also arrange a reciprocal deal to work for them on a recording of theirs. The trick here, when you have to rely on free help, is to be able to pick from a wide circle of acquaintances, and not a small closed group.

There is also a type of groupism, which is perhaps just opportunism, that emphasizes contracting (putting in the studio) people who have reached a peak in popularity. For instance, although Dave Sanborn, saxophonist, has been playing successfully for years, suddenly about a year ago his reputation reached a peak, and every performing artist we talked to wanted to have Dave on the next album. Trouble is, after a while the listener gets to know the sound of some of these supersession musicians, who tend to repeat themselves, and a recognizable style is projected out of the album's texture. The success of a particular song may depend on the way it's become a whole greater than the sum of its nonetheless very good parts.

Recording-studio incest breeds musical diseases like "soundalike-itis," which doesn't always help a song. However, it hasn't hurt Motown, and we should point out there are producers who make hits time after time using studio musicians who have identifiable sounds. They latch onto a familiar sound and, with a good singer and a good song, they produce hit after hit.

Often there are good reasons why some musicians have huge reputations, but no musician can be all things to every producer. Musicians with a talent for bringing out the best in a specific artist or material should get first consideration. A producer who has a gift for this kind of selective process is really exciting. Sometimes the results can be pretty far out, such as when a personal enemy turns out to be the best one for eliciting just the right flair in a performer. It's said of F. Scott Fitzgerald that he wrote his best when he convinced himself that his audience was composed of Hemingways, his enemy. Patti Smith said she was fighting for her life working with producer John Cale, and that it made for a good album.

Session people love to put producers on. Dave Sanborn tells of the time a producer asked him to repeat a passage, because there had been something missing. So Dave played it again, exactly the same way; he only acted different. The producer felt it was now perfect.

Alan Abrahams, as a very savvy studio dude, told us in a rapid-fire monologue, "I am a drummer, and having come up from being in a group and being on the street level, I know infinitely more people. . . . Yes, of course, Richard Tee is incredible, and Gordon is incredible and Steve Gadd is incredible [all prime N.Y.C. session men], but I know twenty, thirty, forty other guys that I could use, and do use. There's this guy, Ted, I use on keyboards. No one knows Richard Crooks, and Richard is in Steve's league. . . . There's this bass player by the name of Larry Paxton. Now, no one will have heard of him. A group from Ohio sent me a tape, and I went out and saw the group, and this bass player killed me. I brought him in . . . he did great. Just a couple of weeks ago, a friend turns him on to a gig with the Allman Brothers. Bang, like that. There's a certain attitude that certain of the New York players have that is a heavy attitude to deal with! 'Hey, I've done everything. I've been with everybody, you kidding me? Two to five. Show up late. Don't give me any bullshit. I'll show up late.' That's the attitude with some of these hundred-thousand-a-year players. . . . Certain players think that they're more important than the product! They've had that thing, that ego, where their name is on every record. People can't deal with it. I don't let that type of thing go down with me because, again, I really hit them where they're coming from. I don't care what they're making — and if you're not going to be on time, bullshit!"

Whoever you are dealing with should have the stuff to deliver what you want with a minimum of hassle. People are willing to put up with the star because the dividends can be so enormous. So in the end it's a matter of weighing your emotional durability against potential gain.

Wealth and Well-being

Many producers, like the artists they produce, use lawyers to negotiate the contracts with both the performer-writer and the record company. Contracts with artists can be as involved as when artists sign record company contracts; so can the contracts drawn up to protect the producer when he signs with a record company. The producer is looking to get into his contract clauses that will earn him points (percentage of mechanical royalties), fees, options to record particular artists (maybe the next record of the artist whose present album is being covered by the contract), plus guarantees that the record will definitely be released and within a specific period of time. Lately the producer has been asking for a stipulation in the contract that his name be featured on the album cover, on the label, and in promotion artwork. And as Michael Sukin pointed out, producers like to tie up artists for seven years, longer than record companies.

Then there's the other end of the rainbow, where a new-comer, unheralded, untried, has only the drive to produce. The record company might be willing to advance a below-subsistence amount, barely enough to see what kind of quality the producer is able to bring in, and usually it will be for an act that the producer has brought to the attention of the record company.

The economic rewards to a producer can be fantastic. *Gallery* magazine reported that the producing team of Medress and Appell "split over $500,000 in royalties this year [1975] alone." Additional profits probably come from production fees, song publishing, and management, but producers keep pretty low profiles and the general music-minded public knows little or nothing about them. As Dorn puts it, "There is a brokerage function for art." By which he means that in the dissemination of the creative unit, whether it be a painting, book, movie, sculpture, or song, there are people who are making tremendous amounts in both the creative and the marketing ends.

Fame and fortune aren't everything, even in the moneyed world of music. The producer is in the unique position of being able to fuse the creative-artistic side of music-making with the financial-practical one if he wants to. And, as he selects and blends those special ingredients into a new, more powerful whole, he can look forward to a long, satisfying career. The creative person who is able to look back over a period and talk about how a sustained body of work feels pretty good. Joel Dorn says, "It's a good sensation to look back over fifteen years of producing and see the places I've been, you know. Some might have sold better than others, but . . ." That *but* points to satisfaction.

3

Production Company

THE OUTFITS THAT are in the most enviable position in today's record world are the production companies, many of which have reaped huge amounts of cash in less time than it takes to go through college, while the people who run them are basking in attention from the press, making reputations as savvy business heads, and receiving high compliments for their creative efforts. What do these production companies do? They do everything from producing a record for an act on a one-time basis to functioning as a full-service organization, managing the entire life of a star.

In the early Seventies practically no one had ever heard of a production company. The title "independent producer" was used to denote producers working outside the shelter of the big labels. But by 1976, that title had an old-fashioned ring, like "song plugging" or "organ-grinder." In the meantime the production company has become a force to reckon with, stealing the thunder from record labels, publishers, and top management companies. The concept is so new that the best book on music law and contracts, *This Business of Music,* published in 1971, doesn't even have the term indexed.

The evolution of the production company has been a matter of survival of the fittest. There was a bunch of aggressive young guys, liberated from business tradition by the politics and culture shocks of the Sixties; you could have found them working in all aspects of the record industry. Gradually they saw opportunities to improve their own positions, considering the long-range terms of a career and at the same time relieving those frustrations that come from suffering under the incompetence of one's superiors. *"If you don't like the way we do things here, then start your own company!"* And they did.

So on the one hand there were the ambitions of music-oriented people very much into hacking out artistic-monetary careers on their own terms, and they made themselves presidents of companies; on the other hand there was the direct encouragement to their struggles by the record companies, who were weary from dealing with employee creative types.

Many founders of production companies were independent producers who had belief in their abilities not only to produce important albums but to supervise other music-business operations. Generally these tape-toting pioneers were convinced that producers were not receiving fair monetary rewards or adequate credit for their work. Others who came on the production company bandwagon, notably A & R people, musicians, stars, ex-presidents of record companies, some managers and agents, all saw the golden opportunity in this kind of mini–record company, and within four years it came to be that one of the more prestigious positions in the business was to head a production company.

Production companies range in size, starting with the push-cart operation where one person does everything from a rented desk, or the free street, and the "president" may never have produced a record. At the opposite end is CAM-USA, Victor Benedetto's production company, housed in an impressive suite of offices on Fifth Avenue, which has a department to service almost every need for its performers. On the West Coast, David Robinson and Friends is a fair-sized production company that handles all aspects of studio production, plus career management, TV packaging, tours, publishing, publicity, the writing of bios, press kits, and even songs — and probably ties shoelaces, though it's not on the letterhead. Production companies promote concerts and festivals, sign talent, supervise artwork and liner notes for album jackets, sell masters to the major labels, in short will do anything with music. Most of them, however, specialize in producing albums.

Even though studio production is the focus around which production companies originally came into being, they quickly borrowed experience from management and record companies, incorporating other functions as the need arose. Functions they have steered away from, with a few exceptions, are physical production of the vinyl discs, marketing-selling, and "the collections," defined as getting money owed from the wholesalers and retailers. Jerry Schoenbaum, who has been president of Polydor, started Verve Forecast years ago, and now operates his own production company, says that only the majors can handle collections successfully, which is the main obstacle keeping production companies from becoming record companies.

David Robinson expresses a human reason for the evolution of his production company: "Because anything you leave to anybody else will get screwed up." Joe Pellegrino, an executive at CAM, feels that record companies have gotten very lazy. And too, record companies were often at a loss in dealing with all the crazies who became big time in music. It was easier for the businessman to concentrate on factory production, marketing-selling, and collections, the traditional provinces of business, and to farm out some of the creative work to small companies, thereby lessening his involvement with the nuts and notes of stardom. So A & R departments dwindled, and in some companies were practically abandoned.

Joe Pellegrino expressed the decline in the importance of in-house A & R departments like this: "I don't think they felt close enough to what was happening in the world. I don't think they could get the kind of individual who was able to recognize or go with gut instinct or gut feeling as to what was happening in the street. . . . It was almost like the labels got lazy, and these people [producers] recognized the chance . . . and said I'm not about to sit around here and watch these people who are slow in making decisions. At least I know how to make a record . . . and they were success-ful . . . and the production companies started to really be-come very powerful."

Today some labels will consider buying only complete mas-ters. Others, feeling the double loss (creative and economic) from having an inactive A & R staff, are beginning to build that department up again.

Contracts with the Record Company

An important — meaning powerful — production company will probably have a contract with a record company entitling the production company to produce major acts — its own acts and/or the major acts belonging to the label. The reason why the label will assign the production company the production of its major money-making stars is that it's after the talents of the company's producers. The production company's goal in the bargain may be an agreement to assign to the record com-pany for distribution one or some of its major acts, which can bring significant income to the record company.

The record company needs to have a constant supply of records that sell well; the production company wants to cast its acts with the most appropriate label, and it wants to ensure its producers a steady supply of production work at the best fees obtainable. Of course there are all kinds of ramifications of the above, additional clauses specifying time, publishing rights, and so on, but essentially the production company that operates primarily as a corporation for producers has the goal of making money for the producer and the producer's acts.

Sometimes, when the record company has sufficient faith in the taste of the production company, it will, under pressure, agree to an open-ended contract, which means that the record company agrees to accept one or more productions from the production company *without* the right to approve the artist being recorded. This is typically part of what's called a package deal, the promise to produce certain specific artists, with the privilege to produce one to a few unnamed artists at the discretion of the production company. Open-ended contracts are usually made with the larger production companies.

With production companies of all sizes, typically the main point of negotiation is the advance obtained from the record company to produce a master. Since most albums are *not* financial successes (in fact, record companies like to claim that most records lose money, thus giving the record companies an image of being generous philanthropists), the record companies will want all kinds of checks in the contract, depending on their level of excitement for the act and their favorable past relations with the production company. And with production companies that have practically no track record and/or work with an unrecorded artist, the contract can be a tough one, as hard-assed as the record company can make it.

The other day a friend, head of a production company without too much clout, brought an unrecorded act to Atlantic Records. Our friend has a history of putting together ventures that make fortunes for other people, Atlantic being the beneficiary of one of these fortunes. Atlantic was interested in putting the act on its catalog, but, according to our friend, the terms of the contract weren't favorable, and he would have to return to the "table" several times to push the terms up. Negotiating contracts like this is work, and past success doesn't necessarily make a difference, as our friend found out when he said, "Come on, have a heart, you guys already made millions off me," and longtime potentate of Atlantic, Ahmet Ertegun, only smiled behind a pair of glasses.

From a production company's point of view the ideal contract is one that entitles the company to produce those acts it likes best over a given period. This guarantees it good advance and regular chunks of cash as the units are delivered. There's great comfort in being able to count on a guaranteed income, knowing that your work is presold. This can be utopia for a creative person, whose efforts are so often expended on speculation.

The contracts with smaller production companies, without staff producers, might not stipulate a particular producer, but the record company, wanting to be kept apprised of how things are going, will have in the contract certain rights: the right to check the quality of studio work as it progresses; the right to approve producer, material, and session musicians; the right to reject the product and pull out at any time; the right to recoup its losses from the production company if the product isn't delivered on time or not at all, all of which combined would make a tough contract from a production company's point of view.

A production company's future naturally depends on the success its products have with the public. So theoretically the production company is eager to do the best job it can within its budget, and a contract is there to remind everyone of these obligations.

Contracts with Artists

We've known some smaller production companies whose method of operation is very vague. Such a company might represent one or a number of artists on a nonexclusive basis, where the agreement is a verbal one. The producer feels there is a chance of getting a recording contract for the artist, so the producer will spend a limited amount of time and cash presenting the tape to record companies, feeling out their reaction. When it's positive, a contract between the producer and the artist can then be worked out. These contracts are as long and as involved as a recording company contract.

In these contracts the artist is almost always the property of the production company. The artist agrees to be produced by the producer chosen by the production company, and along with him often comes a whole team of studio professionals — arranger, engineer, musicians, backup singers. The artist can be sold to other companies, either a record or a production company (the way a professional baseball star is sold) and can be assigned to any label determined by the company. From this it is easy to see that the production company's aim is to exercise as much control as it can over its acts, just as the record company wants to control the production company.

Very often the performer, being vulnerable, unrecorded, desperate, will sign anything to get that first break. But since the contract is so one-sided, the artist is usually the first to break it, which results in expensive litigation.

With the small- to medium-sized companies, standard agreements today provide for an equitable division of the profit from the advance received from the record company. Say a production company receives $25,000 guaranteed on delivery of a master and the expenses are $15,000, then the difference, $10,000, is divided as profit between the production company and the artist, *more or less.*

Selling the Product

Usually there exists between artist and production company either verbal or contractual agreement to make a demo of good enough quality to present the artist's work favorably. When that's done, the meetings with record company executives begin; these are part of the production company's job. The demo is not always used first time around. If the artist looks best in a live performance, the production company will arrange for a live audition in an audition hall, studio, office, or club.

The production company solicits a response first from those companies with which it has a working relationship. We know of one company that places three or four acts a year and spreads the acts out among many companies, on both East and West coasts, believing that too many eggs in one geographic basket is dangerous. A smaller company is happy to place one egg in any basket!

The smallest, most struggling, poorest production company will have to decide on the quality of the demo it can afford. The better it is, the easier it will be to sell. If the artist is really an attractive person — and the trend is toward signing people who look good up there on stage — then either a press kit or the flesh itself is taken to the offices. This can sometimes be a problem because artists want to be appreciated for their talent first; but as business people know, the clincher, the decisive element in formulating the decision to sign an act, can sometimes be pretty far removed from pure appreciation of the musical talent. The first presentation must be as good as it possibly can because it is likely to take a record company a good six months or year before it will be willing to listen to the artist again.

Often the more the production company has at stake, the harder it will try to sell the artist. A company that owns the artist's publishing rights, manages him or her personally, and generally has potential income coming from every which direction will obviously try harder.

The artist who likes to determine her or his own aesthetics with only minimal help and advice from a production staff might have a strained working relationship with any producer. The producer's position of power, supported by the tough contract in his favor, will tend to make him look on the artist as a means to the expression of his own vision. "It's my album! It's all mine!" as one producer is quoted as saying, is a reflection of the "Age of Me." Even with the protection of a production company, that kind of exaggerated self-importance will probably eventually alienate the company and the stars. Everybody in the music business wants to have some share in the credit for hits.

No matter how hot a producer gets, he's got that problem of remaining hot. Today as a producer makes successful records, he is usually either absorbed into a production company or forms his own. When he's really hot, record companies will look on him as though he were an evangelist able to cure the lame. A record company may have a well-known act whose sales have dropped to an incredibly low figure. Big name but no sales; only the record company knows just how low. The record company is eager to take one more chance on salvaging the artist and approaches a star producer for the miracle cure. The offer might be twice or more what the producer is accustomed to; but say the producer has a proven affinity for blues, and the record company is after him to produce an MOR singer of ballads, then the producer has to weigh the risk against the rewards. A failure is a failure, and a hot producer will soon cool after a string of failures. The production company has to worry about its producers being persuaded to take on acts and material that are in opposition to the wisdom of market experience and intuition, which, Joe Pellegrino believes, is at the heart of being a good producer. For in the case of the production company, a producer's reputation is not only his own, but that of the company as well.

Many production companies, of all sizes, maintain a publishing arm. Material comes from professional managers, performers-writers, or just from writers — anyone looking to get a song recorded. Occasionally a production company will give an advance on a song it feels it can place. In any case, the company will be the publisher and receive all or some of the publishing rights to those songs it buys for its catalog, the writer retaining the writer's benefits. (Details are found in the songwriting and publishing chapters.)

The big advantage to the production company of having an in-house publishing department is that it can cover songs in its own catalog with its own acts, chalking up additional income. One can be sure that when the producer has a need for material, the company's own catalog is the first one scrutinized, and the last to be passed on.

It's easy to conclude that the production company is in competition with the major labels. Joe Pellegrino feels that when the time comes that a production company is having a tough time selling the kinds of product that it really believes in artistically and commercially, then it will gamble on putting out records under its own label. Seldom is a company in a financial position to make this gamble, but here and there some production companies are making a stab at becoming total record companies. Besides collection problems, the one thing that will hold some back is the fact that under the present system a number of star producers are making far more than typical record company presidents make.

4

Studio Engineer

WE HAVE DEFINITELY landed in an electronic age! Everyone is crazy for electronics. Scientific foundations and music endowments are pooling their dollars to fund research in programming electronic sound. More and more researchers have backgrounds in both music and science. Eventually digital systems (computers) with a far greater capability for precision recording will replace studios as we know them today.

Some artists and producers will want to make use of all the features that a well-equipped studio can give them, and some won't need to use half its potential. For instance, if an engineer is expected to use the full range and potentialities of the studio equipment, he can. On the other hand, the engineer who may be required to leave the studio and record in a barn because a group or an artist wants to work in a situation much like the one they rehearse in will find himself basically just sitting in the corner and recording them. For John Holbrook, the engineer at Bearsville Studios, such artists are purists; when they come into the studio and say they just want to play and have it go on tape, he tells them to get a 2-track machine and record at home. He sees the studio as a place of complexity where an artist can come in and employ it all. He thinks of the studio as some would a synthesizer; it is an audio process. When Roger Powell, who is the synthesizer performer in Todd Rundgren's *Utopia,* records his own albums, he sees all the technology in the studio as an extension of his synthesizer. "Instead of drawing the line at the output of the synthesizer, because it can be connected by a patch cord to every instrument in the studio, the synthesizer becomes part of the instruments."

In any fully equipped studio there is plenty of technology available that is not always needed. After all this time Dylan is just finally getting started using uptown studio effects, even though essentially his sound is suited to simple recording techniques. Rob Stoner, his current bassman, says that Dylan likes to start out each session by kind of jamming and playing old rock and roll and country tunes, and then let the tape roll. Many recording artists and critics feel that this is the only way to achieve spontaneity. And, too, some singers, such as Dylan, like to sing *with* the band, while others like to come in and "overdub," which means performing one part over another part that has already been recorded so that when played back both parts *seem* as if they were done together at the same time.

Chet Atkins, who claims a preference for such simple methods, said he could kick Les Paul, who talked Ampex into building the 4-track and then the 8-track machine. Atkins misses those days back when he made recordings on a 2-track machine. There was spontaneity in it. For when you compare an arranged, overdubbed, mixed tune with one that was done live, you will see that there is a certain rough edge that is more vital and "lives" with more immediacy than the kind of sophisticated sound produced in most studios today.

It seems that the requisite attitude toward studio sound today is to put in all the quality, refinement, and expertise possible, resulting in a smooth and slick sound. And this is done without questioning, without analysis. Somehow it's what everybody wants. Competing with that sound is almost a necessity and it is the sound we are most likely to have around for a while, made possible by the half-a-million-dollar studio.

So whether an engineer is working with a group that wants to be recorded live, with people who want all the so-called advantages of electronic sound, or with people who want to discover new sounds, what an engineer in all cases has to do is to translate live instruments into what is essentially a dead medium. Then he has to build an atmosphere around those instruments, especially if they're acoustic instruments, so that they come across without losing too much. Dave Charles, an engineer, producer, and artist, said in a *Melody Maker* article that he feels, as most engineers do, the producer's and engineer's job is to get the talent of the artist channeled through "the board" so that the initial talent is on tape. The engineer sits there at the console pushing the right buttons and switches so that there is no distortion, no mistakes — for instance, if the level of something isn't high enough or someone didn't push the button and the producer wants it played back . . . and it ain't there! Essentially, an engineer has to be adept at seeing that the basic things are down on tape with good fidelity, and that they're clean.

It seems that the increase in the number of tracks used by most of the professional recording studios may be leveling off. Most people seem satisfied with twenty-four tracks. Lots of music doesn't need anywhere near that many tracks to record properly. One set of drums can take four to six or more tracks in themselves, though a string quartet may use only two or four tracks. If there is a basic four- or five-piece band, with a minimum amount of overdubbing, an engineer can get by with an 8-track setup. But if later you want to add violins, backup voices, or horns to the tape more tracks for the overdubbing are needed.

A lot of people with no studio experience think that because they can't work a cassette tape recorder, they could never work in a studio, or that because of a certain fear, fear of electricity, for example, they could never be an engineer. It's like someone who is afraid of broken glass feeling that he could never work in the stained-glass medium.

But the quantity of tracks used today shouldn't scare you, because it really isn't all that much more complicated than simple one-track recording. Tracks just accumulate. If you've got one channel to record on, you just add to that, sixteen or twenty-four times.

Part of what has kept the technology in this constant state of expansion has been the demands of the recording artists and producers themselves. Besides the "bigger is better" attraction, musicians have been dazzled by all those lights and gauges and hardware.

Then, there's also been a search for creative freedom. The way it works is this. Musicians almost always have a vision in their mind, and as an engineer you don't want to have to speculate on how you'll have to mix the whole thing down to four tracks so that you can free up another track if necessary. So if you operate a 16-track studio, musicians can try things out and you won't have to erase. Anything can be put on an extra track as an experiment, and if the artists or producers don't like it, it can be scratched.

Although there isn't the same demand as before for more tracks, there are still designers coming out with the "latest" (read "biggest") board. John Holbrook is looking forward to a nice smooth digital system that will work without a lot of hassle. "After a certain point there is only a certain amount of buttons and knobs you can handle." Roger Powell has a rapport with engineering because he uses synthesizers. Roger feels that it's becoming obvious that the big board can't be manipulated all at once, and also that it ceases to be elegant-looking.

How to Get into It

Engineers come from all kinds of backgrounds; they aren't all radio and wire freaks, or born tinkerers. Nancy Daking, the wife of Geof Daking, chief engineer for Sound Ideas, a recording studio in New York City, feels the essence of what it takes is "a mind that hasn't been intimidated into believing it can't do something." Therefore, she feels that the possibility of women getting into engineering is blocked only by the commonly held prejudice that women can't do mechanical things. Geof agrees and also feels that it takes a mentality and attitude that will sit down and cope with the language and technology without backing down when things get complicated. Very few studio engineers were ever teenage ham radio operators, or kids who loved to take apart old Zeniths or wristwatches or frogs. Many have some background in music, or a father who played piano in some Rainbow Room.

The most prevalent way a person becomes an engineer is to work either for a record company that has studios, or for an independent studio as a "go-for." Since most studios love free help (how can they refuse?), asking for a job as apprentice to the engineer might land you inside the door. Eventually you may become an assistant, sometimes called a "tapie," and you'll go on salary. This is probably the best way to learn. Working without pay for three months costs less than going to most colleges, particularly professional colleges. After that, working for minimal pay until a break comes around is a realistic and direct way to learn how to run the board.

Many studios hire people who have gone to one of the few schools around that teach recording engineering. If a studio suddenly needs an assistant and no one's around, they call the school. However, engineers we talked to feel that these people fail to deliver much in the way of practical, useful knowledge, and also tell us that some of these schools that teach audio engineering charge an excessive amount of money. One in New York City has no equipment, uses a blackboard, charges $400 for a six-week, eighteen-hour-a-week course, with thirty or more students in the class. So when you look for courses in your area, be sure to size up any class beforehand. The Recording Institute of America has branches all over, enabling it to go into areas, usually into the biggest studio in town, for six weeks, holding weekly or bi-weekly classes in engineering. (Its New York City address is 15 Columbus Circle, New York, NY 10023.)

Dave Charles feels that a producer or an engineer can't really be taught how to do the job, and that natural flair is all-important. And speaking of natural flair, the way Geof Daking got his first job as an engineer is kind of inspiring. Geof was the drummer for The Blues Magoos, so he was somewhat familiar with the studio from the artist's end. The Magoos had just broken up, and Geof was broke too. So he decided to get himself a job as an engineer. We had just gone with Geof to an exhibition of studio equipment in the Americana Hotel, and Geof spent the whole afternoon tinkering with one console in particular. (The Audio Engineering Society holds conventions in New York and Los Angeles about six months apart, and professional equipment is on view.) After the exhibit, he called up the manufacturer of that particular console and asked if he could have the names of studios in the New York area who had placed orders. He got a diagram of the equipment from the manufacturer and spent considerable time studying the schematics. When he had the design mastered in his head, he went over to a studio that had *just* placed an order for the console he studied and liked so well. He told the owner how much he loved the console and showed off his knowledge. To the owner it seemed that Geof knew the new console like the back of his hand. Since that moment, Geof has been the main man in that studio. Everything has been relegated to him, even designing and installing the air conditioning, and eventually designing and ordering equipment for a second huge studio. The studio room Geof designed is two floors high. In the sound booth the carpet is not only wall-to-wall, but floor-to-ceiling, a cheap way to decorate a wall, when you consider it costs $10 a yard and needs only vacuum maintenance. It seems to be there to absorb sound — an illusion, since we found out that all the walls are doubled, with six inches of soundproofing insulation between them. The studio room is in part paneled with battleship-gray undulating foam rubber, another illusionary acoustical material which makes you feel as if it's keeping the sound from bouncing around. What you can't see, the six-inch insulation, keeps the place from echoing like a 100-foot-long greenhouse, plus isolating the studio from the roar of the city.

Small speakers are hanging all over the ceiling, painted and camouflaged in mat black. Ah, but there are two special speakers, looking like Martian moose trophies, also mat black, designed and executed by the same Jack Weisberg who designed his first large speaker system in a house Dylan bought in Woodstock.

But when it comes to outfitting a studio, decor is cheap. The money is in that equipment, the speakers, the board, the tape decks, the mikes, even if some of it is housed in metal as thin and shaky as a cheap kitchen cabinet.

Access is the major problem in learning. Dave Charles got access to the studio equipment back in the days when the studio protocol was very loose and electronics were a bit more simple. Being a musician and knowing a lot of people in the studio, he used to have a go at the board on his own when the engineer stepped out for a sandwich or something. "That's a good way of finding your way around," he says, and today he is an engineer, a producer, and also a performer.

For Roger Powell, the synthesizer fulfilled a yearning. When he was ten years old, after a year of piano lessons, his parents gave him a tape recorder to record himself. "I really liked music," he told us, "but I was intrigued with gadgets. I began to see that I could turn the tape upside down and could speed it up and that kind of thing." Roger calls himself a professional musician and an amateur engineer; although when working in a recording studio in Atlanta, Georgia, where he "learned to deal with the sound in a studio," Roger engineered the hit "Games People Play." He had access to the studio synthesizer and began to record little demos of himself. Since it was still fairly unknown, he gave lectures on behalf of an English manufacturer about its synthesizer. Later Roger gave lectures around the country for Arp out of Boston, worked with Bob Runstein (whose book we recommend) at Intermedia in Boston, and was one of the original designers of the basic system Emerson uses onstage. "The major problem for people today who want to be involved in contemporary means of expression, video, and so forth, is somehow having access to the equipment."

John Holbrook wishes he'd combined his two interests a long time ago. He was studying to be an electrical engineer, but couldn't sustain it. Music was an outlet for him at school. He got a job in London as a disc cutter (transferring the tape to disc), and now is using a combination of his earlier interests in his work as a recording engineer.

Maintenance and Ordering Equipment

The main thing to keep in mind is that there are many levels of awareness you can have about the equipment you're working with. Kent Duncan began five years ago as a five-dollar-an-hour mastering engineer in San Fernando Valley. Now he owns his own two-studio operation, Kendun Recorders. With the help of people he knew who were good at electronic design he decided to work on improving equipment he had rather than buy all new equipment. "We feel the best thing to do is improve to your own specifics," he says. He has two 24-track consoles, one used as a fail safe in case of equipment malfunction in a large live session.

David Shaw, a drummer in many bands including a long gig for Van Morrison, used to have an 8-track studio. Jean, his wife, learned to operate the board because no one else was around, which freed him to play drums on occasion. She later engineered a Van Morrison album, but when we asked her if she was going to make a career of engineering, she told us that she felt she wasn't a "real" engineer because she didn't know how to repair the equipment. But we've talked with engineers who tell us that good ones sometimes know nothing about repairing equipment, they know only what the buttons will do. Others insist that you don't have to know circuit design or how a transistor works to be able to troubleshoot and maintain the equipment. Just by working with it you get familiar with all the little things that can happen and you learn to fix them in a limited way or else how to bypass the problem temporarily.

Some studios have full-time personnel who maintain the equipment. Geof insists that it's a matter of wanting to learn, and if a person is going to be overwhelmed by a maze of wires, a wall of rejection will be set up. For that person who is afraid or put off at the prospect of finding the one wire out of ten thousand that is shorting out somewhere, take solace from everyone who's done it, it's not as difficult as it looks. It is a matter of getting in there and concentrating. Reading repair manuals, accepting the inevitability of breakdowns precisely at the worst possible moments also help you to be able to anticipate problems by recognizing warnings that often appear before the actual breakdown.

There's not much point in being guilt-ridden because one isn't an expert on repair. In technical fields there is probably an overemphasis on being a specialist, meaning that one has to maintain an ego as *well* as the equipment. "You don't actually fix anything," says Geof, whose attitude seems healthy. "You have this tremendously complex system of components that are all doing this job, and if an individual component fails, and you have a basic understanding of the system, you can find another way of getting from point a to point b. You don't necessarily have to be able to take the component apart and replace a transistor or even know what a transistor is. But you can know how to step around it, to continue at any cost. The show must go on." Sometimes equipment failure occurs just before or during a session and you can't "step around it" and continue. What happens then is that the studio has to pay the musicians for their time. And what's worse for the engineer is that the studio employees hate it because they've become the butt of all kinds of derogatory comments that the musicians invariably make, which doesn't help the situation.

The criteria for the kind of equipment ordered are usually determined by the engineer and the studio owner. The problem complained about most is a company's inability to deliver on time. At any one time in the United States there are probably not more than half a dozen manufacturers of the best and largest multitrack consoles that can deliver on time with all the particular specs that the studio has ordered incorporated.

There are always small companies making customized equipment, but often they are deeply involved in research and development (R & D) and are not yet really into the business of delivering the product. Thus they could go bankrupt in the middle of putting a piece of equipment together, so they're naturally a bad risk.

Some magazines to look at are: *Recording Engineer Producer; Journal of Audio Engineering Society;* and *Studio Sound* (British); and a very good book with diagrams, used all over the industry by the pros, is Robert E. Runstein's *Modern Recording Techniques,* published in 1974 by Howard W. Sams & Co., Inc., distributed by the Bobbs-Merrill Co., Inc., at $9.95.

Being a Diplomat

It's sometimes hard for people who have preconceived ideas about the "togetherness" that is supposed to happen in the studio suddenly to realize that it's really a business world with a strict pecking order and some rigid definitions of function. The necessity of being a diplomat is usually the farthest thing from one's mind as one gravitates toward an engineering career. But, one's reputation and consequently the job depends on being diplomatic, not to mention one's salary.

The control booth is really headed by the engineer. Although he is *not* the boss of the session, he is head of the studio and has to be in control of everything and everyone. This is a responsibility that takes some psychological know-how and finesse, something one doesn't ordinarily think about when considering the actual job of engineering. All the people in the studio make demands on the engineer. The artists need the right word of encouragement at the right time, the producer has to have confidence in what's going on, the hangers-on have to be told to be quiet, the studio owner has to be set at ease, the record company A & R people will have criticisms that have to be dealt with, and all this can be occurring simultaneously within the engineer's realm of authority.

Within the trade an engineer is often judged more on his effectiveness as a diplomat than on his ability to perform the actual functions. For example, an engineer might be working on an album with one artist for a solid month, and perhaps the producer is the kind of person who is totally, maybe even overly, open to all suggestions from the engineer to the point of being entirely dependent on him. That producer might spread the word around that the engineer was a right-on professional, but the next day the engineer might make similar suggestions to a different producer who didn't want his suggestions at all and who later tells people that the engineer is the worst in the business!

There is an unspoken rule in the studio that musicians must stay out of the control room; it isn't their province. Essentially the engineer works directly with the producer, who tells the engineer what he wants. But should an engineer work with a group who want him to sit there and cover most of the producing roles, he will record them and also tell them what he thinks, whether it sounded rough, or whatever. That is, he'll do the basic producing chores. This happens when a group is essentially producing itself. However, the rule is that an engineer must fill whatever job isn't being covered by anyone else.

And there are many combination engineers-producers, such as Tommy Dowd, who records a lot of top artists such as Rod Stewart. There is a theory that you can't be objective about the music if you take on too many functions such as performing, producing, and engineering at the same time, but since some are doing it and doing it successfully, like Todd Rundgren — there seems to be no reason why this can't be also a good combination for those who know they can handle it.

Engineers realize that many of the people they work with don't know just what it is engineers do or can do. Even producers with well-respected names in the industry sometimes don't know half the things studio technology is capable of. They want some effect but aren't sure how they're going to get it. It's like shooting in the dark; they might have only the vaguest notion of what they're asking the engineer to do. And the industry is rich in catch-phrases that stem from a lack of exact knowledge. Roger Powell says the phrase he never tires of hearing and one that's used a lot when a producer is working with musicians and can't precisely express himself is, "get friendly with it." Say a drummer is not really into what he's doing, a producer will say, "It's not right, it's not right, get friendly with it!" Or a producer will say to the musicians, "One, two, three, cook!" Or he could say, "Make it sound different," which is like telling someone to "say something brilliant." That can have the opposite effect of being too much of a challenge and can turn off creative efforts.

When you visit a session for the first time, the studio sounds like another world. We were at a session where the trombonist was alone in the studio, having problems, going over his few measures again and again. Someone in the booth wanted to know if "it was in that one?" The answer was, "No, it was in the overdub." Someone else asked, "Could you punch that one in?" "But where is it," asked another, "bar nineteen?" The engineer said, "Just give me a bomp-da-bomp, that's all I need." Which he received from the trombonist; and then he said, "OK, keep rolling 'em." They work incessantly like this to get the trombone down the way those in the control booth wanted it. "Let me get the tempo." One of the guys in jeans, the producer, wanted to go in the studio with the trombonist for a minute. The automatic sliding glass door slickly and silently was sucked back into the wall. After the producer passed into the studio, the door closed. It was like "Star Trek" in there, and we discovered that this uncomfortable feeling of being either shut out or shut in has a three-fold purpose. Impressive it is; it ensures that control-room noise won't leak into the studio; and it's a diplomatic way of giving the people in the control room the privacy they need in which to comment, criticize, and generally carry on without the musicians and singer listening in.

In the control booth someone was saying, "Bring up the guitar" (on the playback). After they heard the trombonist with the brought-up guitar, the producer said, "Do you know this little trick? Record the trombone at a slower speed, and when you speed it up, it will go an octave higher and sound like a trumpet, like a slide trumpet." The trombone was recorded slower, but when it was played back, they still didn't like it. It was recorded again, played back again. The engineer was instructed to "bring it down" to integrate it with the rhythm track, but the arranger warned, "It's going to blow the tweeter right out." The engineer glanced at the alarm light and said, "The bulb hasn't blown yet."

Since the producer directs the musicians and the engineer and is the boss, John Holbrook pointed out, an engineer has to be more flexible than a producer, and much more diplomatic. Also, he cannot put as much ego into a project; it's just not his function. Although a producer's job in the studio is to get a thing accomplished as quickly and as best he can, and to cut away all the time loss that happens in a recording session, sometimes he can be the one who generates it the most.

The producer's job is to make the musicians at ease and comfortable in the studio; but John feels that a lot of the difficulty a producer has is the fault of the studio itself, which is, in turn, the domain of the engineer in charge of it. Of course, an engineer can't eliminate headphones and things like that. But an innovation John has thought of to ease the shock musicians experience when the red light comes on and they know they're "on" is to install a switch (a manual override over the red recording light) so that he can have a red light on when they're *not* recording and off when they *are* recording. Because when that red light comes on, it means, "Bang, go on, do your thing!" The musicians feel like, "Who, me? You mean, go on *now*?" Another modification to eliminate the suddenness of realizing the red light is ON is the trick of making the red light fade up, like a rheostat. You start recording and the light comes on full within about five seconds of the start. This helps to troubleshoot an area that is really the domain of the producer, which is: to overcome difficulties in order to get what he wants from the musicians more easily. Every studio has its little inventions and innovations. Geof's studio had an alarm light bulb somehow attached to a speaker, so that the bulb would blow before the tweeters blew in the speakers, one of the constant studio nuisances.

Mixing

After the recording, there is the mix. If the producer wants more echo on the drums or vocals, the engineer can put it in at the exact time it should be there. If the vocals aren't loud enough, they are "brought up." If a vocal is weak in one small section, the producer may want it drowned out or may want any number of things, all available through the mixing process. There's a slogan in the industry: "Fix it in the mix." Mixing usually takes a long time. Many times the producer will instruct the engineer in metaphors during the mixing too. He may say, "Make it a little bit more yellow," and it's up to the engineer to interpret that yellow is a more happy sound, or maybe a lighter sound. And it's up to the engineer to know what to put where.

Engineers we've talked to feel that when producers say at the recording session, "Don't worry, guys, we'll fix it in the mix," it is a poor producer's cop-out. Both Geof and John insist that it's all on the tape, you can't change that, and that mainly the mixing is where you bring out what is already on the tape in the most favorable light. If the bass isn't recorded right or if the musicians make mistakes, it's all on the tape, and that's what you have to work with and that's all you're *going* to have to work with.

You often hear that a good cut was lost in a mix, or that the mix made it good. Essentially you have a limited amount of things you can do to the tape on a mixing board. It's up to the producer's ears to tell the engineer what to do, or to the engineer's own ears if it's he who's doing the mixing. One way to get a smooth sound is to bring up the instruments and vocals in a balanced way, so that if you listen to the tape on earphones, both ears are taking in the same quality and quantity of sound.

In England the procedure generally followed is that the engineer who begins a project typically follows it through the mechanical phases from the beginning through the mixing and on to the final mastering of the disc recording. In the United States each process might be handled by a different person. An album might be recorded in several different studios and mixed in another, and so on.

An example of what good mixing can do is what happened to Dylan's *Basement Tapes*. *The Basement Tapes* were originally recorded on a 2-track machine like a Revox. Then eight years later, when those tapes were to be released to the public, they were sent to a studio and electronically rechanneled, cleaned up, and cosmeticized. Taking out noise on a tape can be done to a certain extent by using a device called a Bruwin (or similar equipment). Tapes are edited, equalized (more treble or less, more bass or less; what is known as tone control), and then filtered. The process is similar to the reproduction of a photograph. You can soak different papers with different chemicals for varying lengths of time, in order to bring out different effects, but you are always working from the original negative.

Equipment can only do so much in controlling sounds. When a tape slows down ("oooooOOOOOOooooo OOOOOO") and there's flutter (an erratic nervous sound on tape), it can't be eliminated. There are some flaws that are irreparable. If the frequency response is bad, that's it. That's why the quality of the initial recording is so important.

Judgments as to how the piece is getting recorded are being made all the time by the engineer-mixer and the producer. And it's these decisions to make the basic track sound right that are the most challenging.

Editing

This is another function of the engineer: when he cuts out what isn't wanted and then splices the tape back together, that's editing. You might have made twelve takes of one passage and want to use only the twelfth take, so the tape is physically cut and patched and taped together again. The tempo has to match up right, and there are other criteria for editing. After sequencing decisions are made (what songs will go on what side of the record, and in what order), then the master-mixed tape is spliced accordingly. The length of time between the end of one cut and the beginning of the next shouldn't be more than two to six seconds, depending on the difference in mood between the two songs. These decisions are up to the artists and producers but if you as an engineer ever do get involved, the guidelines to consider are similar to what a radio programmer takes into account when he schedules one song after another. Of course, the best song is usually the first cut on an album and the best songs are on side one.

The next step is to provide a 7½ inch per second (i.p.s.), ¼-track tape for all those who want one, so that they can hear and approve it before the record is pressed. A copy for the studio file is made at 15 i.p.s. before the master leaves the studio.

Overdubbing

Overdubbing allows one to record a track on tape that has had track or tracks recorded on it already. When it is played back, it sounds as if both or all were recorded simultaneously. Most people with an interest in recording and its processes know that a record can be made without the backup singers ever meeting the lead vocalist, which was what happened when Tony Orlando made the first record with Dawn. After he dubbed in his vocal on a tape that already had the instrumentals down, that tape went on to Chicago (or Detroit) to another studio for the two backup singers to dub in their part. In this case, it's reported that Tony Orlando was nervous about meeting the women he'd never seen when, after the success of the record, he wanted them to join him as a group.

Overdubbing is modus operandi in the studio. Some people speak of adding parts to basic recorded tracks as "sweetening." Others think of the overdub as a creative function where one can pick and choose, like making a collage, until everything works. John Cale, for instance, will record in one take to get the spontaneity that can't be duplicated any other way. Then sometimes he will spend $2,000 on four or five overdubs to add to the original recording. Finding that after the mix he likes the sound better without the overdubs, he starts over with the live track. There is always that someone, like Paul McCartney, who wants to do everything himself. Obviously it's physically impossible for an artist to play all the instruments simultaneously. That's where overdubbing really comes in.

Overdubbing is great when you need it. If one musician is not with it during one recording session, for example, the track can be taken out and overdubbed when he *is* with it, or else another musician can add the track instead. Many tracks are redone and many musicians get the reputation of being able to troubleshoot by overdubbing a bad track when the first one couldn't cut it.

Hours

The big subject of conversation in the recording studios is alimony ("Don't send my checks to the old address because my wife will cash them!" and "How much is So-and-so paying So-and-so?"). The divorce rate among engineers is high and some tell us they feel it's probably because of the hours they work. Not only are the hours long, but they're erratic. Many album sessions don't start until late (9 P.M.) and go on until dawn or exhaustion, whichever comes first. Musicians are envied for being able to be independent and freakish with their working hours, and the studio owners prefer that studios run eighteen to twenty-four hours a day to utilize fully the expensive equipment.

Besides the time spent in a session, there are big hours spent keeping the hardware in shape, checking out the piece of equipment that has a mysterious, unpredictable, ever so slightly audible "click." There may be strange hums from nowhere, a weird short in one of the mike cords, and all this takes hours — all away from home. For many engineers the studio is a home away from home and the attention it needs is endless. Some will manicure the studio into a near perfect specimen.

The regular schedule of a busy engineer is two to three sessions of four hours each a day, with time out for an apple somewhere toward the late afternoon.

Pay

Being busy and keeping long hours has a lot to do with how much money you can make, too. Many staff (permanent) engineers are not on salary, but are paid according to the number of hours they work; many are put on basically to cover the studio and don't actually work all that many hours. They may only make $150 a week even when there is a heavy week of dates if it's the kind of production that brings in its own engineer. A really good yearly take is around $30,000, with the average around $15,000 to $20,000.

The *freelance* engineer has as clients producers and/or artists who have found it successful to work with him. He usually gets paid well, typically receiving 20 percent of the fee paid to the studio for studio time. If a producer likes a certain engineer and likes to work with him a lot, that guarantees him that many more sessions to work on.

In a large, busy studio with A, B, and C studios, there is likely to be a chief engineer who seldom, if ever, does the actual work on dates. He's on salary, because he is there to oversee all the recording and all the maintenance of the equipment.

Rarely, but it does happen, engineers get points, or percentages (royalty) of the income from the eventual sale of the record. This is negotiated between the engineer and the producer and/or the record company.

Recognition

When you see an engineer's name on the album, it isn't necessarily there because the engineer has a reputation as a hit-maker. The Beatles, for example, had some of the biggest hits ever, yet the engineers on those early hits never received any notice at all. Within the industry people know and spread the word about engineers and they get a reputation and consequent recognition. Engineers like Phil Ramone, Tom Dowd, and Eddy Cramer are famous in the industry whether they get credit on an album or not.

Women as Engineers

We have used the unmodern "he" and "him" because if we'd discussed this subject with anything but males in mind we'd be hypocritical. Engineering is an almost exclusively male-dominated function. One reason given for this is that most producers are used to working with men, so if they walk into a studio and see that the engineer is a woman, it would take some adjustment, if they managed to adjust at all. Obviously there would be no need to, if such blatant sexism weren't so thoroughly accepted by everyone in the music business. But additional prejudices make the field of engineering a hard one to crack: technology is associated with "brains," with "science," and with the "unemotional control" that goes with it, and these are believed to be the exclusive domain of men. It may seem odd that women have an *easier* time getting assistant-to-the-engineer jobs in studios, but it really is the "secretary" thing all over again. Women look good and can provide relief to the male-dominated atmosphere of most studios, not to mention the fact that they tend to be good workers and can handle well the down-to-earth details of managing a studio.

A female assistant we talked to several years ago, when she was in her early twenties, had gotten into engineering because at the time she was living with a guitarist and used to help him set up his equipment, splice broken cords, and perform other jobs. Another young woman went from being an assistant in a New York studio to engineering for Cat Stevens and Billy Preston, but we heard she is constantly running into antifeminist attitudes, especially in studio owners. And then Jean Shaw, whom we mentioned before, who doesn't consider herself an engineer, did Van Morrison's album in the early Seventies.

As more women get jobs as assistants, learn to operate the board, and use the equipment, eventually there will be a lot of knowledgeable females available, and the studios will be forced to give them positions of responsibility commensurate with their abilities. When they are hired as engineers, and people realize there is no sexual bias in technological know-how, then the stigma will wear off.

5

Session Men

STUDIO MUSICIAN, session man, sideman, backup man —
whatever he's called, his job is to play someone else's music
whenever, wherever, and however needed. He may sometimes do as many as two to four sessions a day, each with different people and different music. And because session men
have to have the versatility and skill necessary to be able to
pick up quickly what is required of them, other musicians respect them immensely.

There are groups of session men clustered about the
various recording centers of the country who are experts at
bringing about a certain sound — *super*session men — and
they thus attract stars to record with them: Dylan has gone to
Nashville, for example; Joni Mitchell uses the L.A. Express.
There are New York supersession soul musicians, Gordon
Edwards, Richard Tee, Steve Gadd, and Bernard Purdie,
among others, who have been playing the kind of rhythm and
blues that was made especially popular in the Sixties by
prominent English rockers and who are the sound behind
many famous people both out on tour and on records.

Having played on so many hits in the past, such supersession groups are used again and again, because they can play what's required and/or bring a sound with them that people are familiar with and associate with hits, and certain producers come to understand their psychology and don't have to second-guess problems. Even so, supersession people are only just beginning to acquire some status and personal recognition such as they've never had up to now. The New York–based supersoul musicians who went out on Joe Cocker's 1976 tour got at times better press than Cocker did himself. It seems that every singer and producer wants them on their albums, and the unfortunate side effect is a narrowing down of the kinds of sounds there are to hear. Some stars are able to see this happening, like Maria Muldaur, who is more interested in artistic growth than she is in counting on a certain sound. She told us that there's pressure from all the producers in Los Angeles to use famous session men and that what has happened is that the sound on the albums coming from L.A. is all the same.

Naturally, producers would encourage singers to use supersession men. After all, they have to keep up with everyone else; it's a safe, cozy, and dependable choice; and also, by the way, they know that studies have proved that when these better known session men are credited on an album, it further boosts sales, especially if they are used with unknown artists (which means, of course, that the public is coming to recognize and look for their names).

Some of these better known session groups have made their own albums, for instance, the crème de la crème of the Nashville studio men, who've turned out two *Area Code 615* albums. A more recent example is Gordon Edwards' *Stuff* album. But in the fact that even these relatively famous musicians will be likely to play any date that comes to them when their time is free, to do anything from making commercials to recording tracks behind a very bad vocalist, the essential nature of studio work is revealed. The musicians' union scale is at the moment $110 for three hours' work. And if you have an extra three hours unbooked, it is irrelevant what kind of music you play or whom you play with. This is the reason that, of all working musicians, it is the studio musician who habitually refers to it as "a job." While Gordon Edwards can say of himself, as he did in a recent publication, that though he is not a quarterback, he plays on the winning team, he, like all studio musicians, is still basically an employee who executes what another creates. And while his success may be measured by the number of hits he has to his credit, it's never really *his* hit.

Sidemen also go out on tours with singers. Supersession drummer Bernard Purdie, sideman for many famous singers such as Aretha Franklin, went out on Jeff Beck's last tour, but prefers to work behind a female. "Females are much more expressive, facially and bodily. I get an extra thing from the ladies. You can take from the line of the dress, or the pants, or her hand movements . . . you follow her movement. Watching them, you are able to hit them, when the time comes, at the right time, whenever it's necessary." This is especially necessary for drummers, because lead singers listen only to the drum and bass, in order to get the freedom they need to sing lead freely. In *Janis,* David Dalton's book, there is an interview with Joplin and Bonnie (of Bonnie & Delaney) in which they talked about drummers. They both agreed that as lead singers they listen to the bottom, that that is the kick you need. Janis said, "I did a kick with my ass to the right, and the drummer went bam! with a rim shot, and I turned around and said, 'Where did you learn to play behind singers like that?' and he said, 'I used to back strippers.' That's how you learn to play, man." Working behind males can be more difficult. "Males are harder," Bernard says. "They're always coming off romantic, and the romantic part for them is always expressed in the chest and shoulders, so I never get a chance to see that part of their body and see what it's doing. The male is always out front. He gets down on his knees and all that kind of stuff, but I never get to see it. I love it, though, because it's a challenge to me to find out what he's doing. It really is."

Getting In

Connections is the name of the game when it comes to studio work. Without them it just can't happen. First among them is the producer, who is the main hiring agent of studio musicians, and who usually schedules only those whose work he knows. Sometimes the artist will want particular musicians; sometimes the arranger insists or is asked to get the musicians for the date; or one musician may get all the others together. Whoever gets the musicians together is called a "contractor" and makes double scale at the session. Decisions on who gets hired are often made way outside of the pure considerations of musical ability: favors are owed; favoritism is played; deals are made on a "you hire me, I'll hire you the next time" basis. It's politics, it's cronyism; but more subtly, it seems to be a method of self-protection against the ever-surging newcomers, always a threat to the in crowd. In order for a hopeful young musician to land even his first few breaks as a session man, he's got to push, and keep on pushing for more breaks. Most musicians feel threatened, whether consciously or not, by younger musicians, who someday may be taking their place, and their insecurity is aggravated by the fact that the music industry of the Seventies has tightened up economically. This is also an age of ego, or as Tom Wolfe describes it, the "Age of Me." Musicians are more into themselves. This wasn't so true back in the Sixties, when the youth movement was such a driving force, and mutuality and sharing had more of a hold. So when you are trying to make your way into studio work, it would be wise to remember that underneath that glad hand may lie a person who feels that there is a survival battle going on, and who will not go to any big effort to help you. It's an all-too-human trait not to want to

87

extend oneself to others for fear that they may soon go beyond, and we're not passing judgments. We're just suggesting that you use your common sense as well as your wishful expectations, so you can move into the job market without too much paranoia.

Bernard Purdie says, "Most of the time you don't get there unless somebody takes you — but it's really essential to go out and ask for jobs yourself, to stay on people's backs until you get what you want. If you are trying to break in, getting no for an answer can be very discouraging; it can wear you down." But Bernard has a street-wise attitude about the word *no:* "*No* doesn't mean anything. *No* is temporary. *No* stands for now. Say to yourself, 'I'm going back tomorrow and ask for a job. Eventually somebody's going to give me a shot.' "

Most first chances come about because of some catastrophe or because of other people's mistakes. Someone isn't playing well, or perhaps doesn't show up for a job.

Bernard Purdie himself got his first break by being persistent and by making sure he was seen. As a kid he came up to New York City from the South and proceeded to haunt places like Charlie's, C & D's on Fiftieth Street, or the Turf Club, where all the studio musicians hung out. He'd practice his drums early in the day, then would hang out from nine to five, and, as if it were a regular job, would try to beat the rush hour at five, like any other working man. He would ask for jobs of Buddy Lucus, who was the number-one saxophone player in the city, and Barney Richman, a bass player, who was the number-one contractor. Consistently for six months he asked them. They got tired of looking at him and would say, "Here comes that crazy drummer." They never heard him play in all that time. One day the drummer didn't show up for a date, but Bernard was right around the corner, so he got his big chance. Although they liked him and asked him to play again, they told him that he was too loud and that everything he had done was wrong. What he had done was to put ten years of drumming into three minutes to show what he could do.

Part of the politics of getting studio jobs sometimes involves becoming buddies with a star or someone influential. And it does work, though each individual approaches it differently. Now that Bernard has paid his dues, so to speak, he feels today that if there was no other way to get jobs than to maintain that after-hours personalism, if he had to hang out with someone day in and day out to get a job, he'd be very dissatisfied. "I don't smoke. I sit and have some bitter lemon or whatever, but I'm not going to sit here in the bar for no two, three hours at a time while you're getting yourself stoned, plastered, to cater to getting a job. Even somewhat established people do that, [but] most of them drink anyway. It doesn't necessarily have anything to do with a lack of confidence. And you get buddy-buddy. You start talking about your personal business. But I've found it's best to leave my personal business personal. It's mine. I don't have the problem of my personality or my ego getting in the way. I get along with people and I can get good at my job when it comes down to being good. And that's all that really matters: doing the job."

Finding a gimmick that will help you promote yourself can be useful, and if an idea comes to you, consider it thoughtfully. Bernard's friend Jim Tyrell (now a vice president at Epic) suggested fifteen years ago that he put up a sign in all the studios he played advertising himself. Bernard's sign read, "Pretty Purdie, Little Old Hit Maker," a self-assertion on the order of Muhammad Ali's "I'm the greatest," and made four years before. It worked. Although he had played on a few songs that had become hits, he feels it was his sign, which became familiar in the recording studios, that quickly made him one of the most successful drummers in New York City.

Contracting

As we mentioned above, studio musicians themselves sometimes contract other players for studio dates and collect double scale for doing so, as they almost always play on the date too. They also put bands together for stars who are going out on tour. Bernard likes to contract, because he gets a chance to put some of his students into the studio or on tours. For instance, having just played on Ralph Palmer's album, Bernard was asked by Palmer to get together a group who could go out on tour with him, younger musicians he could afford, rather than the ones he knew right then who, because of their reputations, would be almost twice as expensive.

When Rob Stoner was offered the job of playing bass for Dylan's album *Desire,* Rob suggested the drummer who had played with him for years. "Bass players and drummers come in pairs, and Bob knew this. He dug my playing and figured that the drummer I was using would only enhance that. And he did dig it to the extent that we were the core of his band for two tours. All the versions of my group have come and gone, but Howie, my drummer, and I have stayed together." Bernard confirms Rob's observation from his own experience, saying that drummers and bass players are the most secure members of the band. There just are not that many of them around in the first place, and they seem to be innately capable, because of the nature of their instruments, of taking a supporting role. The other players are much more competitive. "They're all trying to get the number-one spot, it's that simple," says Bernard. When the rest of the band picks up on how cooperative and cooled out the bass and drummer are together, they usually settle down and start getting along better with each other too. Producers tend to be more considerate of the bass and drummer, because they are hard to keep and hard to find.

All about Reading Music

To be a successful sideman you need to do more than "practice on your ax." As Bernard says, "Make sure that when you go to do a job, you can do it, *plus!*" When he started, he knew what he could do and couldn't do. "I didn't have the technical knowledge that was needed to sustain, but I knew I could play. That's all the difference between night and day, knowing what you can do best and what you can't do."

Most people agree that the ability to read music is one of the first qualifications for studio work. You have to be able to scan or flash on the charts (musical notations prepared by the arranger) as quickly as possible. There are studio musicians who do not know how to read and yet work regularly, but they are the exception.

"Music is read the way you read a book — with understanding," Bernard says. "Do you read it fluently, do you skip, do you use key words to make knowledge of what it is? When you look at a note, you also know how you're going to interpret that note because of the preceding notes. You find out it gets easier and easier to understand what you have and what you don't have on the charts. It doesn't matter what kind. I can go from Count Basie to Jack Jones to Led Zeppelin for interpretation."

Reading has always been a source of anxiety to musicians who can't do it. Many musicians first learn their craft by picking riffs off their favorite records, and do not have the patience and prudence necessary to learn to read notes, play chords, practice scales, and study music composition and theory. They may have had the early experience of finding out that when they read, the sounds came out cold and unexpressive, and they couldn't relate to them as they felt they should. This might be the reason why many musicians get the idea that "when you read music, you lose your soul." But "don't worry about it," says Bernard, "it's not true. Reading is the best part of what music is, because it is the simplest."

If you are a musician who is self-taught, and you want to learn to read, you should expect to find it frustrating at first. Your playing abilities will far outstrip your reading abilities. But when you pass a certain point, it will begin to feed back to you. Perhaps you'll go beyond yourself, and the frustration will leave you, and you will realize that you still have a soul!

Being in Syntony

Besides knowing how to read, you also have to be able to follow whoever is conducting and have empathy with the other musicians around in the studio and the people in the booth. Warren Bernhardt, a piano player, told us that you have to be able to be "what used to be called in school 'in syntony.'" Our dictionary defines the word as being in resonance; also, in agreement. Warren explains the term: "The more you're tuned into what's happening around you, the more you're in syntony." And the more you're called back.

Diplomacy and Psyching out What the Producer Wants

Bernard takes his students into recording sessions when he can. He understands the word "technical" to include finding out what is involved in the realm of the studio — "how you have to act, how you have to control yourself, how you have to 'button your lip,' how you have to learn to speak up when someone is undermining you, how you have to learn to control most of your emotions, which is number one!"

Obviously, the studio isn't a place where you can go in like gangbusters, or even be carefree and natural. Bernard considers this kind of advice on the need for grooming one's own ego "technical." "Before you can even get involved with the engineer, you've got to bring yourself to a certain frame of mind, because you've got somebody dictating to you all the time."

The producer is the boss of the session, and he wants the respect due a boss. Once, at dinner with producer Alan

Douglas and Michael Cuscuna (Bonnie Raitt's producer), Bernard related some of his early indiscretions in the studio, such as how he'd yell across the studio to a horn player that he was off-key. This is the producer's job, and Cuscuna became very serious as he said, "You're not supposed to do that, especially if you're a drummer." And then he added, "Musicians should show respect." Though many people who are "top dog" actually get obedience out of fear, true studio diplomacy is a matter of mutual respect and knowing what your function is in a given situation. Even Cuscuna, whose job it is to direct the session, is thinking of not speaking to the musicians over the speakers from the control booth anymore. It's not the most delicate way to correct someone.

Bernard explains what it's like working with producers: "This man calls you for one reason — to get what he has in his mind out, so he can hear it, because he can't do the job himself. That's what you are, a tool."

Understanding this, he has found it easy to psych out what producers want, and it's usually what they've heard on somebody else's record. "They ask you if you know So-and-so's record. But you have to be ahead of the producer, because he may really want the opposite kind of thing, or something 'in the vein' of the record he's pointed out. You have to pick out things he says, because he can't pick *your* brain, and, eventually, if you let him talk long enough, he gets down to articulating what he wants."

What we want to stress is that things are not always perfectly clear in the music business, nothing is regimented, nothing is particularly consistent or laid out clearly for you every time. Warren Bernhardt has gone into the studio when the producer has had a definite idea in mind of what he wants to go on tape. Sometimes the producer even tells him the feeling he wants to go along with the music, which might be all written out as completely as a Bach prelude. At other times Warren walks in and the producer says, "We're going to have to make this one up." When this happens, Warren likes it, though he'd also like to get the credit and the money for doing the arranging, which doesn't always happen. He might work with an artist or producer in the studio, for example, developing ideas on the piano and overdubbing tracks. When later a song was orchestrated, several of Warren's ideas got in there, but credit did not. However, for Warren the opposite can be even worse: if the ideas he puts into the music are then taken out again, then he really feels "squashed." So any way you look at it, there's a chance of feeling deflated or exploited, and it's just one of those things that makes hired work like that of the studio musician potentially dissatisfying for some people.

Session Cats' Discontent

Professional studio musicians are sometimes referred to as "you studio cats," implying that they can do anything well. But if you have a drive to play your own music or want to develop something personal or even *keep* something personal, there are many drawbacks in this work.

Many musicians do studio work solely for the money. Some feel it's like doing piecework. Leon Russell, who was a studio musician for years, called it "glorified factory work."

"A lot of it is just a big money game," says Warren. "You always feel there's a big corporation running it all, whether it's a disco or a jingle you're doing. There's always a guy from Exxon, plus a guy from the advertising agency Exxon deals with, in the studio with you."

Sidemen feel they have to accept all dates offered them so they'll continue to be called. They might have only one date booked, for which they'll nonetheless have to travel whatever distance it is to the studio, or they might have a full day's booking of maybe four or five sessions. And they may not know what they're going to be playing until they get there or even whether it's a demo or an album (which means more money).

Many session people talk about cutting loose, but the talk never materializes into action because it's hard to get something else going for yourself when you're so busy being a session musician. One reason some don't feel it's gratifying work is that they rarely get to play what they want in the studios; always doing what others want, they feel, tends to destroy their individuality. Also, they usually play so many different kinds of music that it's hard to move into a true personal direction. Drummers have slightly different problems in that though they may not have as many people telling them what to do, they have to maintain a lot of emotional control. Even so, a drummer may be able to express himself to a greater extent than an instrumentalist can.

Some musicians try not to do studio work exclusively or for long periods of time because of the way it cuts in on their personal creativity or interests. Warren comes home from studio work and plays classical music alone or jazz in a group of friends or at clubs. He warns that when you start to feel like a guy on the assembly line in Detroit, each one tightening a bolt, you can also get into that same feeling about your instrument. Something you once had a lot of affection for begins to turn into a mechanical device for making money.

Being a sideman not only categorizes you professionally, it can put a label on you in terms of only one kind of music you're capable of, a real stigma. You get typecast, and this can become one of the pressures dangerous to the individuality of the musician. Next thing you know, you go into the studio to do your own thing and you're lost, because you don't have someone telling you what to do.

Rob Stoner told us how much more satisfaction and ego gratification he gets from being up in front of a live audience, with people knowing who he is, instead of being in "the invisible role of a studio musician," which he was for several years. "But it was like stopping and starting all over [again], when I decided I was going to be a band leader. It is less lucrative at first, of course, and my reputation and experience in the studio field didn't do me much good at all to become a draw, and

95

attract people into the club I was working in." This is true for all but the biggest session men, who *can* draw an audience when they play out in a band of their own.

Bernard tells us that many sidemen have been offered contracts for their own music, but aren't able really to rise to the challenge, or to sustain their efforts. Their problem is precisely that they have grown so good at being sidemen. Their talent and skill lie in being able to bring other people out front. "It's a different ball game to be an artist in the background and one that's out front." And session men are conditioned to lay back. "You can be outstanding on this record and that," says Bernard, "but what happens when you put all of them together? Somebody has to be head man.

"Of course, there are some sidemen who have become leaders, but they are few — Marvin Gaye, who backed-up on drums, and Stevie Wonder, who was a drummer when he was twelve or fourteen, and some others. It's almost unheard of to go backward from being a leader to playing as a sideman."

Another element of studio work that some musicians find emotionally unsatisfying is the practice of overdubbing. Today overdubbing is the most prevalent method of recording, and it means that the studio musician is sometimes virtually alone in the studio, adding his track to the tape and listening to the rest of the music over headphones. Some studio musicians find this process too depersonalized. When we discussed this with Rob Stoner, he observed that most instrumentalists prefer to record live and feel they play best that way. Live means all together, at the same time. "A jazz record is never over-dubbed," Rob says, "because the basis of that whole thing is improvisation, the guys interacting off each other." In fact, the dream recording-studio situation for many musicians is to record live in the studio with a small audience present, to get that electricity happening. As Warren puts it, "You tend to lose it somewhere along the line [in an overdubbed session]. You begin to realize that a million people are going to hear that record, but you can't connect with any of them."

Rob Stoner himself is one of those musicians who doesn't have any strong personal preferences about whether he's doing live or overdubbed work. He likes to focus on the intent of the recording. He recorded live on Dylan's *Desire* album because Dylan's intent was documentation. "Dylan is into capturing the moment in the room more than he's into making a perfect record and having the notes correct. Dylan does everything all at once and refuses to have his mistakes touched up." Rob did admit that recording live has more spontaneity and real feeling than you get from putting the tracks on one by one, but he adds that even playing live in the studio can't approach playing with other people in your living room, since you're still listening to each other over earphones, even though you might all be in the same room together.

Warren Bernhardt only recently met for the first time a baritone player who had been on a lot of records with him. "You don't know who you're playing with when you're overdubbing. The record's released and you haven't even met the other people on the record. You haven't communicated with each other in any kind of way."

Warren prefers recording live because then he has more opportunity for artistic freedom. Rob says you'd probably find that producers and singers often prefer the overdub method because it gives *them* more freedom. "A singer doesn't have to interact that much," and a producer has a lot more control, with a lot more leeway to change the recording when it's overdubbed. And people who like to do everything on a record naturally prefer overdubbing — they have to!

Warren likes to play live on tours and club gigs with a band before they go in to record an album. By the time they get to the studio, they have the material together and can "really cook on it."

Some studio musicians don't mind overdubbing, they may even prefer it. But if you're thinking of working in the studios as a profession, especially if you're an instrumentalist, you should be forewarned that overdubbing is the method you will be using the most.

Session Man as Troubleshooter

Bernard Purdie (like other good session men) is so accomplished that he does a lot of overdubs for producers who have already completed a record, but feel that the drummer was not really that good, so they call him in to do it over.

"What I do, I'm called a troubleshooter. If you're in trouble, call Purdie and he'll fix it up. That's what I do in the business. I fix up records that weren't in the best of shape. If a record fails, a lot of the time it's the drum track. I have to go back to the original as if I'd been on the date from the very beginning and make all that's on there sound good." Bernard listens to the original drummer, and at the same time turns him off and does what he wants to do. "I take the essential thing out of the record that I feel is the thing it needs, based on how it's being done. I take the main ingredient and I make that happen."

When the young, white, self-contained bands of the Sixties started making their albums, and before even the best of them could record with the necessary precision, people like Purdie were called in to lay down another track of whatever was needed. The public at large remains unaware of this. Geoffrey Stokes describes an intricate situation in his book *Star-Making Machinery,* when the studio musician Roger Kellaway was called in to redo a piano part on a Commander Cody album. Just Kellaway's left hand played a piano part on one track, while Cody's own piano player, Frayne, overdubbed the right hand on another track. Stokes describes the respect given to Kellaway by the band. And one can imagine how it must feel to be the man that can save an album!

6

Making Jingles

CREATING MUSIC FOR commercials is the most understated, as well as the most lucrative, part of the music business. It is surrounded with secrecy. When you see a lady about twenty-two years old, dressed in old jeans and T-shirt, going in and out of recording studios all day without fanfare and with just a manager in tow, and you know that she makes two million a year singing commercials, just how understated can the lifestyle be? The truth is, no one wants anyone to know how much money is actually involved in the jingle jungle, and competition is not encouraged.

Since there is essentially no glamour in the commercial industry, the people who get into it for the most part have previously been in some aspect of the music business and then backed (or sneaked) into commercial making. For instance, a singer might have tried the star syndrome and found it wasn't working out; then she got exposed to the commercial field and probably said to herself, "Why should I break my neck and burn myself out for something that might never happen when there is this? I can go in and sing every day for a year and make a million dollars!"

99

Stu Kuby, a producer of jingles for Dancer-Fitzgerald-Sampler, Inc. (one of the few advertising agencies that has an in-house production team for making commercials), told us, "It's hard to land something secure. When it's good, it's a steady and very high-paying job. In records, you often have to put your own money into it in a gamble that you might never see it again, but you may be fortunate to place a master and get your investment back. If the release is not successful, that's it! You break even. Plus, it takes another year to get money coming in even if you are successful. So it's much riskier. The people [jingle people] we work with in the studio are much more successful financially, do much better, than the recording artists, excepting the superstars like Elton John, but the people you see on the charts all the time don't make anywhere near what the jingle singers make. They stay in the background, and that's intentional. They maintain a low profile, in contrast to the pop singer who is the *star*."

Breaking in is easier for a singer than for either an instrumentalist or a producer. The singer comes in to put down her track and if it doesn't work out, it's not that difficult to overdub another voice. So producers and sponsors can afford to experiment somewhat.

But in contrast to a star, who may "burn out" and then make a comeback, the commercial singer has the problem of getting overexposed. Like the employers of a fashion model who tire of a "look," the advertising agencies that buy commercials tire of a singer's "sound." These singers will make a bundle in the five or six years they work, and that's it! Pop singers sometimes become commercial singers as a fill-in before they make their comebacks, such as Barry Manilow, who did all right turning out a very popular McDonald's commercial.

Stu Kuby has a very realistic opinion of the best way to break into the business. He suggests doing the same thing with your commercial concept that also works best in breaking into the recording field as an artist, that is, you've got to make as professional a demo as possible, both in arrangement and performance, and send it to the agencies and/or independent production houses that furnish arrangers and composers for commercials, such as Tom Dawes Productions, Inc., Kevin Gavin Productions (of McDonald's fame), Herman Edel Associates, Inc., and a lot more.

A newcomer, whether in commercials or in writing and singing songs for the pop market, is expected to provide more than the professionals themselves, because the professionals usually have a lot of available people helping them — arrangers, producers, and capable musicians — not to mention the money to pay for all this in advance. But there it is. As a friend once told us, "If you're looking for fairness, you're not going to find it."

There are a few schools that teach commercial producing, one in Toronto, Canada, and one in Boston, the Berklee College of Music. But it's really not taking a single course in school that's going to make you. It's either full-time and a total commitment or nothing, and most often, Stu thinks, it's nothing.

Though we've been told that most agencies do not want to listen to unsolicited tapes for fear of a suit if the person sending it comes to believe that the agency ripped off either his tune or his lyrics, at some agencies tapes that get sent in actually do get heard. Agencies get tapes from individuals all the time. The melodies are rarely used, but sometimes a talent for lyrics may be spotted, and the agency will contact the person who sent in the tape and may assign him a job. Stu Kuby says they are looking for new people constantly, but frankly, he says, "The new people we work with are really not new; just new to *us!*" Well, that's familiar too. The record industry parallels the jingle field, which also like to know in advance all the possible eventualities before working with someone.

Producers want to get things done fast and with some degree of predictability. One agency made two hundred commercials in six months, mostly with the same set of singers every day, twice a day, for months on end. A producer gets to know what each talent can do. The challenge then is to come up with a different sound each time, have the new production sound different from the last, and be interesting. Not always, but mostly. Because everyone is always using the same people, taking from a pool of around fifty suppliers of singers, composers, and arrangers, says Stu, there tends to be a pervasive sameness to the sound. So it's a problem.

If producers were to take on new people based merely on talent and not on experience, they feel they'd be doing some heavy gambling. They wouldn't know whether untried people can produce steadily or whether they are going to be able to "pick up on the politics," which means getting along with other people and so on. But they are always looking — for new sounds, and they do need new material and new people to work with. What will work is somewhat a matter of the right timing and of putting yourself out there in their world. For instance, when a producer for a Pepsi jingle needed a character with a country feel, who had to be genuine, who would come across in a good light, it was necessary to go out to clubs and screen a lot of people. Seventy-five people were found and auditioned in front of a camera, and one was used. But the agency made contacts with about ten of the others to work on other projects. Once Tommy Dawes called Mike Young, who has never done commercials, to send down his tapes because Toyota wanted a rock and roll voice and he thought Mike might be right. Mike sent his tapes by bus to the city from Woodstock, N.Y. Since it was a rush, someone else was found in the city. Later, people close to the business told Mike, "When Tommy called you should have jumped in your car and driven down with the tapes. Apparently singing on a Toyota commercial can bring the singer $50,000 in residuals!

If you send in a tape, it's best to call first, says Stu, "announce your existence," and say you'd like to send your tape.

Letters are OK, but not as good in the busy music world as sound. Obviously with the schedules these producers have, it's hard for them to really respond to an unknown and to contribute anything in the way of criticism or advice. They can listen and if there is something that turns up on a tape, hopefully they will set up an appointment. The foot is in the door.

We asked around to see if one way to break into big-time commercial producing would be to start out in small or medium-sized cities and found that this is where the people who *were* on top finally end up, and not the other way around. It seems that when the pros are tired of commuting or don't like the pressure and the pace, they go to the country.

In the late Sixties, the go-go years on Wall Street and Madison Avenue, when the bright youth were infiltrating the business world, becoming creative directors of ad agencies and investor mavens on Wall Street, the rock and roll sound was just starting to emerge slowly in the jingle jungle. At the time, rock musicians were too interested in pop music's expanding field to get involved in commercial making, just as poets rarely got into writing song lyrics. But just as a few poets did start writing song lyrics, a few rock and roll musicians got into the jingle field. Sometimes at first it was just to be able to support their band, which was their main love.

Those who were involved with the beginning expansion of the youth music (subculture sound) into jingle making got in on the ground floor and soon became aware of how lucrative it really was. They got busier and busier, and now they seem to be overworked completely. People like Tommy Dawes are reported to be busy almost twenty hours a day.

Now that everyone in the field seems to be stacked to the hilt with work, and you hear that commercials are being put out so fast, by so few people, and that there is a lack of both preparation and creative contribution, it seems logical to assume that there *is* room in the jingle-making business. It's also realistic to assume that you're going to have to fight your way in, because those producers, performers, arrangers who are already established have an interest in keeping it a closed field.

One really good advantage someone new to the field has is *in* being new. Since most jingle veterans concentrate on specific knowledge and experience, over a long period they tend to turn out repetitive products. Someone new, who is not intimidated by the prevalent styles dominating commercial making, and yet understands the essential aspects of what a jingle should do, might have the fresh twist agencies are looking for. Someone who is not rushed for time, someone who can make sure a jingle is logical, musically, in interpreting the message could be far more expressive of ideas and thus add to the pulse of the ad itself — and, too, introduce new musical ideas. But since sound is the last thing people not really into music are sensitive to, one will have to convince business heads of its relevance. The stress is on consistency of copy, and what is apparently accepted as the prime criterion is, "Does it sound professional?" An easy standard to apply, perhaps, but not necessarily the only way to re-create the product or improve the ad.

Functions of a Jingle Producer

First a company with a product typically hires an advertising agency to handle all its advertising. The advertising agency gets a 15 percent commission of the cost of all ads and commercials they place, the cost of producing them, plus a contingency to cover markups — and everything is marked up. Since television networks charge sponsors $100,000 a minute for prime time and the agency makes 15 percent each time the commercial runs, with an average of sixty times for many of them, you can't beat TV for the big and easy commission. Cheaper forms of advertising, newspaper and magazine ads, take just as much agency time to produce, so many people claim that agencies push for TV coverage too often and too hard. Others claim that TV is easy to push because clients love any involvement in "show biz." Many clients spend $30 million a year which gives the agency nearly $6 million plus fees. Some ad agencies won't take an account unless it earns over $750,000 a year in commissions. The research and accounting heads determine production costs, and $80,000 to $100,000 is spent on making a network TV commercial, more or less.

If the agency does not have in-house producers, and most of them don't, they hire independent producers, one to handle the filming end of the commercial, and one to handle the sound. Producers work on many commercials simultaneously; each one is finished in about three days to a week from the moment of assignment. That's a lot to cope with and a lot of money invested. If the commercial is for TV, the total expense will be even greater than the $5,000 it costs to do a typical radio ten-second or thirty-second spot.

The sound-track producer is the first one to get the copy for the commercial. If it is a TV commercial, he is also given a story board. This is a board with simple drawings of what's happening on the screen while the copy is being sung and/or read. There are notations like "SFX" for natural sound effects (such as the clinking of silverware) when needed. Many times the original copy will not fit a musical idea and the composer will have to change a word or come up with whole new copy. When that happens, it all has to be screened by a lawyer to make sure it is not offensive and that all the product claims are met. Once an agency cast a Santa Claus in a diet commercial who never saw his efforts on TV, because he was too thin. This commercial, which cost $80,000 to produce, never ran because one can't claim diet products cause weight loss, and it was implied that Santa became thin using the product. The continuity clearance departments of the networks are very strict, so the agencies have to be careful.

Along with the copy given to the producer come the demographics, a description of whom the commercial is aimed at, such as housewives or kids. Some products are for everyone, like toilet paper; everyone "tries" it. But mostly there are two categories: sex and age. If it is for teenagers, then the sound is geared to them. In car ads today a country flavor is sought because demographics show that the next crop of new car buyers will be attracted by a country sound. Once in a while music is geared to blacks, a soul sound is created, and the commercial will be programmed heavily in black areas.

A producer's job is to get into the spirit and aim of the project. Then he calls in a composer (sometimes the producer is the composer) he thinks can work well in the style best suiting the commercial. In a few days the composer comes back with the melody, and if that is acceptable, then an arranger is called in (if the composer can't arrange) who is good at the type of arranging wanted, and he in turn will often hire the available musicians because it is the arranger who usually conducts the performance. The producer knows everybody's forte and weakness (since as we said before, in the commercial business there are relatively few musicians and singers working daily anyway) and will usually agree with the arranger's choice. A producer can suggest a particular bass player, for example, and it is here that the producer has to make the right choice, make sure that he knows what the client is looking for.

Then studio time is booked. There is usually someone from the agency's creative group, and the copywriter, who is also at the session. We were at a session when the client himself was there with a man from his advertising department.

The producer sits inside the control booth with the engineer, while on the other side of the booth the arranger works with the musicians. When the producer wants to comment about something, he communicates through speakers directly to the arranger, who can then know best how to get what the producer wants from the musicians. A jingle producer, like any music producer, is basically a coordinator, and has control of the session by directing and leading it, and making the final judgment when something is "right" on the tape . . . or not.

Usually, the singers and musicians have a chart (score) to read by, but it is not necessarily true that *all* singers and musicians read music. Some of them hear something twice and know it, some even once.

Recalling the tension at one session we listened in on, we commented on the sense of achievement a producer must have when he's managed to get everything he wants out of everybody in such a short amount of time and "it's in the can." How much fun is it? "Seventy-five percent is fun, the other twenty-five percent is pretty heavy," Stu Kuby told us. "It's hard because it's very political. There's always somebody to answer to." And we could understand, thinking back on a session (not from Stu's company) we witnessed. After going over the whole vocal part half a dozen times, the engineer started putting the singer's voice on tape. There was a sudden interruption in the booth. One of the men in suits commented to the producer, "She's got an operatic quality, too much vibrato, it seems a little inappropriate here." The producer answered back that she was operatically trained. The arranger suggested they bring in another voice. The agency man said, "On the demo we heard a male voice. This is not the sound we want." He was firm. The producer pushed for the girl, saying, "Let's give her a chance." But the agency man took control and told the producer in no uncertain terms, "We have a choice; put it down and don't use it. It's a quality we don't want. No use wasting time; let's get the announcer and do the singer later." The tension was incredible.

Stu says, "It's also difficult for us, because we want to make a contribution to the music too, and the concept held by a writer or a creative director or the film producer might be different from what we have in mind musically. They are in a position where they get involved with what *we* do, but we don't get involved with what *they* do. So we don't stand over their shoulders and say this is what you should write, or this is how you should cut your film, whereas when it gets to the music which is the final stage, there they are, telling us do this, do that, this is what I feel. If we make a move, we have to be able to back it up, so if it's something you really believe in and it's something *they* don't want, you have to really assert yourself and take the consequences if it's not successful. In records it doesn't exist that way, that much. A film producer comes to the recording session a lot and feels that it's his baby, but we feel that way too. Film producers feel we're infringing, and they try to take control of the recording session and they might not have any recording and musical knowledge or techniques, and they can make it very difficult. They'll hear music in the stages that it takes to record something, and they might come to a conclusion very early in its formation, but it's the wrong conclusion. They don't know what the final sound is going to be. A producer's job is to try and hear the total before, and then try to put it all together. There are times when a film producer may think a recording is going in one direction and he will be very vocal about it, and he can upset and destroy the atmosphere and distract the sound producer from his goal."

Stu continues: "It's difficult, and you ask, 'Is it fun?' You really have to do away with any ego because you have to judge how important it is to get your ideas across, how to get the balance back into the session because you don't want that wasted. If you feel that what you want is soundwise the best, commercially, no matter who's there and no matter what they say, I have to go with my judgment. Unless my point is really strong to me, I usually feel it is better, psychologically, to go with the other opinion, but if any sound producer feels their point is really essential, then it's their responsibility to stand by it. Because, if you give in to the other opinion and it *doesn't* work out and it *isn't* successful, the responsibility is yours, not theirs!" Sometimes things blow up.

"The record experience [producing albums] is much more relaxed, you can take a lot more time, it is not as strict, and the budgets are elastic and the atmosphere is much more creative. Making an album, you can really be a maverick. You have to be, to be successful. Whereas here there is just a little touch of that maverick, but it's more of an aping situation, it's more of being aware of what's successful soundwise on the market in records, and trying to achieve that sound, and maybe go one better. Constantly we are aware of the top forty, singles are for teenage girls, albums are for a different market, then there are the country charts and a bit of jazz."

Producers rarely get feedback. They produce for the client, try to make them happy, give them what they want. Stu told us, "I've been at this agency for six months and done more than 200 commercials and only once I got feedback from the company on how that commercial changed the product's sales." The reason for this is no doubt because so many things depend on the commercials' success. An "idea" that is right in the total concept of the commercial may be the reason for a dramatic increase in sales. A clever idea stemming from market research can focus in on an area not exploited by anyone else. (This formula is called "positioning.") When the idea is conceived around a claim about the product that really stands out, it is called "pre-empting." So, the most important part of the commercial is what it says and how it says it, in words and in visuals. The *last* to be really important is the musical concept — or sound track. Precisely to isolate the contribution of the music in a commercial to the product's success is a difficult task. It is also hard to tell whether the commercial is successful, for the product itself may be on an upswing because people like it or going down because people don't like it. So, when awards are given in the field, Cleo Awards (the national awards), the Andy, and the Gold Medal, they are based on a panel's personal favorites, not on amount of airplay or on consumer research.

Producing the Jingle

From a lifetime of listening everyone is aware of the more obvious aspects of commercial making. Such guidelines as

"Be sure the product's name is always the high point of any commercial" are already truisms.

But a concept such as "fool the listener so that he thinks he's listening to anything but a commercial" is less obvious, and we can all remember watching a commercial on TV and thinking for a moment that it was part of the program. For instance, we're watching the news, the commercial comes on, and some guy is spieling off a "message" while standing in front of the White House, and what's more, looking like the typical anchorman.

Being aware of the commercial from the vantage point of an analyst is the best way to learn how it's made.

Sometimes the problem in commercial production is in keeping too tight a lid on for fear of going too far out. One of the standard prerequisites in this business is that a producer should be conservative. The commercial can't offend anybody. No doubt that is why it's not customary to hire people from the "outside" to add inspiration and freshness. Creative directors are supposed to fill this role. But we have heard of one creative director who practically snatches people off the street, types who haven't been working in an office all day, day in and day out, to give *him* inspiration! Sometimes he just wants to hear their talk. No matter how much of a maverick a person may have been at first, after a term of routine work one loses touch with the beat of the outside world, and thus can lose the quirk that makes one's work fresh and new. Even IBM employs people to stir things up, to keep people on their toes; they're sort of creative troublemakers. So the point is that a producer should be aware of the conservative nature of the jingle business, and at the same time check on himself to see how jaded his ideas may be as a result of routine, school, or whatever.

A producer should be aware of the techniques used in both writing the music and recording it, even if he isn't an engineer, writer, arranger, vocalist, or instrumentalist. Some producers *are* the composers and arrangers, and may also serve as vocalist or in the many other functions. There's no set formula. Income increases with each role filled.

The inability to read music isn't an absolute drawback. Musicians who can't read music still create many of today's albums. Similarly, it is entirely possible to produce a commercial with only a working knowledge of music.

Here are some practical points. First is an awareness of time. The seconds count! If it's a thirty-second TV spot, you have to make the whole commercial fit into twenty-eight seconds. (There should be a second on each end for leeway and relief.) You have to do some figuring, but there is no mystery in this process, it only *seems* to depend on mathematical expertise. There are conversion charts that break everything down into beats per second. For instance, you decide upon the tempo you want. If it is 4/4 time and quarter notes, it will break down into 1 beat per second, or 60 beats a minute, which will break down to 15 measures. If, on the other hand, you use 3/4 time, there will be 20 measures. If you use a fast tempo, you will have 2 beats per second or 120 beats per minute.

Whether composing for a ten-second, thirty-second, or sixty-second commercial, you are dealing with exact timing. A stopwatch is especially useful in the studio.

Standard radio commercials are sixty seconds. Usually they are produced in three parts: (1) a twenty-second "front" usually sung by the soloist or vocal group; (2) a thirty-second "bridge," which the announcer reads, usually with a variation of the music used in the front material; (3) a ten-second "tag" with vocal recapitulation.

When composing, you have to think about what the copy is saying, the age of the market, and its sex, especially if the product is nationally advertised. If it is a fifty- to sixty-year-old market you are appealing to (iron, tonic, and so on) some nostalgic music that that age group would respond to is often simulated. If the product is aimed at youth, a voice that sounds young is used. On breakfast-food spots children's voices are used if the ad is played after three o'clock, when children are home from school. Breakfast-food spots heard earlier in the day, when women are home, use voices that will capture the young adult female.

When you listen, see what instruments are often used with the female voice and which ones are used with the male voice. A disco beat is used more at the moment we're writing this chapter than the rock and roll beat. If you want a sexy sound, a sax is usually used (though not with a strip beat, which would be a bit too much of a statement for a commercial and would take the romance and emphasis right out of the product). A pretty bossa nova might create a relaxed feel. Strings also give an easy-listening effect. Most of the top forty use strings, and they are used on commercials too. They give a cooled-out expansiveness that relaxes. If it has a catchy melodic line, if the group sound is good, and if the contemporary requirements for success are met, chances are the jingle will be successful.

Rarely is commercial music sad. Chord changes affect moods, minor chords don't usually come across as very happy. Plato, the Greek philosopher, was the first to state that people can be directed through music. And that's what one has to think about: the message of the ad, and how to promote it through sound.

Musical passages that are played in conjunction with the name of the product are marked "ID," which stands for identification with the product. When people hear that musical passage, they relate it instantly with the product. You also may have noticed that some commercials use pop songs that have been hits. Well, the client pays a lot for the rights to this so that every time that song is heard outside the context of the commercial, in its original pop-music form, people will identify it with the product in the commercial.

When arranging the tone for instruments, the key to coming up with the right blend is to think of each sound that's desired and how best to bring it out. The voice is the only instrument that can naturally adapt itself to several timbres. For instance, the flute is not heard unless it is supported by a reed played below the C above middle C. It gets absorbed into the other instruments. You have to be able to distinguish the different sounds you hear so it's worthless to use instruments that get lost when used with certain other instruments. Instruments that go well with the flute are vibes, piano, and acoustic or electric guitars. Amplified effects are countless when using devices such as the wawa, fuzz tone, or phaser. Attachments for woodwinds and brasses create different sounds. Synthesizers are capable of almost any sound. Commercials, remember, are full of sound effects as well as music. Actually, serious musicians picked up on the use of synthesizers as a result of their early use in commercial making; the novelty of the synthesized sound attracted their attention. Synthesizers are used on the Eastern Airlines commercial to get the sound of soaring. Roger Powell, Utopia's synthesizer player, told us the sound of an onion going bad in your refrigerator (like "OOUUAHAHugua") was achieved through the use of a synthesizer. Half the effects on commercials, anything from street noises to musical sounds, come from the synthesizer. Stu works with a special-effects wizard who has a recorded collection of thousands of sounds, everything from walking on gravel to the pop of a cork. He's very much into theater so he is good at casting actors and announcers. Once this special-effects genius produced the sound of a bear running through the woods by crumpling up some old tape in front of a mike. It was just what the client wanted.

Everything to do with the sound, such as sound effects and the announcer's voice, is recorded on the music tape. You'll notice that when the announcer's voice comes on in the "bridge" section in the center, the music is usually in the background. So that attention isn't drawn away from the announcer the vocals fade off, and something else has to "hold up" the music. Many times horns are brought in for the bridge, or violins, lead guitars, trombones, and so on — some new, interesting sounds. Musically they call this the hole in the doughnut!

When you are in the studio with the engineer, you'll notice that just as in the bands you hear playing out in clubs and in bars, the last beat before playing is silent; it is not counted off. For instance, if you are to begin on the fourth beat, you say one, two, then there is a silent beat and the players begin. In the studio there is a real reason for doing this: so that the counting-off won't be heard on the tape in the event that there should be a leak on it.

Sometimes segments of longer commercials are used in other media for shorter commercials of the product. The part taken is usually the "tag," which is the last ten seconds, called a "lift." This may happen when the tape is sent to radio stations throughout the country where the station's announcer has his own copy, individually written for his area, in case a local distributor of the product is mentioned. Radio stations use the 15 i.p.s. tape for better fidelity rather than the 7½ i.p.s. you might be familiar with on reel-to-reel recorders.

The only qualification a musician must have to be used in a commercial is membership in the American Federation of Musicians. Singers and announcers must be members of the American Federation of Television and Radio Artists. (The federations get 7.5 percent of the overall money paid for each session, which goes into the unions' health and welfare funds.)

It's interesting to watch an announcer actually working. One announcer we watched arrived right on time, very sharply dressed and officious. He took off his suit coat and walked into the studio and started to read over the copy. The ad man at the session remarked, "Brings people together, sounds a little fuzzy." There were a few more quick takes and suggestions to the announcer like, "Don, can you pause after the word 'wine'?" and "You have a whole second to do it." Then there was a word change in the copy. The ad man continued directing . . . getting quick response from the announcer, eventually asking for a quarter-wild track, and instructing the announcer to repeat a sentence four times real fast . . . which he did. The ad man said, "That's it." The announcer came into the control booth and everybody thanked him and he left. He had been around the rim and out. It was clockwork, and it was stunning to watch.

If the producer is working with visuals for a TV commercial, he is given the story board, which looks like a black-and-white comic book. Originally, when the film is made, there is a counter on the projector that counts off the frames. When something happens on the film that calls for a sound effect, for instance, the exact period in time when that sound effect should come in is marked on the story board. If someone's facial expression is supposed to respond to a tympanum this is worked in and done in the studio, along with the music and other sound effects. There are 720 frames flashing by in one thirty-second spot. The story board also serves to lay out the story of the commercial so a composer can create around it. Producing a jingle basically comes down to just knowing the techniques, and they aren't so difficult.

Since the film producer and the sound producer are *the* coordinators on a TV commercial, they should be able to get along well and communicate well with one another.

Sometimes sound demos as well as film demos are made as a kind of trial run for the client's approval. A small-scale, low-cost tape gives the film producer an idea, and then he might do a tapographical-filmographical film: cutting the film to go with the sound of the demo. When it comes to the final stage, the film producer might bring along that demo sound track and film to help him get his timing. Then he might edit it, and that means that the sound producer has to look at this edited film and take new timings and go back and record the sound again in a final recording. Once the music is mixed with the film, that's the end!

7

A & R

The A & R Dream

Most people have the notion that the Artist and Repertoire
(A & R) person on the staff of a record company has the best,
most romantic job in the music industry. And no wonder.
Some A & R men have gained overwhelming respect and fantastic reputations in the field. Their discoveries have placed
them in the minds of both the general public and the trade as
real creators and have granted them an association with wise
men, intuitive geniuses, and poets. Can you imagine anyone
else in the industry, other than perhaps some established person like Sinatra, qualifying for the kind of birthday celebra-
tion that was accorded to John Hammond over national TV,
with artists like Dylan joining in to pay tribute?

Jerry Schoenbaum, who heads his own production company today and who has touched several bases in the music
industry, from establishing a chain of retail stores to serving
as president of Polydor Records, began and has functioned in
an A & R capacity for most of his career. He told us that discovering an artist *is* the ultimate reward. "I've been able to

discuss music with artists who really have something to say and I've had the pleasure of finding out that those artists bore out what I always imagined they should be. I was very pleased that Chick Corea and Janis Ian both won Grammy awards. I signed them to their first record contracts. These things are pleasurable."

The A & R person is supposed to have creative foresight, with the ability to anticipate trends ahead of everyone else in the business. Jerry's Verve Forecast presented the first recordings of Tim Hardin, Laura Nyro, Richie Havens, Dave Van Ronk, James Cotton Blues Band, Frank Zappa and the Mothers Of Invention, The Velvet Underground. But Jerry states: "It's not just saying, 'Here's a wonderful new artist that we're going to present to you.' A & R is not just going out and finding a great new talent. As one looks at the music business, it's kind of fascinating, the idea of finding talent, putting it in the studio, surrounding it with the right elements, the right songs, recognizing these things, making a record, and Wow! But there's a lot more to it than that. It's very difficult to lay business and creativity side by side. They just don't work well together. You have to put alongside of that ultimate reward, the problem that you have to deal with that big establishment: what am I going to do with this artist and how are they [the public] going to react to this artist once a deal is made? Making a deal is difficult in itself."

The Realities

The A & R staff actually has to perform many functions besides the finding of talent, which may be only a small part of the job. In a medium-to-large company the A & R staff meets with the board of directors, the sales and marketing departments, and the president of the company to discuss and break down the budget for the next calendar year. The history of sales is analyzed, the artist roster is examined, and projections are made for the coming year for their current stars and for the people they hope will be stars. Then maybe some part of the budget is allocated for research and development, which is called A & R in the music industry.

It is the A & R person's job to oversee the fulfillment of the company's commitments to the artists it already has, and in turn make sure that they deliver a certain amount of product to the company. Artists have to be chased, according to Jerry, to get the product out of them so that it can be delivered on schedule. "Perhaps the marketing department is saying, 'Hey, what's happening?' and the sales department says, 'We need X million units in this first quarter, how come we haven't gotten an album from A, B, or C?'" So the A & R man has to make sure of the delivery, or else the year's budget is not going to be met.

Finding Material

The A & R staff has the big job of finding songs for those of their artists who are not self-contained. Finding a good song can open things up for an artist, which is what happened to Barry Manilow. When Clive Davis didn't hear that "career-marching" hit song for the AM radio, Bob Feiden, head of Arista's A & R, told us Clive submitted the song "Mandy" to Manilow. Feiden reminds us that the primary concern of almost everyone in the business is the finding of hit songs — not just good songs. "The only thing you're looking for in outside material," says Feiden, "is the hit, and people send you all kinds of things that aren't hits." The A & R man also has the problem of diplomatically convincing a particular artist or group to use a certain song. "This is very touchy, because artists have egos, and the first reflex is defensive, because they feel that you are telling them you don't like what they're doing, because why else would you be bringing them outside property?" Which may not really be the case. Sometimes certain outside material might bring them acceptance with a wider audience.

There is another way that artists and material get matched. Sometimes the A & R people have a song that is such a sure shot it becomes their overriding concern to find a singer for it. They like the song, record the music track, and then decide what singer would go best with what they have. This happened at Midland International, when they found Carol Douglas to sing one of the first successful discos. They had been calling people in the business to tell them what kind of a voice they wanted. Singers auditioned and so did Douglas, whose manager had sent her over to sing a few songs accompanying herself on guitar. She'd been out of the business for quite a few years and wanted to get back in. She just laid her voice down over the tracks that were already there, and Midland gave her a contract for four singles over the following year.

When an artist signs with a record company, usually she/he will be required to permit the record company to choose the compositions to be recorded. Sidney Shemel and William Krasilovsky point out in their book *This Business of Music* that the "mature" artist will try to have the right to approve any choices, *including* "a provision made for resolving impasses." The right to approve *only* may destroy the essence of the agreement! Shemel and Krasilovsky explain that the big artists, like Presley and The Beatles, who have their own publishing companies, will favor material that they have a financial interest in. And this becomes an important factor in the selection of material; making it is not all that objective; the best song doesn't always win. A record company with its own publishing company will naturally tend to pick material from its own catalog. And Shemel and Krasilovsky point out: "In fact, some record firms make special incentive payments to artist and repertoire people who do obtain publishing rights to material recorded." Artists can sometimes be convinced to record a song owned by an independent publishing company, if that company will assign part of the publishing rights to the artist's record company. This happens even when the artist is one who *never* writes his or her own material. Sometimes A & R men are offered a percentage, paid through a third party, for pushing a song and getting it recorded. The final decision to record a song might have quite a powerful and complicated body of deal-making governing it.

Jerry Schoenbaum says, "The trouble with the music business is that it is a business. It is a business that deals with immediacy, human emotions, a certain amount of creativity and business, and those elements don't work too well together."

Most material comes to the A & R through publishers who know A & R is looking for material for a certain artist. Bob Feiden says that the bulk of unsolicited material that comes — usually with a "Dear Sir" or "Dear A & R" — he's never cared for very much. "We get hundreds of tapes that way, and we do listen. Arista also gets material from managers, agents, and attorneys in the business. Sometimes your hopes are up, depending on who submitted the tape, because the person might have a good track record, as far as their associations with talent." Of course, top professionals in the business are passed on by A & R as well.

In contrast to this situation, Michael Lang, who produced the famous Woodstock Festival when he was twenty-one years old, liked a tape sent to him cold by a young group in Los Angeles; but what clinched it for him was their letter, which said simply, "Please help!" He signed them to his production company. So there is just no one way to appeal to a person.

Finding a Producer

A & R is also responsible for finding the right producer. When an artist needs a producer, A & R has to find one who will get along with the artist both in respect to the kind of work each will demand of the other, and also on the level of personality. They ought to meet in advance and get to know each other. "It's hard to find producers that are really good," says Feiden. "Just as you can count on the fingers of one hand the top directors in the film industry, the so-called top producers in the record industry are very few."

Record companies have producers they work with regularly; or the artist may already have an arrangement with a producer, in which case the two are accepted by the company as a package. The reverse is also a possibility. Sometimes the record company receives a tape from an indie producer and likes the artist but not the production. This can be very touchy, and at Arista, when this happens, they call the artist and find out what the relationship with the producer is, hoping no contract is involved. Many times the record company won't sign the artist, because he/she is locked into a producer that the record company doesn't like. Sometimes the company goes along with the artist's choice of producer, and it turns out to be a mistake. Bob Feiden says, "Arista has spent $40,000 on material that will never be used, because twice this artist went in the studio with producers that he felt he owed that [was obligated] to. He's on his third producer now."

Other Functions

If an artist comes to a label without management, the A & R staff may have the job of recommending management too. Sometimes they find themselves working with the artist in the capacity of management, and that's where Feiden says you get those phone calls at two in the morning when the artist is unhappy, things aren't going right, suddenly a record isn't selling well, or the performer is wondering when the next single will be out.

An A & R person is responsible for overseeing many of the noncreative administrative duties as well. Although most companies have an A & R administrator, it's the A & R man's· job in general always to be informed and in touch with what's happening with the acts on the roster. The A & R administrator is that person on the staff of a record company who assists the head of the A & R department, performing top-level functions such as negotiating contracts, but without the responsibility for making final decisions. Without bearing the onus of having the final yes or no, go or stop, in matters of budget and other sensitive points so close to the hearts of all parties concerned, she or he can be particularly effective, from the company's point of view, at diplomatically, graciously, bringing home acceptable contractual terms.

Once an act is accepted, the A & R administrator will be briefed on what kind of contract the company wants to offer. From then on, the administrator negotiates for the record company as its representative in meetings with an act's attorney or manager-agent. Together they'll work out all points of the contract, compromising as necessary to come to some agreement on matters of advance, budget, advertising, and promotion, and all the fine points. The administrator then does the same thing on the contract between the album's producer and the record company.

Next the budget for the studio time will be set (determined by record company executives, but worked out in its details by the administrator), and a studio will be selected. Finally, when the bills start coming in, they'll come through the administrator, who will review them and OK payment.

Barbara Davies has been in the music industry for fifteen years; she was an A & R administrator for Polydor, and now is with Sid Bernstein's management office. Although she didn't make aesthetic judgments, or take part in deciding on which acts to sign, she was in on the total event from then on. "I took care of the act until the record was absolutely shipped. It's a good job, because you get to know the act and everything that's going on with the act."

To figure out a budget, which is part of an administrator's

job, you have to know how many musicians are going to be used. "At $110 for the work of one person for three hours [union scale]," Barbara says, "if you have twenty strings, that's going to bring up your budget." An average recording budget today is about $40,000.

It is a notorious fact that most acts exceed their budget. "If you set the budget at $100,000, anyone should be able to bring it in," says Barbara. And they usually do. But not everyone merits such an outlay in the record company's eyes, and there are so many unpredictable variables that going over the allotted budget becomes everybody's constant problem. It's the administrator's job to oversee such things while the making of an album is in progress, and if Barbara saw that an act was going over budget, she would "have a very serious talk" with them. She found that she was usually willing to be somewhat more cold-hearted about it and hold out in favor of the original figures agreed upon, whereas her A & R director might say, "Look, they're creative, you've got to give a little bit." This can be a cause for some stress, since it's the administrator's job to hold them to the budget, but at the same time it's not his or her ultimate decision.

Though it's not a highly creative job, it can be a very interesting one that allows you to participate in the music business from both ends at once. So if you're a person who wants to be involved in what goes on in a record company and relate in a pivotal way with artists as well, A & R administrator may be your answer.

The A & R man must keep all other departments within the company apprised of the degree of completion of a record. Everything has to be coordinated with the other departments. The sales and merchandising departments especially have to be kept up to date, if the marketing of a record is to be timed right. Space for ads in newspapers and magazines, as well as radio time, have to be bought months in advance and coordinated with both the tour and the record release.

Packaging is another area A & R has a hand in, communicating performers' suggestions to the art staff and giving final approval for designs. Sometimes more time and energy is spent on this than one would think. Jerry Schoenbaum told us a funny story about a singer with a great vocal style whom he once signed to Polydor. The manager at the time wanted his brother, a sculptor, to design the singer's album cover. The guy showed up with a plan to make a cover that resembled raised dough. It was like those topographical maps you used to see in school. Jerry tried to tell him that it wouldn't work, because records are packed so many in a box. And, besides, the record would warp! But this didn't stop the manager, the brother, or the singer herself. All wanted the cover molded to this conception, with grand ideas that the covers would be displayed in stores as mobiles. A & R took over, and the cover came out usable.

Adding to the Roster

Considering all the jobs an A & R person has to do, it becomes obvious that little time is left for discovering talent. Although there have been periods in the past when discovering talent has been a major concern, it's unrealistic to see this as A & R's primary function. A & R actually means the signing and finding of new artists and material. But the word "new" is not taken literally. When we were talking with Eddy O'Laughlin at Midland International about signing *new* people, what came to his mind is how hard they are to find: "When you find people with a lot of talent, they usually want so much money to sign. When I was at Buddah Records, they wanted Harry Chapin, but felt he was asking too much. He asked for six figures."

The A & R people usually do not have the power to sign acts on their own, though they can push for a certain act.

One of the really taboo subjects in the industry is the specifics of advances and offers to artists. The excuse given is that it varies with the person. When pressed, most everyone will come up with some estimate of how low — how *very* low — it can be. For instance, can you believe $500, or maybe $1,000? Maybe just a month's food money. Barbara Davies, however, was unusually direct when we queried her on this (perhaps the companies she has worked for are especially above board on this point), and she told us very firmly that, as far as she knows, an unestablished person coming to a record company for the first time could expect a $10,000 advance, at the lowest figure. (But we have heard of much lower advances.) She also said that because everything has tightened up, three or four years ago it would have been more.

Although there is today a tendency to reduce the size of the artist roster by budgeting out some of the "fat," the record company still has to keep signing new acts to take the place of those dropped or lost for whatever reason. Maintaining a constant quantity of product is a must. What happens for the most part is that there is a competitive struggle to sign acts that are new to the company, but who are already heavy breadwinners at some other company. This is called "label-raiding," and is part of the manipulation that goes on in seducing and acquiring artists. Whoever in the company is behind that switchover achieves status and lots of credit and salary increases. Jerry Schoenbaum explained an aspect of label-raiding that may account for the tremendous, perhaps even the ultimate, power that lawyers have in the record world today: "Outside the record company there are a great many lawyers on both sides of this continent who have an enormous amount of power in deal-making. Many record companies depend on lawyers to bring them artists, or to make them aware that artists' contracts are coming up for renewal — and then there is a bidding war."

Label-raiding may not come down exclusively to who makes the biggest offer. Bob Feiden says of Arista president Clive Davis: "Another way you get talent, which is something Clive Davis did so brilliantly when he was at Columbia, is label-raiding. You are always keeping your eyes open for other acts, to see when their contracts are up, what might be breaking. And the maintaining of friendships with artists on other labels can eventually turn into profit in a sense, even though you might not be looking for it. Today I find that the judgment made by many artists as to which label to sign with is really for them [the artists] a matter of personality. They really, very often, want to be with a given person."

What this amounts to is expressed in more direct terms by Alan Abrahams, who, having done almost everything else in the business, is about to go into an A & R job on the West Coast: "Just this past weekend a friend of mine was in town with Carole King. He's keyboard, her musical director, Clarence MacDonald. But like it started out, we were doing each other favors. And if a record label wanted him, they couldn't buy him. He's getting a lot of money a week and his songs are now being recorded. But he now comes and does arrangements for me for nothing, and he'll come and do a demo for me for nothing because of stuff I've turned him onto. I'm saying that it's very rare that I've done somebody a favor where they've turned around and shoved it up my ass. And if it happens, then it happens. That's the percentages. But I feel that all the nice things that have been happening to me are usually all from friendship and all from favors."

A record company may sign someone who is selling well but not great, so as to avoid having to compete in an expensive bidding situation, with the hope that the artist's record sales will improve; a company can sign a group or singer not fabulously successful and invest thousands into making them superstars, as we write about in the chapter on merchandising a record. In an interview for *Gallery* magazine with Steve Popovich, head of West Coast A & R for Epic, Meridee Mercer says, "Epic is currently riding big with newly broken artists like Michael Murphey, Minnie Riperton, Labelle, and Fogelberg." These are all people who have been around a long time and plenty of money is being spent to "break" them, that is, get them further into the public consciousness.

A & R people acquire artists with reputations whose sales have slipped and build them up again. However, unless you are on the inside track in terms of actually knowing what the last sales were, you could mistakenly sign an artist with a big past reputation who will have sold only 5,000 copies of the last album! Which is a sale that has more than just "slipped." Promotion men know that sales pick up fast when artists are rolling again and getting exposure every day. Frank Sinatra drew one of the poorest crowds in Saratoga during the summer of 1974, while Jefferson Starship had the largest. Later on in the year Sinatra's attendance figures picked up until he sold out at Madison Square Garden.

Available talent also comes to the attention of A & R through important people in the business, from promoters, managers, agents, producers, lawyers. Sometimes the publishers are looking for a record deal for their singer-writer because there is more money in it for them as publishers when the songs are recorded. "Recommendations come from friends and other artists in the business," says Feiden. "Most of the artists I hear about that I am excited about pursuing I don't first hear about in my office, but at dinners or in people's homes. Artists tend to congregate and know each other first, and I know that three or four years ago Jackson Browne and Glenn Fry, who's one of the leaders of The Eagles, they told me about a writer they know who had written two songs The Eagles recorded. I wanted to meet him for about a year and a half and finally on a trip to California they suggested that we have dinner together. We did, and the writer played me his songs, and I loved them. He later formed a group, and Clive signed the group named The Funky Kings."

One of Feiden's finds for Arista came to him this way: "When I came to work for Clive, Peter Rudge, who manages The Rolling Stones, said to me, 'There is a group from the South called The Outlaws I hear is quite good.' He told me he'd manage them himself but they have management already. And coming from the man who managed The Rolling Stones and The Who, that seemed like quite an endorsement.

So I flew south and the following week made another trip with Clive to the South. We signed the band." Feiden continues, "So, wherever you hear about an act, I'll take my lead from anywhere." Peter Rudge isn't from "anywhere," however!

Another way new talent comes to a record company is in the form of "masters" (finished recordings). They can be purchased in many ways, some outright, some for just a percentage of the royalty without a direct reimbursement for the studio costs. Shemel and Krasilovsky say the money these masters are sold for has been greatly reduced. Record companies assign the A & R men to listen to both "hot masters" and untried masters. By "hot masters" Shemel and Krasilovsky mean: "A record, made by a small independent producer . . . being played frequently on radio stations and . . . there is a demand for the record at the consumer level." Masters for forty-fives are acquired this way because the companies realize that the singles market is one of fads, styles, and whimsies and that no one has a corner on the flexibility necessary to meet the demands of the market. The record companies obtain the rights and distribute them. Then the job is to get them out and around quickly before the fad changes. In fact any new rage is not really considered part of any long-range plans. For instance, at the time when Dick Fox, at the William Morris Agency, talked to us about booking, we learned that they couldn't always book someone even as well-known as Melissa Manchester was at that time more than two months in advance because if it were any longer, the promoter would be afraid the public might cool on the artist and the date would bomb.

From Underground to Establishment

It's amazing, really, that rock music ever made it considering all the prejudices that came out against it in the beginning. Jerry tells us that when he and Tom Wilson brought Frank Zappa and the Mothers Of Invention into Verve Forecast (Blue Verve they called it), there was a meeting at MGM, and a minor executive there said, "I wouldn't bring those records home to my children." "The president of MGM then was extremely leery about what Frank Zappa was putting on his records, and there were censorship fights constantly." Once Jerry took the whole staff of MGM executives down to a little place Zappa was working in for a live performance, and their reaction was violent. "They had no understanding about what he had to say, which was tongue-in-cheek about society. We had the same problem with The Velvet Underground." Now Lou Reed is a big star, but in those days, when Jerry and Tom Wilson brought him into Blue Verve, there were problems.

What amuses Jerry is that after the establishment accepts the true underground, it becomes good business, and all of a sudden they all rush in and say, "Where's *our* artist?" and that's when Jerry feels the creativity falls on its face.

Most people in the business who want to be in on the beginning of movements in music believe that the success of a record company is determined by how quickly it picks up on what's happening in the street. Jerry's opinion is, "When the establishment accepts something, it's no longer the underground; it becomes commercially viable. It wasn't until the late Sixties that the majors got into those folk people in the Village full force. That really started in Sixty-four–Sixty-five when only three companies emerged in the rising folk elements into the pop field: Vanguard, Electra, and Verve Forecast."

There is always the unpredictability of the level of success some artists can have. "I laugh when I think of the people — and maybe I'm one of them," Bob Feiden says, "who were ready to write off Linda Ronstadt, Neil Sedaka. Ronstadt was around nine years making records that didn't sell very well. She had a cult following. She had one or two hits spaced apart by four years. All of a sudden her albums, all gold."

What A & R Looks For

The A & R heads today are mostly looking for the *song.* They study the top forty, have their staff listen to album releases within and outside of the company, and they're also looking for a good live act.

Almost everyone we talked to in the business at the time, including Jerry Schoenbaum and Bob Feiden, reflected what is true *at that moment:* that instrumental virtuosity was not important, and that you must have a hit song to make it. Feiden remarked: "If virtuosity were to jump off the demo, I would pursue it, but if it's not there it doesn't make me think any the less of what I'm listening to. . . . From a record company's point of view, it is a dwindling concern, because the public has become much more song-oriented. The kind of Jimi Hendrix virtuosos were important to the late Sixties, when FM radio played a large part in breaking new acts — which it doesn't today but with rare exceptions." He thought that virtuosity in someone like John McLaughlin helps him sell records to the people with "progressive consciousness."

But in just a few months since their comments, the pattern of slick, tight 2.6-minute tunes, which dominated the charts for a couple of years almost exclusively, was broken by Frampton, who suddenly had the all-time best-selling album, from which a raw-sounding song (live) became an AM hit. It is three-quarters instrumental, about eight minutes long. At the same time, another song, by Heart, emerged on AM, also extremely long and comparatively raw-sounding by previous standards, and it too was dominated by long instrumentals. Then from an unheard-of band's first album a long single became an AM hit, also primarily instrumental. The band is called Boston.

It is interesting that Frampton's success was totally unpredicted, and that both groups' first albums reached unexpected heights . . . Heart, on a small Canadian label — having what became a platinum album turned down by American companies, now with three hits from it, and Boston, whose leader went through six years of rejection from the music industry — his hit was written five years ago. This reminds one that a needed change can come out of left field. And it should silence those industry people who say there is no good material around, no good new artists.

But although this music has since been proved valid by public acceptance, dramatically indicating that the conservative hit song isn't going to obliterate or totally replace artistic and innovative "sound," Clive Davis is quoted in an April 24, 1977, *New York Times Magazine* article by Geoffrey Stokes as saying essentially the same thing Bob Feiden told us a year earlier: "I think the return of the song as a dominant factor is one of the most important aspects of the current music business," and "In the late 1960's and early 1970's a lot of groups broke [achieved commercial success] from their performances and not from their songs. In fact the long guitar solos sometimes tended to obliterate the song."

If all of this is beginning to impress you that A & R can be interesting and creative, but that business is business — you're right. Today, talk of one's favorites is not so aesthetically descriptive. It goes mostly like this: Ron Delsener, the New York City concert promoter, expresses the times perfectly in his interview in *Gig* magazine: "One of my favorite performers is Wings, Paul McCartney. There are lots of classy performers. I like classy people, Chicago, Paul Simon, The Beach Boys, Elton John, those in that special class. The crème de la crème."

Of course, though the freezing out of new talent and capitalizing on known names (which guarantee sales) may help to cut down on the risks the industry takes, it may also cut down the flow of vitality and youth into music careers and, following that, the general public's interest in popular music may drop off. One hopes that more changes will appear, as they have recently, and a loosening up will take place.

The Job That Never Ends

The A & R person also has an eye on what's happening in the recording studio. Besides approving the material, the producer, and everything else, he might make the choice between two or three mixes, and also make judgments about the final sequencing. Clive Davis takes credit in his book *Clive* for being good at this. Feiden agrees, telling us how adept Davis is, and says, "Sequencing is to records what film editing is to film, and they say the judge of a good film editor is that when you're watching, you're not aware of the editing. Well, the same is true in sequencing." The reason why the best songs are usually put on the first side of the album, with the best song the first cut, is to catch people's attention so they will listen to the rest, especially the radio-station program director.

Artists have an amazing amount of loyalty to people who have first given them a break, gotten them studio time, and helped them out. So very often artists and A & R people have long-standing relationships. In the last analysis if there is one sure answer to the quest for an opening in the imposing wall of music business, it is in agent Dick Fox's advice: "Go out and find talent yourself, become a singer's manager, booking agent, promotion person, anything. This country is swarming with talent; it's all too cheap, unfortunately. Talent can be developed, and in the process of helping bring some of those undiscovered young stars into visibility, you will make it too." And of course, that *is* how it happens. When there is a flow of new artists into the industry it follows that there will be a flow of new people in other capacities who will also gain a foothold.

8

Merchandising a Record

"MERCHANDISERS IN THE RECORD world can come out of any discipline," says Jim Tyrell, vice president for sales and merchandising for Epic Records. Good merchandisers have to have a salesman's instinct and desire to make things happen, and since they work closely with the sales force that goes out and pushes the records, they have to be experts at preparing both their package and their salesmen.

Carole Jaspar, Epic's manager for sales of singles (forty-fives), comes from a background that proves Tyrell's point. Though she didn't know music, Epic hired her because of her recent success as an organizer for the antismokers' organization SmokEnders, for which she held seminars in New York City and turned many corporate executives into ex-smokers through her coaching. Understanding coaching and selling, she now has the responsibility at Epic of supervising and training the salesmen who sell singles. She gives them the pitch they will use to promote the records, as well as determining priorities such as which records should get preferential treatment.

Tyrell oversees it all, including Epic's in-house art, advertising, and promotion departments, among others. He must be ready and able to pass judgment on such creative things as liner notes, artwork, and promotion-campaign ideas.

Artwork and Liner Notes

As merchandising manager with the responsibility of approving all record cover art, Tyrell keeps himself informed of the latest trends by visiting galleries and looking at art books. Even so, he says, the value of cover art for sales is questionable since no studies show any direct correlation with impulse buying. However, it's been our personal observation that some things do catch the young buyer's eye. One of these is photographs of the artist or group. And though art nouveau has come and gone, the one aesthetic influence that seems to have stayed with us ever since the advent of LSD is surrealistic and fantastic art.

And since you've got to keep the star happy, within reason — which qualification would exclude that singer who wanted to have a sculptured record jacket — whatever he or she wants will have something to do with what the cover looks like, and will, of course, have to be thrashed out with the merchandising manager.

Merchandisers know, from studies that have been made, that liner notes are responsible for sales to some of the public when they are not previously familiar with an artist. The deciding factor is sometimes the presence of studio musicians' names with which they *have* become familiar.

Making Talent Sell

When a company really decides to get behind an act, a lot of money can go into breaking it into a top sales bracket.

Some record companies have a policy of promoting artists who are already established, attempting to make them even bigger.

Labelle, for example, had been around for many years and were known but not big. Epic got behind them because they dug their costumes, their staging theatrics, and their general flair for presenting their act, and therefore sensed Labelle could really make it. So Epic spent $25,000 promoting Labelle, including a costume party and concert for them at Avery Fisher Hall, with the idea that not only Labelle but everyone there would be adding to the visual feast — and thus make for better press coverage. Although some of the press put Labelle down after the concert, the excitement caused by the party enabled Epic promotion people to bring pressure to bear on radio program directors — they simply could not ignore Labelle now — to give the act that single most important exposure in the business: radio play. Surveys show most people buy records after hearing them on the radio so record companies will try anything to get airplay.

Determining the Pressing

The merchandising manager is also the one who determines the quantity of records that are to be pressed. To make intelligent decisions, ones that will not set the company back by allowing overstocks, he's got to gather extensive background information. Aside from having the basic facts, such as what type of an act it is and the fame of its individual members, he's got to read advance reports from the sales force and the booking agent and be apprised of the intended advertising campaign and also recent sales of similar acts. Even further than that, the manager has to have a knowledge of the current tendency of the public to spend or to save money. He or she will need to know the larger accounts' billing and credit records and what particular problems of theirs he'll need to be aware of, such as inventory reduction, debts, closing of fiscal years, floor tax (in some states retailers have to pay a tax on their inventory on a certain day, so they won't be adding to it around that time). Computers can store some of this information. In fact, the merchandising manager's knowledge has to be so wide that it includes what's happening in all fields of music and how each one is selling in particular markets. All of this influences the marketing of a new act.

The real key to getting a record sold, however, is making sure that there is immediate delivery to the stores when the record is breaking. If a customer comes into the store to buy that record and it's not there, he'll forget about it and buy another one that *is* in the store. This is a fact of essential importance in selling and is acknowledged as top priority by people in the record business. Jim Tyrell uses three record manufacturing and shipping plants, which can, in an emergency, turn out a million LPs in a week. Book merchandising managers are light-years away from the music industry's ability to turn around on a dime and get merchandise into the stores when necessary. Clive Davis couldn't believe how primitive book publishing is in relation to the music industry when he experienced the lack of marketing-merchandising by his own book publisher.

How Records Are Sold

Epic's projected sales for 1976 were $60 million. As part of CBS, it has eighty national salesmen operating out of twenty regional sales offices. They go out on the road with a catalog of albums distributed by CBS to present to the retail buyer, and they'll visit big outlets once every two weeks, when an inventory clerk will count all the outlet's records by hand to find out the rate of flow and other things. Epic concentrates its efforts on the big stores, so the smaller, more out-of-the-way retailers may never get to see a salesman.

This is only one of the ways it's done, however. "Sy Leslie was one of the first people to sell records in supermarkets, variety stores, and other outlets other than the regular record shop or department store record department," reports *Gallery* magazine. This led to rack jobbing (when the wholesaler stacks the racks in chain retail outlets) fifteen years ago. Leslie is the founder of Pickwick International, and his corporation owns 240 record stores. Pickwick, he told *Gallery,* will make $120 million from rack jobbing, and his whole music conglomerate makes $225 million a year.

Alan Douglas, the producer best known for being the man behind the 1975 Jimi Hendrix album, told us that he thinks the whole industry is governed by its returns policy. Retail outlets have *a year* in which to make returns, sending back records that don't sell, from which they receive credit toward the purchase of new records. "If they took three years," says Douglas, "What's the difference?" But the result of this pressure to cash in on credit due the stores is that as last year's deadline draws near the stores begin returning records in exchange for the newest hits. Douglas told us that Clive Davis was the only one in the business who showed shrewdness in this area, an important factor in his success at Columbia. As soon as he got an indication that returns were coming in on a particular record, he would order production of that record to stop, even though there might not be enough inventory at the time to meet current orders. Such an apparently obvious measure must have been more difficult to accomplish than it seems. Recently a major record company experienced a loss of millions. It was caused by a huge inventory of records for which the market had collapsed; it seems that the company had no way of warning itself that returns were coming in at the same time that more of those same records were being produced. So all over the country warehouses were full of dead merchandise.

Sometimes the cause of problems is within the sales department. A salesman can oversell his accounts and distort the general sales trends that the company uses to order new pressings. In such cases an awful lot of mistakes can be made, resulting in overstocked warehouses.

Many merchandising managers like to see their salesmen obtain orders of from one to several copies of every title in the catalog rather than hundreds of one title. Record stores won't bother to return a few copies of one title. Sooner or later everything sells, and such orders are good for all the artists in the catalog.

Who Buys the Records

Many people in the business feel that young women form the bulk of the record buying public. Some claim that it's preteen girls who buy the singles and twelve- to twenty-year-old males who buy the most albums. Lynn Goldsmith, who is a professional image-maker and very conscious of exactly who the audience is for every act she is working for, told us that audiences have changed, and these days all she sees in the front rows grabbing at the clothing of the stars are males. Drummer Bernard Purdie observed mostly women at Aretha Franklin's concerts. Producer Michael Cuscuna (who works with Bonnie Raitt) claims that women buy Streisand, but only when dragged to performances will men see her. It's common knowledge in the trade, however, that women tend to attend concerts featuring male artists. Jim Tyrell adds a further dissonant note when he tells us that while it's true that John Denver and Elton John are bought by young girls, the rock and roll bands have always been marketed for males.

When it really comes down to it, there seems to be no *reliable* consensus on the age and sex of record buyers, though studies do show some correlation with race and income level. The merchandising manager, if he or she is to be at all effective in the job, must be not only aware of but ahead of all these things.

9

Program and Musical Directors

SONGS BECOME HITS through extensive radio play, which presents them to a large segment of the public. Whether a new release is to receive this extensive exposure is often a life-or-death decision: no airplay, no sales. The people who make this decision — who "break" the tune — are the radio stations' program and musical directors.

The strict definition of a program director (PD) is "the person responsible for everything that goes on the air." Since the rates a station charges its advertisers are primarily determined by the size of its audience, its PD is expected to schedule programming that will attract the greatest number of regular listeners. Not all stations appeal to the same market. Many small stations attract audiences by offering them programming not played on the big stations (for example, soul tunes). So most program orientation isn't necessarily centered around the top forty playlists. The heart of American radio is found when a station knows its audience intimately and can afford to take a few flings in its musical programming.

Program directors are responsible for everything that's heard over their stations: music, interviews, news, commercials, weather. Every second of air time has to be filled with a sound that will keep the public tuned in, turned on, entertained, and informed. Because of this, many considerations, besides musical taste, affect the PD's decision whether or not to "break" a new tune. Size — of both station and audience — often determines the amount of leeway. Typically, before the large stations play a new release (other than an obvious hit), there is always evidence that the single or album is selling well. Also, many small and medium-sized stations have usually played the tune long before the big stations air it. If, for example, a new record starts to sell in Des Moines, a small station in that area may begin to play it. This increases sales. Sales and airplay go hand in hand, and you can't always be sure which comes first. But as this process builds, other local stations, encouraged by requests for the tune, will pick it up and begin to play it. All PDs look for new trends and new songs to add to their playlists. Hopefully, the new release, through added airplay and larger local record sales, will receive recognition of its regional popularity in a trade magazine. Such recognition in the trades can have a major affect on a PD's decision to air the tune. Favorable reviews in more general publications, like *The Village Voice, Rolling Stone,* and *The New York Times,* also help a new record.

In most cases, a station with a looser playlist (one that gives the PD more freedom to choose a greater variety and larger number of tunes) has a smaller audience and fewer sponsors. Such a station might play a tune that is moving up at the bottom end of a top-100 chart. But for the major stations a tune has to be a national top-forty hit before it's programmed, in most cases. And even though not all tunes are played on the smaller to medium-sized stations before the top-forty and the even more restricted top-twenty stations will program it, these secondary stations have a significant influence. When, eventually, major market PDs consider a cut for their outlets, a tune is most likely being aired several times a day on a majority of the smaller stations in the country. Finally, a station like

New York City's WABC, with over a million listeners (21 million potential) will program the tune many times a day. It then becomes one of the top ten on all the charts and "goes gold," or becomes a "monster" and "goes platinum." The record company will then give WABC a gold award for making that tune a hit. But often enough, large stations only harvested what the smaller stations sowed!

What a Program Director Does

Many PDs fill multiple roles: deejay (the personality on the air), musical director (the person exclusively concerned with what records will be played and at what hour), and station manager (the person who oversees the entire station operation). Some PDs also moonlight in the evenings on a sister FM station.

Every moment in radio has to be accounted for. Every song, commercial, or newscast aired is logged in — written down in a book much like a diary. A look at the log will tell you how often a song was played during a given week and during what hours. The log helps avoid excessive repetition, shows omissions, provides proof to sponsors that their commercials were aired, and presents a complete picture of airplay to the examiners of the Federal Communications Commission.

The log is also used by the station to study sequencing, called in the business "segue" (pronounced "segway"). Segue is the art of moving from record to record, from record to commercial, or whatever, and back again. This procedure is, to a great extent, what gives the station its image — cool, dignified, hyper, ethnic, and so on. Through segue the station both achieves and communicates its life pulse, the rhythm through which it relates to its audience. To foster and supervise this relationship is the PD's responsibility. In smaller stations deejays may have some voice in the sequencing. But on a big station like WABC deejays have practically nothing to say about what gets played. They are "talent" — hired to project a personality.

PDs control their programming in different, often unique ways, lending personal qualities to what is played and to the sequencing. Richard Fusco operates single-handedly a cable-vision FM channel with no commercials. He might have an all–Rolling Stones afternoon, for example, moving from record to record with a little nostalgia, but letting the tunes speak for themselves. (Another station, in contrast, might feature a more intense announcer, who constantly reminds the audience that The Stones' is a "today sound.") Fusco approaches the sequencing of tunes on his show intellectually. If one song ends in a special downbeat or on an interesting note, he will look for a tune that begins with the same beat or note, though maybe with a change from guitar to horn or vice versa. He discovered, for instance, that one of the songs on Simon's album *Still Crazy After All These Years* ends with the same choir that sang on an earlier cut by Dylan called "Knockin' on Heaven's Door." He used this sound to establish his segue.

The mood of a show, when there is leeway in the programming, can suit the day, be it rainy or sunny, morning or night, the season, or even the phase of the moon. Some PDs say that during the twenty-four hours of a full moon they definitely program a more relaxing playlist. Every year in the Northeast, in late winter, you hear the stations playing Fred Neil's song about going to Florida, "Everyone's Talking," because that's when Northeasterners get that obsession for sun and surf. When you perform all functions on a station the way Fusco does, and think of your work as a hobby, you can "sit there having fun, just a lot of fun, putting out your ideas through a combination of records. You'll be sitting there listening and suddenly you'll be inspired, like a flash, and the next song will come to your mind."

John Betaudier sees things differently. Betaudier is a West Indian PD living and working in Kingston, New York, on a station with something like 10,000 to 20,000 listeners a week. Since all his programs are commercially sponsored, he sees segue as "the art of playing music that is attractive to the listener *and* conducive to commercials." He feels that his station is pretty loose, a place to have some fun. It doesn't have the problem of those big-market signals, which have an "A" playlist of twenty to thirty tunes that they have to play over and over and over without seeming to, with their deejays sounding alive, fresh, and current, while presenting "intense, new musical discoveries" every three minutes.

Small-market stations, many of which operate in direct competition with the big-city signals that travel a hundred or more miles, have to have a larger playlist to attract those listeners who are not exclusively top-forty fans. A typical middle-of-the-road (MOR), small- to medium-market station might have a musical programming that runs something like this: "A" list, top-forty tunes; "B" list, potential top-forty tunes chosen from recent releases; "C" list, oldies — hits popular five to ten years ago. With a playlist like this a station offers more variety.

A program director has a lot of information coming to him in different forms to aid his programming. Promotion men from record companies visit stations (particularly the larger stations) constantly. They spend fifteen to twenty minutes with the PD playing one or two songs they think will hit, or point out how their tunes are moving up on the charts and show local or national sales figures. Bob Bruno, PD on giant WNEW-FM, New York, feels promotion men don't recognize the value of grass-roots radio. They will work New York City to break a record, but never get in their cars to drive out to Long Island or New Jersey. He feels that if they concentrated their efforts "out there," they could force a break in the city. "These guys [small-market program directors]," he says, "get frustrated from lack of contact with record companies."

It's the record company promotion man's job to get his company's product airplay. Way back in radio history, promotion men (pluggers) from publishing companies would slip the big bandleaders a hundred dollars to get a song performed on network radio. Many program directors feel that "payola" (bribing) still influences chart action. From the Fifties until today promotion men have been accused of bribing radio station personnel (today usually PDs) to play certain tunes. For instance, when a seasoned PD receives an "A" side, is positive that it does not have a sound warranting airplay and, furthermore, knows that no other stations in the area have "gone on it," and later picks up a trade magazine and sees that that song is in the top fifty, he may well be suspicious of record company influence — fixing the charts, in the same way people try to fix races.

In an article for *The New York Times Magazine* of April 24, 1977, Geoffrey Stokes points out that "record companies strive — legally, for the most part — to get their product played. Some, it turns out, strive illegally. Something — cash, airline tickets, quantities of salable 'promotional' records, or even drugs — changes hands. And a record gets played."

PDs will tell you that good promotion men are useful to a station and fulfill a need, especially when they respect the image the station wants to maintain. Clive Davis, ex-president of Columbia Records, in his book *Clive,* places a surprisingly big value on the effectiveness of promotion men, knowing that program directors have the incredible power in the music world of being able to make or destroy a record. But, as Bob Bruno points out, to be overly impressed with one's position as PD places one in a vulnerable position, because promotion men have learned to become skillful ego inflators.

In his book *Star-Making Machinery,* Geoffrey Stokes writes about a large record company's promotion department. Controlled by the home office, which gathers and computerizes all possible information about every record, it has conference calls regularly with all promotion men in the field, operating like a military strategist.

Besides the promotion men who work on the PD, pointing

out the tunes they think the station should play, there are tip-sheet services whose self-appointed experts claim an ability to pick hits first, and advise stations on tunes that are breaking in isolated markets. The trade magazines also provide regional statistics on new releases. Then there are the listener requests that come into stations all the time, the number depending on the appeal of the deejays, the size of the market, and the age group the station's programming appeals to. The largest number of requests come from the young girls. In network and other large-market operations it takes a lot of calls to get a reaction from the PD; but in medium to small stations fewer calls are necessary to get a response. The really small stations sometimes will take even one request, or complaint, seriously.

Some Programming Concepts

It's difficult to define MOR programming. Unlike rock and roll, country and western, jazz, or soul, all with pretty identifiable sounds, MOR can and does cross over into all the pop-music categories, from soft rock to country and western. As an MOR program director, Bob Bruno feels that much of popular music comes within the MOR category. Hard or acid rock is avoided, as are novelty tunes like "Convoy." MOR music is generally used by conservative stations with conservative sponsors and/or owners. A rock listener, Bruno points out, is more vociferous, and will call up and complain right away if she or he disapproves of a sound. The MOR listener, on the other hand, typically won't say much, but will just turn the dial. Sometimes, when programming gets "too rock" or "too country" for MOR listeners, they will write in. But Bruno advises the aware musical director to pick up on the programming switch through a sixth sense long before the letters and calls start arriving.

Some people claim that when there isn't an exciting new

trend afoot, radio always falls back on MOR. Some stations find it hard to shift when there is a vital trend happening. For instance, we know of one MOR station owner who refused to let his employees play any rock and roll from 1965 to 1974. During this time, the station's ratings fell off from the number-one position in the market to nearly last. We know another PD who is currently working under pressure to program disco music, which he personally can't stand and claims is boring. The younger deejays on the station maintained that their audiences wanted it. When he finally did allow the introduction of some disco in the P.M. hours, he found that it attracted a whole new raft of sponsors.

The problem for any musical or program director when a new fad comes along, Bruno suggests, is that it doesn't take long before the fad overwhelms the programming, and the station finds itself acquiring a new image, one it might not be looking for. So a tendency to run with a fad has to be examined carefully to make sure it doesn't dominate "the mix" — the composite of all the tunes played.

Program directors are also, as we said, in charge of nonmusical programs: news, interviews, sportscasting, talk shows, and so on. But most stations are run on 90 percent music. With 7,400 stations in the United States there is a lot of air space for many PDs to thrive on, whether it be in cable channels, FM college stations, small- and medium-city and town stations, or the more competitive and coveted big-city stations.

The biggest current threat to *personal* programming, however, is the appearance on the scene of companies that sell prerecorded program tapes to stations. At this time, about 20 percent of all radio time is automatic programming subscribed to by stations, and it's on the increase. Naturally, it's the deejays, and to a lesser extent the program and musical directors, who are hardest hit by these tapes.

The theory behind automated programming is that a lot of people basically tune in for background music, are comfortable with a pretty rigid playlist, and don't mind hearing the same tunes and the same type of music over and over. Many station owners love these automated tapes. They are saved the expense of live deejays, and feel that specialists are choosing the music that will win their station the widest possible audience. Also, the risk of anything offensive accidentally slipping into the programming is lessened.

Promotion men know that automated programming playlists are tight, resulting in less air time for new releases. Potent tape-service companies like T.M. out of Dallas, Texas, consequently, cause record promotion people to wonder about the security of their own jobs. Tight playlists, ones governed by a top-forty concept, often have a domino effect on other stations in the market, forcing all to tighten up their playlists, since all are competing for the mass audiences.

John Betaudier criticizes the automated tapes, saying, "They don't live enough. They cut a station's personality." Bob Bruno, working on a million-listener-a-week station, says of these tapes, "The industry [radio-broadcasting companies] is abdicating its position to the handful of people who dictate for the whole country what will and will not be played. You have a little station in Podunk, Iowa. You take an automatic service out of New York or Los Angeles . . . I'm sorry, but New York or L.A. is *not* Podunk. You have to be sensitive to your market, to people that you're servicing, the community, and you have a responsibility, and that responsibility includes properly programming your station to fill your audience needs. Tape services aren't particular."

Richard Fusco estimates his audience, depending on what else is going on in town, to be from twenty-five to one hundred listeners a day. As we emphasize in the chapter on the deejay, Fusco is in total agreement with Cousin Brucie of powerful NBC in New York City, when he says of prerecorded programming, "They play these tapes over and over, until a sensitive ear gets nauseous, and you sense that the announcer is trying to appeal to the widest possible audience. But it has nothing to do with local concerns. So after a few months' exposure, you tend to switch that station off for lack of contact. Radio personalities are important. You're riding along in your car listening to the radio, and you don't hear the announcer say anything about what a good day it is or anything! No human contact!"

Ways of Getting into the Field

Because positions of influence appeal to so many talented people, there is a lot of competition today for important posts in radio. Salaries, however, especially in the early years, do not provide the principal incentive. A U.S. Department of Commerce report on salaries indicates that one of the most underpaid professions is radio work. Pay runs from a minimum of around $5,000 a year at small stations to $50,000 at the huge ones.

Not too many people back into radio, as they do into other areas of the musical field. The usual ways of becoming a musical or program director are pretty conventional. Most PDs have been deejays and/or straight announcers. And before that they spent some time in one of the many formal radio schools located in the major cities, or in communications courses offered in colleges and universities. Some staff people get their jobs by answering help-wanted ads in the trade magazines. (And nationally a few women are landing spots as PDs.)

The best training, and the least formal, is to work on a local college FM station. It is a no-pay situation, but one where you can learn everything from engineering to management. It's curious, but much of the free labor on the college stations comes from people who live near the campus, who hear of the need, and volunteer. Listener-supported stations like WBAI, New York, since they also thrive on volunteer everything, offer another opportunity for those who can afford some free time during the learning process.

Once people have some experience in radio, it seems to get

into their blood, and they have careers in the medium that are much longer generally than those in other fields. From PD a person might move into station management, or into packaging shows, and from there on over into television, where the salaries are higher, the pressures greater.

10

Deejay

THERE ARE ABOUT 7,400 radio stations in the United States. Not all of them program the same music, observe the same policies, or appeal to the same audiences. So the management of most stations restricts deejays' freedom in selecting songs much more than it seems. The deejay's job is to present music to the station's audience. Music is the backbone of radio, not the deejay, even though the jock (another word for deejay) may take up a lot of radio time reading commercials, giving the time, weather, news, and so on. Some jocks do everything to produce their own programs: hustle up sponsors, cut the commercials, choose the songs, and arrange the segues. At times they function as engineers and actually put the records on the turntable, or punch in the cartridges used at the big-market stations. Above all, they are expected to project an audience-winning personality.

Personality, in radio, *is* the talent. It can earn the person behind it $300,000 a year and more. In Allan Jeffreys' and Bill Owen's novel *DJ* the main subjects of professional conversation with the radio executives were the public appeal of the jocks and the incredible fees these personalities were getting.

The deejay with the right personality becomes a highly desirable commodity, with a following of fans (listeners) just like a star performer.

It's a lot easier to get a start in radio through any of the ways we covered in the previous chapter than by trying to create a winning personality. A beginning, though, is to work on affections for both people and music, and hopefully some of those feelings will be communicated to the audience.

Richard Fusco, partially a frustrated musician who'd loved the music he grew up on in the Sixties, would sleep with the radio on. He, like so many, is really into records, and he knows a great deal about them. He plays records on radio on a "hobby" level, as he calls it, while commercial radio is far removed from that kind of involvement. Nationally known Cousin Brucie, for instance, is projecting his image, personality and humanness, but on his shows music is not selected because of his "personal taste."

Richard first went to a station with 10,000 listeners and told them he wanted radio time to play records. He sold spots for his own three-hour program and produced the commercials; he played music that none of the other stations was playing.

One day Richard heard about a channel on cable radio in Woodstock, N.Y., that was available at no cost. In order for the local cablevision company to get permission to serve the town with commercial radio and television, it had to give the town a channel for its own TV station; and in this case the audio (radio) part came across on the FM radio. Richard went to the town board and said he wanted to use the channel to play music . . . four hours every afternoon. It wouldn't cost them a thing, because Richard had his own stereo equipment and it was nothing to hook it up to the cable. He had his own records, and those he didn't have, he could borrow. The town board OK'd his plan, and Richard began to broadcast.

"What I'm doing," Richard explains, "is as free as you can get on radio. Even freer than the college stations. The town board is all I have to answer to, so I exercise discretion. But I've slipped in a few things . . . like Eric Andersen's song, which says, 'They've heard the same old shit before.' You can't play basic profanity. One complaint to the FCC and that's it."

So, as deejay-producer, Richard will put in a variety of material — from a Firesign Theatre song about a cigarette, fading into a segment from "Sanford and Son" about giving up smoking. Here he doesn't have to be bothered with things that he's not regularly involved in, like commercials. He is the engineer, the program director, deejay, all in one. He works around things like what kind of a day it is, what's happening in the area to inspire the choice of music and segues. He feels very comfortable with the microphone now, but he doesn't want to develop into a personality.

Then there is Bruce Morrow, or Cousin Brucie, or Supermouth (his new handle), who today looks like a cowboy in factory-faded blue denims. He is strictly a Deejay Personality. Working now for NBC, Brucie sits inside a glass enclosure with his engineer, Bob Massell — who was there before with Wolfman Jack — facing him, working from the log. Prepared by the music and program directors, the log indicates what will happen during every second on the air. The log will say 504 . . . and Brucie will turn to the rack of cartridges nearest him and pull out 504. He will place it in the slot and it will play — in the case of 504, a Rolling Stones number. The log tells him when and what commercial to read. Besides these scheduled items, he may interrupt the program with spots about traffic, weather news, or other — little items that have just come in on the teletype. In addition to being "on the case," Brucie must also work in his charm, his personality, his upbeat tempo — feeding the audiences what he thinks radio is all about. "Radio," he believes, "is tomfoolery, if you want. Having a good time . . . that's what radio is."

Brucie began by taking engineering and communications courses at New York University. Bob Massell also started as an undergraduate, working at a college station. Brucie explains why he doesn't choose any of the tunes he plays. "Our program and musical directors," he explains, "know probably better than I know what I need for the show, because my whole career has changed quite a bit." He used to listen to a hundred records a week when he was a kid. Later, when he was on a station in Bermuda, he chose the records he wanted to play. But now there is no time.

"The whole attitude of NBC is different than my former employers', where I worked for thirteen years," Brucie told us. "At NBC they want to use their people properly. My whole image has changed, and a television career opened up. The radio career leads to all these other things." Wolfman Jack, for example, has done everything, including acting in movies. Many deejays have written books, and a number of them have gone into producing records or into top spots in record companies. Johnny Hyde, longtime small-town California deejay, now program director of a station in Sacramento, freelances TV features.

An interesting trait of Brucie's, which might be an asset gone unacclaimed, is the way he paces himself. Sitting at the microphone, he is alert to *everything:* his log, his engineer, people who come in to tell him something, the stopwatch, and especially to his audience when he is "on." An indication of this quickness in his work is the way he smoothly fits in reactions to things going on around him. He relates to the kids on a field trip from New Jersey, who are looking through the glass at him. He makes a big thing about kissing the glass between him and a little girl, who blushes and is thrilled. He asks us questions about our book. Whatever it is, he's "on the case" — at a pace that is almost computerized. When he's off the air, he continues the same pace. He is alert to and takes part in every single piece of stimuli happening around him — including a visit from his wife, who runs an antique shop in the area, and who stopped in to look at some candles someone at the station had made that Brucie wanted to show her.

This evenness in his energy doesn't fluctuate in the slightest degree, whether there's a lot going on or a little, whether he's on the air or off. It might be the secret to his success — that up-tempo evenness, and an ability to ad lib and relate to his listeners as a human being. "I'm not compressed into a situation where I just do time and weather," Brucie says. "I can say whatever I want. Radio is a very human medium, and that's what's happening to radio today: they're forgetting it's a human being — it's an extension. Most radio stations today, they take time and weather and they think that's it. But that's not what radio is about. That's a jukebox. Radio is a human being." Naturally, he "hates" computerized programming. "It makes me nauseous. Take the human element out of radio and you have nothing."

Developing a radio personality takes a little time. An aspiring deejay has to develop microphone assurance — the ability to ad lib at will, while not forgetting the names of things. He must correct stutters, avoid disturbing pauses; and, most of all, he must rise above that awful style of public speaking encouraged by high school English and social studies teachers. Brucie has mastered all these skills, to the extent that his mistakes are part of his act, making him even *more* human. He slurs over words the way most people who are excited do. He makes deliberate repeats.

John Betaudier, whom we talked about in the chapter on program director, says that becoming a successful personality means "flipping to the B side . . . where one loses one's stiff, more formal self — where a natural, more loose personality can flow." When Brucie told us, however, that he can say whatever he wants to say, he must mean that in two ways. Either he can express himself within the limits of what the listeners want to hear and in a way the station wants him to say it, or he means that he has arranged his personality so completely around what's accepted in radio that there is no conflict, and he doesn't have to edit as he talks.

Most live shows are run through an eight-second delay, so

that if anyone slips (profanity is not allowed on the air), it can be taken out. But the not so obvious taboos must also be understood and respected. If a jock should happen to say something off-base about religion or politics, immediately the station knows it has to come down on him. "One doesn't have to wait for the vibrations to come from outside," Betaudier says. About compromise he says, "Deejays have to respect their mix, but they aren't going to love everything they play. But the program directors don't love everything they program either."

Getting the personality is something else. A woman deejay in Seattle said she didn't want to take on a personality that connoted a psychology she didn't either believe in or relate to. One of the most famous disc jockeys of all time was a woman, Tokyo Rose. During World War II, she was heard on American servicemen's radios throughout the Pacific Ocean. The program played popular American music, and her message was propaganda directed at undermining American morale. But her pitch was delivered and hyped in such an extremely sexy voice that her program did very little damage to GI morale. Instead, she became the brunt of jokes and ridicule, and her program actually gave the GIs therapeutic relief. The point is, the personality chosen by the Japanese High Command was so extreme that it lost credibility.

Lisa Karlin, a part-time disc jockey in Boston, said, "I won't fall into the trap that some people try to push me into. They'd have me talk more softly, make on-the-air sexual inferences, or be a pinup girl on the air. I use my full name for the same reason — to avoid the audio pinup girl syndrome. I have a complete identity, and a first and last name is part of that. I also feel that there is a natural sexuality that any good announcer, be it male or female, communicates through the rest of their on-the-air personality. This is achieved without making one's voice breathy, talking low, or any other affectations."

Since females make up both half the population and way

over half the national radio audience, it would be a really interesting experiment if radio management used teenage female jocks on the right program. It's teenagers, after all, who have always made record shows so popular, and built their high ratings. And it's these ratings that make possible the station's and the stars' huge incomes. Historically, one of the first and most important personality deejay shows was aired in Hollywood, California, during the Forties, called "Peter Potter and his Platter Parade." You could walk the two-mile stretch of Santa Monica beach — popular with all the high school kids — and you wouldn't miss one tune, because all the portable radios were turned on to the Platter Parade!

Although every station is different in its programming and appeal, small-market stations typically tend to be more conservative than the big-city stations, because their audiences are more conservative. When the community tends to be conservative, the station owner and his or her set of friends in the area are conservative, and when the local business people who supply the station's economic support are conservative, then the station's natural conservative tastes build a wall of objection toward any tendency to try to reach an audience in the area that may not have those same tastes. All station employees, including the deejay, are careful not to offend their listeners, their sponsors, or their boss.

A deejay, consequently, with progressive musical tastes, or one with controversial opinions or an open outlook, will typically have a hard time maintaining an even and happy relationship with the directors of a small-market station. An audience lets a station know what it likes and what it doesn't like! And stations worry when complaints come in. But this catering to their audiences' preferences by small-market stations does not, by contrast, imply that the big stations in the cities are "progressive." They're not. The reality of broadcasting is that progressive radio, with few exceptions, is found in the metropolitan areas. Usually it's on FM — often where FM is part of the Public Broadcasting System (PBS), or what's referred to as noncommercial radio. And, of course, it's on college stations. Often music-business history, and music-business success, come about through the sweat and blood of adventurous spirits who go against the established grain by committing themselves to a sound that has little acceptance, or about which there is a prejudice.

Writing for *Billboard*, Rudy Garcia talked about how the college FM stations were filling a vacuum created by the absence of commercial Latin (Spanish-speaking) FM outlets in the New York City market. "Two college stations making a particular effort in this regard," he wrote, "are WKCR-FM of Columbia University in New York and WBJB-FM of Brookdale Community College in Lincroft, N.J." Richard Hansen, WBJB station manager, said, "The response to our Latin programming was really quite phenomenal. When we started, we inadvertently went into competition with a local commercial station." WRLV of Long Branch, N.J., which was experimenting with Latin music programming, also entered the competition. Being an educational station, it had no commercial interruptions, so it drew off listeners from commercial stations.

Much of FM today, however, is like AM. "What young people especially forget," Brucie tells us, "is that radio is in business to make money. We [AM] are here, and so is FM. At first FM was not into making money, because they didn't have the listeners. If you don't have listeners, you don't get commercials. As you gain listeners, you get commercials. Sponsors don't come on the radio because they like my thing, they come on because they know we have listeners, and that's the same with the FM stations. They're becoming commercial because they have listeners, and in order to keep your listeners you've got to become pretty commercial. They were able to play newer records that were not as popular as the ones we can play, because they didn't have a huge audience. So they attracted a special audience in the beginning. But as they got a little bit more successful, they got a little bit more greedy. Success makes you greedy. So they had to change their format to keep this large audience."

What will take their place? "New stations will come on, and new formats will be tried," Brucie explains. "As they get more successful, they keep trying to develop that sound. They have to try to do things that other stations aren't doing — such as exposing new records." And this suggests, perhaps, a way to break in as a deejay: be a maverick and provide a service not on the other stations.

Johnny Walker (who is credited with being the first deejay personality in England, rather than merely a disc spinner and commercial reader), operated from a "pirate" station in the mid-Sixties. His, and other stations like it, transmitted from ships anchored three miles out at sea, where they could legally broadcast without the usual government licensing. These pirate deejays were guided by their own personal musical tastes. They presented discs they chose with sincerity, and expressed a believable commitment to the music, which brought excitement and a feeling of necessity to pop music. They boosted new artists, and provided exposure and demand for records that helped new record companies and producers to come into being. There were 100 to 130 pirate deejays covering the English radio; for the first time in that country music was on the air all day and all night.

Naturally, these pirates were taking power away from the music establishment. During the period of the pirates' activity, sales were spread over a greater number of artists than during the previous period, when fewer artists were getting the bulk of the exposure and sales. A BBC Radio special, "The History of Rock and Roll," said that these pirates provided for new music; and they broke up the power structure that previously had virtually monopolized the music-business scene. Legal charges were brought against the pirates; when they agreed to pay performing rights organizations the fees due the artists, no terms were reached, because the power structure did not want to settle and let the pirate stations continue to broadcast. By then, however, the pirates' practice of projecting their personalities and playing the new sounds had been picked up by BBC, and ex-pirate Tony Blackburn, along with six or seven others, started the famous music program "BBC One."

In the United States a similar effect was achieved through FM and noncommercial programming. But the swing is definitely back toward a more conservative programming. And probably one of the reasons that U.S. radio is getting more conservative is that the deejays have so little to say about the music they play.

Brucie claims that payola scandals caused the deejay to lose power by denying him a strong say-so in the choice of records. "The stations, in order to protect themselves," Brucie says, "and the personality had to meet somewhere in the middle." Dick Fox at William Morris Agency agrees. He believes that is why stations are reluctant to add new records. "Years ago," Fox says, "you could get anything played if you gave the guy a hundred bucks. Can't do that anymore." Just being suspected of taking a payola is enough to put a deejay's career in jeopardy.

Tape services, covered in the previous chapter, present a big threat to the deejay profession. They take the feeling of experimentation out of the station's programming. They are most regimented when it comes to adhering to the hits-and-hits-only rule. Tape services reflect the tendency in contemporary radio to knock down the deejay, to keep him or her from becoming one of those irreplaceable personalities. The automatic tape service pressure will probably ease off a little as the station owners find out that the computer will never replace the personality — particularly individuals like Brucie, Fusco, and Betaudier. Betaudier hangs out in parks and laundromats, where he can hear *living* language. He heard, for instance, a little girl say, "Let's pretend that you are me and I was you" — which he promptly used as an ad-lib one-liner on his program. And the deejays who concentrate on building their radio personalities — through clever phrases, or by relating to audiences in human terms, or by charm, or through whatever means — build followings that attract the attention of larger stations, and the larger salaries.

11

Songwriter

SONGWRITING IS one of the most purely creative functions in the music business; and since, as with the novelist or the painter, the internal motivation has got to come from some place within you, it's hard to write about the process. But it's also a craft, and as such it can be learned. There are various ways to approach it — as a singer-songwriter, a professional songwriter, or as a songwriting team.

Singer-Songwriter

The singer-songwriter has the advantage of being able to perform and record his or her own songs. The credibility this personal presentation establishes with audiences is invaluable. The music and the mood come across as authentic — because of a personal connection with the particular song.

Today's charts are loaded with singer-songwriters, so there's no mistaking their appeal. Gerry Goffin, onetime songwriting partner of Carole King, says in *In Their Own Words,* "After the Beatles started to grow and get real good, it suddenly didn't appear that going in and writing songs for whoever you were writing songs for was the way anymore." About his own response to this shift he says, "Groups are writing now for their own personal feeling — it's a whole different thing. To me that's a little more honest — not that I didn't enjoy what I was doing."

Singer-songwriters can try out their material with an audience almost while they create it, getting valuable feedback. Besides this helpful exposure, they have another immediate advantage over less all-around talents. Even if their own recordings never make the charts, in the process of performing new songs they automatically provide a showcase for them. This can get other artists interested in covering them, which nets them, as writers, additional royalties. The Beatles' song "Yesterday" has been recorded by hundreds of people throughout the world. Earning potential can be enormous. Fred Neil, author of the theme song for *Midnight Cowboy,* and many other well-known writers, make most of their income from royalties earned from covers recorded by hit-making singers who don't write.

Hoyt Axton feels that songwriting and performing are all tied together. In an interview with *Songwriter Magazine* he told a story about John Kaye, ex-dishwasher at the Troubadour, who would come out of the kitchen every time Axton sang his song "The Pusher." When Kaye formed Steppenwolf, "The Pusher" was the tune most identified with the group in their early days.

Often the first time a songwriter's song is recorded by another artist nothing much happens. Then perhaps another recording artist picks it up. The song "After Midnight" by J. J. Cale was first recorded in 1965 by Snuff Garrett. In a *Melody Maker* interview Cale said, "When Clapton recorded that song [in 1970], it created a demand."

There is no rule that says a singer-songwriter can't write songs with another singer in mind. No longer bound to your personal emotions, you may even find there's a freeing effect on your creative efforts. In any case, it can be a good experience.

Singer-songwriters sometimes become so popular and so busy with performances and recording sessions that they have little time anymore to sit down and write their own songs. They, too, turn to outside material.

The Songwriter

The songwriter who doesn't perform his or her own material often needs to write with a particular singer in mind, though writers sometimes do create a golden egg before they've come up with a goose to lay it. You'll hear that a particular singer is recording and is looking for songs. Either you or a representative from your publishing company will set up the right contact on the artist's end to present your song. Known writers may get a direct request or assignment to write for a singer or a group. Such songs are often needed in a few days' time. Writers who accept such assignments really have to know how to produce quickly.

Songwriters usually know what age group or market their song should be aimed at when they write. Dick Fox, Neil Sedaka's agent, told us that Sedaka makes a study of the pulse and feelings of the fourteen- to eighteen-year-olds, in order to write his songs from their viewpoint.

The songwriter has to learn thoroughly how to tailor his inspiration to the need. While the singer-songwriter usually writes "from the soul," as the saying goes, and with a drive to release her/himself from a personal emotion, the professional songwriter is not tied to his own mood. "Create your own moods, don't depend upon outside forces to do it for you," advises Tommy Boyce, in his positive book, *How To Write A Hit Song . . . and Sell It.*

Sometimes there's a good voice hiding beneath the writer's songwriting talent, and singers have been known to be "discovered," when record companies or publishers, listening to a presentation tape, like not only the song but the voice singing it. Carole King is only one of many songwriters who wrote for years before deciding to come out and perform herself.

But you don't have to be able to sing well or play an instrument or even know musical notation to be able to write songs. Johnny Mercer, who wrote a large share of songs for Bing Crosby, played piano by the hunt-and-peck method. All you have to do is be able to communicate your song — some way, somehow.

It's probably a good idea to find someone with a better voice, if you feel your own isn't adequate, to sing your song into a tape recorder. This tape will become a kind of rough demo, which you can present to publishers, who may in turn present it to a performer they have in mind. When recording costs were cheaper, this method of selling a song was used a lot more. Many of today's stars once worked as professional singers hired by publishers to record demos in prescribed singing styles. These styles would match those of the artists for whom the tapes were to be played, so that the artists could better imagine themselves recording the songs.

In most big cities there are 8- and 4-track studios that rent for as little as $10 an hour. Check at a large college, university, or radio station for studio rentals. If you or the singer you've hired are well rehearsed, you can go in and do a couple of songs in very little time. Just be sure that the lyrics are sung so that they're easily heard and understood.

The Songwriting Team

Some people only write lyrics, while others only compose melodies. When the two find each other, that is the beginning of collaboration, if their personalities can blend harmoniously, and if they find out it's a mutually dependent situation.

There are those who can write both lyrics and melody, but

find they prefer to collaborate. They find that they produce better when they have another person to bounce ideas off. Although there are obvious advantages to collaborating, a purist may feel that a synthesis can't be reached in these efforts. Singer-songwriter Tim Hardin feels there is a naturalness and unity to a song totally composed by one person that you don't hear in collaborations.

Evolving a Direction

You are probably already set in some sort of musical direction, depending on whose music has influenced you the most. Next you have to get down to developing a personal style, *if* you are going to be a performer-songwriter, or to capturing hot new hit sounds, *if* you are working toward writing hit material, the more restrictive of the two. It may be harder to develop the unique style needed by a singer-songwriter so that his or her albums will give off that instant identifiable sound. People expect a nostalgic one, for instance, from The Band. Although the sound is somewhat contrived, The Band is definitely The Band; no one else sounds like it. And once you've evolved your own style, there's the possibility of a meal ticket. But this is not to say that there won't come a time when you'll feel the need for a change. Pressure to get out of a groove will come from many sources: your own creative urges, your critics, and your audience, too, who, though they'll expect to hear the old familiar sound, will "double-bind" you with a demand for something fresh. Toward the end of their lives Jimi Hendrix and Bix Beiderbecke were both preoccupied with this effort to change.

When performers and songwriters sense that their audience is getting bored, they have to change with the times. Sedaka felt that in his old career he made the mistake of making his songs too predictable. He didn't want that to happen his second time around. In a *Rolling Stone* interview he said,

"I'm really happy with 'Bad Blood' because the lyric line is a little controversial, with words like 'bitch' and such. I was concerned at first because my image was wholesome." Ironically, Sedaka, when working for his comeback, opened for The Carpenters . . . who by their own confession in *People* magazine said they were getting boring. Sedaka upstaged them in all their performances; Dick Fox told us that had The Carpenters only played it cool and sweated out the last gigs where Sedaka was sure to keep on upstaging them, it would have slowed down Sedaka's comeback. As it happened, The Carpenters fired Sedaka, which caused the press to zero in with heavier bad press about *them,* and more good press about Sedaka. The next day, by the way, Dick Fox called Las Vegas and booked Sedaka as the headline act, and for lots more money! So even when one achieves a unique personal style that catapults a singer-songwriter or self-contained group to stardom, development, change, and self-criticism are all *still* part of maintaining the total act.

As a songwriter you've got to also consider what kind of songs you're going to try to fall in with (country, western, rock, and so on). Some writers merge an interesting underground-type song with what is already hit-oriented material. Others try to write songs that "cross over" into other markets, thus widening the song's appeal. Country music, for example, has been crossing over more and more into pop; and when you realize that country accounts for 11.6 percent of dollar volume (as reported by the National Association of Record Merchandisers for 1974), versus the 6.1 percent that goes to contemporary rock, pop, and soul, you can understand the commercial wisdom of crossing over. Some merge a generation of sound into their songs.

A lot of writers yearn for a special slot: the merging of poetry with songwriting. Gerry Goffin says in *In Their Own Words,* "First, it was just sort of pop lyrics. Then all of a sudden poetry got involved. And there's a big difference between being a pop lyricist and being a poet — which blew my head a whole lot. . . . Being a poet is a lot harder; it's really work. I had a desire to write that kind of song — to be a poet — but I wasn't able to, so I gave it up." Of course, everyone knows of the few examples where it's worked successfully, with poets such as Leonard Cohen, Bob Dylan, and Patti Smith. By contrast, when we talked with Joe Pellegrino, publishing head at CAM-USA, Inc., we expressed our feeling that women aren't used enough in the songwriting field. Our attitude was that women know more about how women feel; and most songs contain lyrics which try to elicit young females' emotion. Joe disagreed. "Usually with the girls, the young girls that you speak about," he said, "they're more into poetry. They'd make wonderful poetesses. And poems are not songs, I don't care what anybody tells me, they just don't make good songs. Guys, if they are in that kind of bag, maybe can do it better [write about what women feel] because they're more removed."

Agreeing with Bainbridge Crist's traditionally chauvinistic attitude that women are the inspiration of songs rather than the writers of them, because they are the passive ones, Tommy Boyce tells his readers that most songs about women are written by men, and that very few women write songs about men. Those few include Joni Mitchell, Carole King, Joan Baez, and Mae Axton (Hoyt Axton's mother, whose "Heartbreak Hotel" is about a woman leaving her man). Landy McNeil's recent personal experience while running Chappell's songwriting workshop is interesting: he felt that there were more good female songwriters than male.

What Is A Hit Song?

Most people in the business will tell you that they don't know what a hit is, but that they know one when they hear one. What they really mean is they can tell whether or not a song *sounds like* the songs in the top forty. This may seem like a primitive way to judge hit potential; but in the songwriting field such a statement has far more validity than it does in painting, say, where you hear people say, "I don't know anything about art, but I know what I like." Many people have even said that you can measure how big a hit a song will be by how good it sounds on a cheap car radio! When music business people say they are looking for a hit song that is unique and fresh, they're really saying that they want something "like" current hit material, only "a bit" different.

If you want to know what makes a hit song, the best and easiest way is to constantly keep abreast of the current top forty. Analyze some of them. Hit songs are comprised of the same elements as all songs, only the boundaries are tighter and more limiting. This description is so simple that nobody in the business will admit to it.

Writing hits is a fairly compressed process. Compare the songs on the top ten with those by someone more underground, someone even as popular as Dylan. Although his songs may be recorded by other singers and become hits, they have a more permanent place in American music than tunes with only temporary spots on the top of the charts. It's risky, in terms of the future betterment of popular music, to advise a new writer to emphasize study of the top ten or top forty. It could really hinder original and fresh writing. In all good conscience, because we don't want you to starve, we have to come down to talking about the hit a lot, because that's the one thing the music business *really* cares about. It's the money in the business; and writing hit material is sometimes the quickest or only way to break into songwriting. Almost no one can get a start today, unless someone feels there is hit material in there somewhere . . . regardless of artistic talent.

The industry is not as open as it has been, and underground movements have not raised their heads in the way folk, or folk rock, or the psychedelic sound once did. Strong MOR songs took over the AM radio and the charts. One reflection of this revised focus is seen in *Rolling Stone,* which is turning its attention more than ever toward paying homage to the same superstars over and over again. It tends to be much more into gossip about a few people who are increasingly commercially important. Yet it still remains, in spite of changes, the finest source of independent critical writing on pop music.

"This, then, is the record industry's equivalent of the quest for the Holy Grail: the quest for the hit single. It's a search wired with high tension and hype," writes Meridee Mercer in *Gallery* magazine, "not to mention compromises."

What's in A Song Title?

Pop-song titles — past, present, and probably future — generally have a number of obvious things in common, so obvious that everybody intuitively knows what they are, but it may help you in your own writing if you analyze them. Song titles, as well as the song's lyrics, are usually conversational in tone. Titles set a tone and a premise ("I'm Leaving It All Up To You"). Often some pretty strong feelings are involved; but the title, by neutralizing them somewhat, makes them much more palatable and bearable ("I'm So Lonesome I Could Cry"). When one hears a song about anguish titled in a catchy, clever way ("How Can You Mend A Broken Heart?"), it's a little easier to accept. When you can lighten up a really terrible experience ("Heartaches by the Number") by the way you express the concept, you're going to be taking the edge off anxiety in a way that will make it easier for people to identify with some universal, tough emotions. A title like Frampton's "Do You Feel Like We Do?" asks for audience involvement.

Slang is used a lot in both lyric and title, so that the listener who uses popular speech can quickly identify with the song, and the more sophisticated listener (who accepts slang) will be assured that the song is honest and sincere ("He Don't

Love You Like I Love You"). Some universally felt feelings can be expressed in an almost ludicrously simple and naive form ("Make The World Go Away").

Things can get pretty corny in songs. Corniness seems to make them more easily acceptable, giving the listener an impression that aids and solicits sympathy. Once that is done, one can identify easily, especially when the song deals with universals. Gerry Goffin substantiates this in *In Their Own Words* by saying, "When I was younger, I could write every day. But it all gets corny after a while." However, the corny element underlies much commercial songwriting.

One way of avoiding repetition, while employing catchy slang, is to keep your ears to the ground for new phrases and words used in young people's speech. For example, the word "hooked," first associated with drug usage, was later used acceptably in many ways: "Baby, Baby, Don't Get Hooked On Me," and "Hooked On A Feeling."

Cleverness and wordplay are part of successful titles too. Whereas in the fine arts, artists are warned against resorting to cleverness (Picasso was particularly outspoken against it, though he couldn't resist being clever himself), in popular music, the most mass art form of all, catchiness is highly cultivated. Dylan's songs are not above it: "Motorpsycho Nitemare" is a very clever title. And who could not respond to the economically rendered wordplay of George M. Cohan's classic lyric about World War I, "We won't be back till it's over, over there"? Such skillful wordplay is something songwriters aim for.

Study the hot new titles. Usually you can spot an implicit trend. Try to detect future directions. Make up titles simply as an exercise — phrases that trigger your imagination, that say it all. File them away in a notebook or a card file. Two or three noted ideas combined may become the title and following lines of a lyric.

Bernie Taupin, Elton John's collaborator, tells an interviewer for *Circus* that basically he finds titles before anything else. He likes to think of titles and feels you can construct a whole song that way. If you can make a statement in a few simple but catchy words, you'll have not only your title but your theme and probably one of the first lines of your song all at once.

Theme

It's important to get a good title down from the start, since it states your premise and is often reiterated within the first lines of the song. Thus it becomes your starting point, a way of writing the song line by line from the top down, to get a logical continuity. However you accomplish it, writing the chorus first, with rhyme or without, studded with hook lines or not, you've got to maintain some kind of focal point. Which is what a theme is: the basic idea that you're talking — or rather, singing — about.

Country music affords an exaggerated example of what we mean: it usually tells a complete story. Most songs, however, do this in one way or another. Sometimes just a slice of life is conveyed, often in the form of an analogy. Bernie Taupin's "I Feel Like A Bullet," for instance, describes how someone feels when he breaks up with a lover after years of going steady. Other songs may depict life directly, without analogy, as in "Livin' For The Weekend," Gamble, Huff, and Gilbert's song about the drab middle of the week and what happens on the weekend. In his greatest songs Chuck Berry described teen life as it was then with precision. Totally imaginary visions, some visions based more on reality, images of what's happening around you — they've all been used as themes for songs. When sharp observation is combined with strong personal feelings, you'll often have something that gives an amazingly accurate picture of the time. Tim Hardin says, "If songs were really just personal, they'd bounce off your neurosis, because your personality would be in the way of anything more universal."

Many people get ideas directly from chords they put together that suggest something to them. Or sometimes you'll get an idea from listening to someone else's song, or even from just the "feel" of someone else's song. Alex Harvey and Tommy Boyce are two songwriters who sometimes go to comic books for ideas, because they find there a kind of short-hand similar to the one needed in songwriting.

For any number of reasons, besides realizing it is lucrative, you may want to consider writing the hit song as a goal. You may want to try to bring out the things most people want to hear in a song and *still* slip in something that you personally believe in, or want others to hear, that is perhaps new to them. Lots of writers' songs spell out their philosophy of life. Frank Zappa's ideas are so socially and politically radical that he has had to keep them under restraint for the purposes of commercial songwriting. However, your philosophy of life may not be an obstacle to the medium you are working in. Monkee Mike Nesmith is quoted in *Circus* magazine as saying, "I think I'll always have the philosophy . . . that life is meant to be enjoyed, and we always want to have a good time and sing positive and harmonious and uplifting songs, and that's only been more and more refined in the past few years since we've been meditating and stuff." John Denver at-tributes his mass appeal to the fact that while everybody else is writing about how hard life is, he talks about "how good it is to be alive."

Ideas for songs are literally everywhere. Don't be inhibited about taking an idea from a short story or a movie or some-thing you've seen on TV. Lots of writers have mentioned how some sentence they heard on TV sparked an idea. You might even try an exercise used by some songwriters, which is to create a song around an interpretation of something that's happening on the screen with the sound off — good training, especially for those interested in writing TV and movie scores.

The most common subject matter by far is love. There seems to be no end to how it can be expressed. People can identify with a disappointed love, a love ended, a new love, a first love, a realistic love, a sadistic or a masochistic love, a love-hate; in fact, any variation you can think of will strike a resonant chord in many people — not to mention that most popular theme: the hope of a regained love. Love is expressed a lot these days in terms of friendship, and love of nature or life comes second to love for another human being.

Whatever theme you're attracted to, do as artists in other fields do: keep working. Don't just sit around waiting for flashes and become dejected if nothing comes to you. Unless you are among those who, at a certain time in life, find it easy to sit down and write spontaneously, you will no doubt put a lot of effort into working before the seemingly instant song comes through. It's possible to spend months on a song before it works, and it's possible to write the whole thing in a flash. Simon and Garfunkel were rumored to have spent a year on ten songs.

Ironically, many writers maintain that their best songs are written almost effortlessly. Gerry Goffin is reported as saying that any time it took him a long time to write a song, it usually wasn't too good a song. John Sebastian said, "I wrote 'Welcome Back' in fifteen minutes. Generally, they're hits if you write them fast. The idea that can be put down in fifteen minutes is very often simple enough to be commercial." And John Lennon and David Bowie came up with the number-one single "Fame" in a reported forty-five minutes. Bernie Taupin writes his songs in fifteen to forty-five minutes.

But the idea that comes to you the most easily is often the one that's easiest to forget. Also, things one doesn't work hard for may seem unimportant (our Puritan background makes us put hard work first). So train yourself at these impulsive moments to write down your ideas instantly, no matter where, even if it's on restaurant napkins.

The Hook

One of the standard components of hit songs is the hook line. Usually, it's *the point* of the song. Sometimes it's the climax, and often it's the title as well. Everyone aiming for a hit wants to come up with a strong hook. Some songs have double (two) hooks, or a hook within a hook.

Although most songs have a hook line of some kind, in the hit it is really driven home. The hook statement of Eric Carmen's "All By Myself" *equals* the song's title *equals* the entire emotion of the song. Though instant pickup is the aim of the hook line of a song that is trying to be a hit, there is the danger that the hook will drive so hard it wears the song out. Self-defeating, incessant hooks can create fast saturation in the listener. And on the other hand, "Midnight At The Oasis," which is not dependent on a strong hook, had a year of airplay before it was spread all over the country on AM, and it consequently had a longer lifespan.

However, since the biggest question one asks of a song is "Will it get picked up or not picked up — by radio play?" the faster you can attract attention to your song through the familiarity of a strong hook line, the better. Dick Fox at William Morris Agency feels that not only the song gets accepted through repetition on the radio, but also whole movements in music. "I feel the public and, in particular, kids," Fox says, "are very vulnerable, and can be coerced into liking certain things . . . through repetitions." Other people think of the process in terms of mass hypnosis.

Repetition can be addicting, and whether or not you like a song may have nothing to do with your personal taste. For instance, most people have had the experience of hearing a song over and over again on AM radio, a song they may have at *first* disliked or thought dull, only to end up singing it with zest! Some producers claim that they make all judgments on a first hearing.

Things don't always work the way the establishment thinks they will, however, and when the artist's and audience's tastes meet at the right time, as did Frampton's and his audience, the artist should take his own "event" seriously and concretely. Speaking prematurely, Frampton said that he didn't want to go all the way (in hit writing), but he did want to add to his own writing one of the standard elements in most hits, the incessant hook. In an interview for *Crawdaddy* magazine, after he "came alive," he said, "I'm not going to do anything different this time when I write songs for the next album, except that I want to put more direct hooks in, I want at least one hit single next time."

Song Structure

A typical form songwriters use today is verse, chorus, verse, chorus, verse, chorus. There are also many songs that are written the other way around, starting with the chorus and ending with the verse. Another typical form is verse, chorus, verse, chorus, bridge, verse, chorus. Slight variations of these basic forms are also used; there is no absolute rule to adhere to in any creative work.

Writing your song so that its length is adaptable is also something to think about. It's to your advantage to have a song that can be played at one length for live performance and another, shorter one, for a single. That means that when it's played on the radio, the song can sound complete in under three minutes, but on the album it might continue with further verses and chorus or whatever. There have been several hits lately that run eight minutes, and perhaps flexibility in AM programming will allow songs that run over three minutes more airplay.

The Bridge

The bridge, also called the release, is the section of a song that is sufficiently different from the rest to "release" it from becoming too repetitious or boring. It is used to give relief much as painters use the color gray to give the eye a rest area, and at the same time to set off the other colors, which will seem more alive by contrast. But like the gray in painting, the bridge of a song can't be too dominant; placement and tone must be just right. One of the most common pitfalls is allowing the song to "drop" too much at the release (to lose momentum or excitement). When this happens, you have to work especially hard to bring it back up in the final verse and chorus.

So, depending on the requirements of the song, the bridge can be rather long or very short, exciting (as in lead-guitar instrumentals) or calming, anything so long as it provides that vital contrast.

Exploiting it to the full, you can make the bridge suggest some other kind of sound that you think will help make the song more popular. If you think that a tiny suggestion of jazz, for instance, will add to the interest of a pop song, this could be the place for it, assuming, of course, that it works with the rest of the song. Eric Carmen's Rachmaninoff-type break gave "All By Myself" the relief it needed from its insistent hook, and at the same time added a seriousness to the sentiment. Though to a lot of discerning ears this may seem to be an obvious ploy, with material oriented toward mass listening it nonetheless succeeds.

Lyrics, Mood, and Melody

To the perennial question, "Which comes first, the lyrics or the melody?" the only answer is that every songwriter has his or her own method; there is no other way.

Many people start out first of all with a title, then work on defining a mood that best communicates what the title suggests. Next come the lyrics, and last of all the melody. Some writers speak the words as they might be sung, in rhythm and at a tempo that brings out a rise and fall (upbeats and downbeats), and that captures the emphasis just right. (One can imagine Dylan working this way.) The sound of the words themselves may suggest the melody, and the mood (emotion) may come this way too. "Certain words will not fit with certain other words," says Tim Hardin, who has a rationale for writing words first. "Therefore, because any musical note may go next to any other musical note of any length, notes and melody are less restrictive. You can put one note of any length next to any other note of any length. So it's easier to fit notes to the more restrictive long and short syllables of the words and sentences you write."

Words ending in vowel sounds (*you, they, I*) are usually considered to be of long duration, though they can be notated as short. Consonants are generally assigned short notes.

When writing lyrics, you'll want to use adjectives and adverbs to make strong images. Verbs move a song; any action song will probably have a lot of verbs. You might try going to an old movie magazine like *Hollywood Confidential* to pick up some terminology from the past and revive it. You could find just the right word, something in common usage then that would sound fresh today. Or perhaps a headline will catch your imagination.

Mood often naturally evolves out of the theme and lyrics. Then interesting chords that seem to relate to the mood can be used as a takeoff for the melody. Play a set of chord changes while experimenting with a melody over the chords; try letting the words, naturally spoken, suggest one. Keep making up words until you hear a melody. A set of chords that is unique and interesting has been known literally to make a song, especially if those chords are kept at the beginning of the song.

Most professionals will tell you that a good melody is one that is easily remembered, so if you're working on one that's hard for you to remember, forget it. If your melody is unusual, however, it may really have to be heard a few times in order for people to remember it, and this is why professionals warn against being *too* unusual. You've got to find a balance. In any case, don't feel that you have to take the first thing that comes to you. Experiment. Give yourself a few alternatives, and if you end up thinking the first was best, so what? Chances are, if you make a practice of doing this, especially when you have slight reservations about the song, a new try will make it perfect.

Traditionally, the melody of a song matches its subject matter; sad tunes accompany sad lyrics, and so on. Sometimes, to be sure, the opposite is done with great success. Typically, though, minor chords are used for a sad or melancholy feeling and major chords for a happy or upbeat feeling. A rock beat, too, can give a cheeriness and a lift to an otherwise low-key melody and at the same time "rough-up" the sentimentality so characteristic in many songs. But rock also tends to take out whatever melodic subtleties you may have tried to put into a song, overstating and flattening them. Some songs work better with light rock and with more melodic instrumentation.

Although they say this is the domain of the producer, the right sound is also something to think about, as you begin to work out the melody. Generally, if you are aiming for a hit single, your song has got to have the sound of other hit singles, something that gives it that instantly familiar quality, makes it easily remembered. This is why songwriters copy other people's "feel"; and since the "feel" can't be copyrighted, hit songs use the same one over and over again. It is really all in the arrangement and production.

Which brings us to the final point, that no matter what you initially put into it, the life or death of your song is ultimately in the hands of the people who arrange, produce, perform, and promote it. "There's a certain magic that some records have and that some records don't have," says Gerry Goffin in *In Their Own Words,* "and that's not a quality you can capture unless everything is going right. And that's something that comes and goes and there's no formula for it. . . . There are so many personalities involved, so many variables. Sometimes you could write a mediocre song and it becomes a big hit."

In the same book Buffy Sainte-Marie talks about how the completed song is also the arrangement of it: "Let me tell you something about being a writer and having a band at your disposal. It could be devastating unless you have very generous musicians. As a writer it enables me to be like five writers at once. In other words, when I go in to record a song, it's not only the words and the melody that makes it me, it's the whole arrangement." Tim Hardin will use a band to help him work out his ideas — "paint a sky so he can fly"; but he feels that rhythm is essentially created by what is said, and that the words of a song really shape the melody.

The singer who performs (interprets) your song has a great deal of control over it in terms of phrasing, which is a form of arrangement that you can write into your songs. Dylan is a master at phrasing. He comes in on the beat a fraction of a second late, which is another way of creating expectation in the listener. Phrasing can be dramatic or subtle; and Dylan, when he sings his songs, incorporates both.

So as a songwriter you've got a lot of variables to gain control over: but you can't promise everything. The most you can do is write the best song you are capable of, one that has a melody you can sing and remember, that is of an adaptable length, with instrumentation that is interesting and related, and that conveys clear and simple lyrics with a good hook.

Thoughts on Spontaneity and Discipline

Since songwriting, like all creative functions, has a certain mystique that may cloud one's desire for actual involvement, we'd like to add a few words about "the natural" — a talent who seems to turn out songs effortlessly. What is this automatic ability really all about, and where can it lead?

It's not uncommon for the early songs of some writers to be their best. There have been songwriters who have sat down and written a string of songs that all became hits in one year, and then never attained success anything like that again. The fact that these early triumphs usually come to young people who, without thinking much about it, may write something that becomes a hit (Bobby Charles at fourteen wrote the hit "See You Later, Alligator") makes one *think* that learning songwriting is not what will make songs "happen." Maybe this phenomenon comes about when a person, at just the right time in his or her life, is attracted to the most current sounds and, not being bound by tradition, is instinctively in tune with the times. Without any hesitation or reservation such people then have the impulse to write . . . and they do write their own songs.

It isn't all that mysterious. Sensing what songwriting is all about is simply accepting it just for what it is: ". . . there is a natural outburst that happens when somebody goes into their late teenage years the way I did. . . . I hadn't intended to do it. It was a wonderful thing that came falling out of the sky, so it was a very spontaneous, easy, and thoughtless process, not anything I worried about," said John Sebastian in *In Their Own Words*.

Popular music is the most available mass art form. Most people, including the young, are exposed to it through radio and records, sometimes constantly. Persons with open, receptive minds, operating in all-inclusive ways, may be moved to compose songs of their own. Being influenced by current music is part of the process: Pete Townshend says in *In Their Own Words*, " 'Can't Explain' got into the British charts. It was kind of a lift off the feeling the Kinks had in 'You Really Got Me.' " In the same book Sebastian says, "It's not hard to write now, although it is harder than it was during my eighteenth year when I had never tried it before, when I knew something about rock'n'roll that nobody else knew, or so it seemed."

Picking up on things happening *other* than the current songs is also part of it. Townshend continues, "Like odd things would give me incredible surprise. I suppose I was surprised by how obviously observant I was, without ever really being conscious of it."

What may begin as automatic and spontaneous may have to be more consciously pursued, if one is to continue writing songs. This process of becoming more conscious probably happens naturally as one gains experience. Songwriters who shy away from analysis may be setting up a block, preventing their natural ability from becoming a conscious tool. At a certain time, this block is a protection, which is good . . . when words and melody are there more or less automatically. It can be confusing to the writer if the writing process is discussed in bits and pieces. Sooner or later, though, the writer has to be open to consciously analyzing what he has been doing all along. Spontaneous effort can't always be depended upon. When the times change, music changes; songwriters, once locked into the times, may not be able to shift. The external stimuli may not be the same. It seems that the Sixties were a period when the social tenor of the times and musical expression were rapidly meeting. There was a subtle vitality waiting for those who wanted to get involved. A lot of writers from the inspirational Sixties aren't heard from today, which is where a more professional approach, involving discipline, comes in. Any writer with longevity in the field has a grasp on what he or she is doing.

Phil Ochs, who committed suicide in 1975, summed up what we're saying in *In Their Own Words:* "For me songwriting was easy from 1961 to 1966 and then it got more and more difficult. . . . Part of the problem was that there was never any pattern to my writing. The point of discipline is to create your own pattern so you can write, and I haven't done that. I always make plans to do that — I'm now thirty-three and I may or may not succeed. But ever since the late Sixties that's constantly on my mind — discipline, training, get it together, clean up your act."

To continue any enterprise in the face of some adversity, which is inevitable, takes more than courage or blind faith; it takes self-assurance, which is best backed by some kind of concrete knowledge. Conscious consideration of what songwriting is all about will allow you to be legitimately confident, for you'll be able to make an intelligent assessment of your own songs that will sustain you if they are rejected.

Think of all those people who have had their songs rejected and have quit the field, never to write again. Their early failure doesn't necessarily mean they didn't "have it"; it only means they didn't have the confidence to persevere.

Possibly the hardest thing to do is to keep plugging songs. But pros in the business write more songs that get rejected than those that get recorded. They also know from years of experience that a lot of the people who are in a position to pass judgment know less than you think they do.

It may be easier to maintain the persistence it takes to get your songs heard, if you realize that even those songwriters publishers revere once pounded the streets, getting as many holes in their "soles" as they did rejections. Gaining a foothold in the business takes hard work and often involves a lot of luck in being in the right place at the right time. Different people look for different things, and until you connect with the right person you'll have to be optimistic.

Felice and Boudleaux Bryant, a country and western husband-and-wife writing team, say in *In Their Own Words,* "One of our biggest songs was shown over thirty times before it was ever cut and that was 'Bye Bye Love.' It was even shown the very morning of the same day the Everly Brothers heard it. . . . The fella said, 'Why don't you show me a good *strong* song?' . . . Nobody really knows what a good song is." Says Boudleaux Bryant of their many rejections and criticisms, "I'd been in the music business long enough to know they weren't lousy songs."

Finally, here's a last bit of advice we feel very strongly about: *don't get into the habit of writing songs that you never finish.* The more work you leave unfinished, the more you will start to feel that you're incapable of finishing anything, and you'll see your confidence dwindle away. If you look at each idea or melody or title or whatever as the best and most exciting thing you have going for you at the moment, then it's worthwhile taking it all the way, even if it means working hard to work it all out. Even if the song is not the best you've ever done, you'll have the experience of knowing you can accomplish something you set out to do. And you will gain confidence. Fear of rejection is generally the reason why people don't complete projects.

Selling Your Songs

The quickest way (but not the most accessible to many) to get your foot in the door is to work with a pro. If you have really good lyrics, try to convince a professional with a track record to collaborate with you. You may ask why one should listen to you. There are a lot of reasons why. Anyone who is creative should understand that freshness comes from someone fresh. Many seasoned pros get stale; and if their egos don't get in the way of their shrewdness, they'd rather listen to what you've got than go to another pro, who may be in the same bind and also demand a better deal. For someone who feels he hasn't got quite as firm a grasp on the times as he used to have, experimenting with new writers is smart. If the pro doesn't provide the inspiration, at least he can add that professional touch to the rough qualities often present in beginning writings. A deal might include the pro's getting more of a percentage of the rights, while doing less of the actual work.

For the most part you'll have to engineer getting a foothold in the profession *entirely* by yourself. The quicker you realize this, the sooner you will get a career going. No one is going to find you — you have to find them. However, nothing is unavoidably one way. We advise you to have your songs ready — you never know when the opportunity may be right around the corner.

The main method of selling is to present what you have to sell, namely, a tape recording of your song. Reel-to-reel is most preferred. Music publishers claim cassettes are all right; but we have the feeling that they are all right only as long as you are as famous as Elton John. So the first thing is getting the song on tape. The second thing is optional: have lead sheets written out, so you can present the written words along with the tape.

Among the people you want to see are the publishing houses, any producer you like and who you think would like your song, any artist or his/her representative for whom your song is especially right. Essentially, you are going to be doing the same thing a professional manager or "song plugger" does for a publishing house (see Chapter 14). Go in person, calling first for an appointment (you may have to call several times). Tell the secretary or the professional manager or whomever that you would rather "show" your tape than send it in. A great part of success in selling is being there to project your own conviction in your songs, your energy, and so on — and you make sure they actually hear your tape. Your attitude should be professional, too. You should seem to be together, someone people can deal with.

You can make the rounds methodically by finding out where publishers are located in the city. Look in *Billboard* or *Cashbox* to find the names of the publishers with the songs that are "hitting," and also the ones who publish the particular kind of music you write. Go to a centrally located phone booth and start making your calls. Tommy Boyce, in his book on songwriting, says that instead of making an appointment far in advance, it's better to ask to see someone right then. Tell them that you're in the city, right in their area, and would love to come up and show them your songs. Boyce says that if you make an appointment for much later, when that time comes, the people who have spoken to you don't even remember who you are, and may not be as open as they were. If they have the time when you call and tell you to come right on over, do it.

"Performing live for a publisher is the worst way of presenting material," says Jim Fragale in *The 1976 Writer's Yearbook*. Also, he says, "Don't mail in your material. I know a lot of writers can't get to publishers, but I've never accepted material through the mail, nor have I run into anyone else who has accepted unsolicited songs." He advises you to go to the main cities where publishing is located, or hire someone to make the rounds for you.

When you set out to make the rounds, have it in your mind to see as many people as possible. If the first two places you go to aren't encouraging, don't let it get you down. Conversely, as Boyce points out, such is human nature that if you get just one favorable reaction, you might use that as an excuse to call it a day. Don't.

If people don't agree with you about your songs, be tactful. You might be able to pin down the disagreement to any number of reasons that can be psyched out by considering where the other person is coming from. Also, remember: everyone has an ego.

If someone is interested and wants to publish your song, but doesn't seem too enthusiastic, don't let that kid you. They want the song or they wouldn't want to publish it. They're playing it cool because they want to negotiate favorable terms for themselves. Always get a lawyer before you sign anything; if the producer, manager, or publisher doesn't want you to get a lawyer, forget him.

Sometimes, professional managers may be really enthusiastic. Even if they take your songs to a board meeting, which rejects them, the managers may still be interested in you, hoping that something favorable will happen to your career, so they can go back to the board and try to get you signed on the strength of that happening. They may also keep you hanging, thinking that they will make their move at the time you start to prove yourself. . . . Someone signs you to a recording contract, your song is accepted by a friend who happens to record hit records . . . and so on.

If you're a newcomer to the music business, it may be easier for you to break in than if you are a has-been trying to make a comeback! It's interesting that the William Morris

Agency wanted no part of Neil Sedaka, when their Dick Fox picked him up. They thought that because he was a person from the Fifties, he was passé, he wasn't what was happening, etc., etc. Fox decided that since there was such a preconceived opinion of him, he would cut a record by Sedaka with a new name, and take it around to record companies. They all liked the record, but wanted to know more about who he was. When Fox told them it was really Sedaka, they all said, "No deal!" and Fox could not land him a contract. Sedaka went to Europe where he had a big, faithful audience, and the support of Elton John, and he got hooked up. That helped when he came back to the United States.

There are songwriting contests that thousands of people enter hoping for a break. For many people the entry costs can be pretty high, when you add up the cost of the cassette, possible multiple submission, or submission of one song in several categories. Thinking you are competing with amateurs who will be sending in amateur home tapes, you might imagine these contests as a way to get into the business. But you have to consider the odds of winning; the contests have sometimes been won by people in reality not so amateur as you'd think, who are represented by people in the music industry, such as major publishers who have paid for both professional production of the tunes and entry fees and sent the entries in on their own stationery.

People in the business itself warn especially against sending in lyrics and such to those advertising in fan magazines. There is no way but the hard way, the professional way, to break into the business . . . and skirting that fact will only delay or stifle your career.

One final suggestion: once you *are* successful in any way, it will open lots of doors for you, and you'll find it much easier to get things to happen. Use this opening to its fullest by *not* lying back on your gratification, but start to build immediately with your first success. Stay on the case; that's what the pros try to do. As Leeds Levy, when he was at ASCAP (the American Society of Composers, Authors and Publishers), told us, "The best way for songs to happen for someone is to have one on the top of the charts, one that just fell off, and one on the way up!"

Once a song is off the charts, things start to get cold again. More than once, a writer has had to start from near zero, because he allowed himself to get cold. So, when you're hot — stay there!

12

Arranger

AN ARRANGEMENT IS all the *color* behind the singer. The arranger writes down (charts) all the notes the musicians will play — charts for the drums, the violins (which are included on most of the top-forty songs you hear today), the guitars, the piano, and so forth. A studio arranger always works as another force between the musicians and the producer and the songwriter, and is the only person who really knows most about what's going on musically — what's going to happen in bar 20, for instance.

In an interview with Robbie Robertson, guitarist and writer for The Band, *Circus* magazine quoted him as saying, "Now, I'm not looking to fill up our albums with a lot of guitar doodling." He meant that although he and Garth Hudson, organist, could play a lot of good instrumentals, it would mean that they would get fewer songs on each album. He likes to do only as much as is necessary for the song. "All of our songs aren't that wordy and there are some that are more instrumental than what I really like to do. That's about as far as I like to take it. Beyond that I think it's 'filler.'"

Horace Ott, an arranger-conductor-composer of movie

scores, commercials, and material for Aretha Franklin and Gladys Knight and the Pips, told us he likes to do his own mixing. He feels that other than the arranger, the engineer is the person who usually creates the "sound." The arrangement can make a song a hit, and conversely can keep a song from becoming a hit.

"When I'm working the initial session, I sometimes have a question like, 'Listen, where I'm going with this, I'd like in the end to run this through a phase setup on the strings, so it comes out phasey-kind-of-hazy-in-and-out-of-this,' and I will ask the engineer, especially if it's a new studio I haven't worked with, just to make sure his head's on straight, and I say, 'Any problems?' and he'll say, 'No, no.' A lot of engineering can really turn around what you've done. You can work your head off, do one heck of an arrangement, and you hear it on the radio and you say, 'Oh, my, they're trying to put me out of business!' A lot of times, too, you hear mistakes on records, and there is no need for it. You can isolate that track and bring it down."

In order to do the best job, the arranger should work with the lyrics, because the arrangement and the melody complement the lyrics. There are no secrets to arranging. Each song is a separate entity. Horace looks at each song and sees what it has to offer. The aim of the arrangement is not always to clarify orchestration and keep things simple. Horace says, "Some songs you gotta come on like gangbusters to make it work." Sometimes, when the singer doesn't really know in what direction the song should go, Horace writes two different types of arrangement. Or he might be asked to write a country arrangement, and the singer says, "I want it a little bit more pop than that." In the studio, arrangers sometimes make up things on the spot that work, but essentially Horace feels that that's not dealing from a position of strength. He feels that an arranger really does his best work when he has time to prepare the music. "You can change things slightly in the studio for the betterment of the music, but basically it's all scored out like a blueprint."

Horace feels, from his long experience in the business, that the biggest problem an arranger has to cope with is the producer. There are producers who are totally involved in the situation, while others leave it in the hands of somebody else. "If a producer's a producer he should produce, that's all. I've had experiences where the guy says, 'I'm recording this act, here are the demos. I think the key is good, but use whatever key you want.' To me that's not dealing from strength. A good producer will say, 'I think this song should have this kind of beginning, and then maybe the vocal group can support the lead singer here.' Concrete ideas and directions. Not just, 'OK, I'll see you next month,' while he goes off to California, as he keeps his fingers crossed, hoping the arranger did his job for him."

An arranger may, at times, become a producer, a writer, or a co-writer. On one occasion, when Horace was helping arrange an album for Nina Simone, one of her writers told him they needed another song. Horace offered them one he'd written, a song he never thought would be played farther away than his home piano. Simone's writers made a few alterations, and she ended up using it. So Horace became a co-writer on a song later recorded not only by Simone, but by The Animals and Joe Cocker.

Recently, a lot of old songs have been reissued with new arrangements incorporating new sounds. Horace has done some of these, including turning "That Old Black Magic" into a disco single by the Softones. "You just look and say, 'Well, this is really a good song, let's do a new sound.' And without trying to negotiate with anybody, you just go ahead and record it; and when you do that, the original writers get all the royalties." Horace goes on, "Everything you did was update — making it contemporary. But I'm sure there are some people who approach it like, 'Listen, I'm *thinking* about doing your song.' If you want to be a slick businessman, and you wanna say, 'I'm thinking about it, with this number-one group that I have,' I'm sure they'd talk business. But I've never done that." In talking with Leeds Levy when he was at

ASCAP, we found that an arranger can go to ASCAP with a new arrangement of an old song, and the ASCAP board will vote on how much of a percentage of the writer's share he should get, depending on how much he changed the song. For the movie *2001* an arranger considerably altered the theme, from Richard Strauss's *Also sprach Zarathustra*. Because of the extent of the arrangement, he got a greater percentage of royalties than arrangers customarily get.

An arranger's fee, and the amount of assignments he gets, depend on his popularity in the business. Horace has always been self-employed. This happens to him a lot: he's walking down the street, typically Broadway, and he sees someone he knows. "By the way," the guy says to him, "how's your time? I'm doing an act in about two weeks, I gotta have some really good arrangements."

"A few years ago I was walking from Forty-ninth Street to Fifty-second Street," Horace recalls, "just three blocks, right? I got stopped three times. When I got finished with the third one, I had to get in my car and drive home. I had the third recording session locked in. Three different people I met in those three blocks. They said, 'I'm looking for ya.' But more often the phone rings, and either an artist who's heard you're good, or a producer, needs an arrangement."

The arranger is a contractor or is constantly in touch with a contractor. Technically, a contractor is a musician too, and, as discussed in the chapter on session men, he calls the appropriate other players for a date. "If I call him [the contractor] and say I need a saxophone thing that's really schmaltzy," Horace says, "he's not goin' to bring me a guy who's really stiff."

13

Music Publishing

MUCH OF THE ECONOMIC power of the music industry is centered in those companies that own the largest quantity of the most important copyrights — that is, the publishers. Awareness of the importance of publishing rights grew very slowly throughout the Sixties. By about 1965 it picked up among groups, solo acts, producers, arrangers, managers, and agents. All of these began to form publishing companies; so that today everyone negotiates to get all or a piece of the publishing rights, if possible, of the music he or she works with. It is even more recently that the film industry has begun to realize the income potential from music publishing rights and demand its share.

The publishing income is derived from the performing rights agencies (ASCAP and Broadcast Music, Inc. — BMI), the mechanical royalty from record companies, the sale of the copyright to other media such as films or jingle producers, and *last* from the sale of sheet music.

Publishing is the easy money in the music business. It involves the least expenditure and the least risk for potentially the greatest income. The pennies earned in royalties add up and a simple three-minute song that becomes a standard can earn the writer and publisher annual income for the length of the copyright. There are literally thousands of songs in that category. Even a song that becomes a modest hit and is then forgotten can earn the writer and publisher twenty to fifty thousand dollars each. The publisher can collect mechanical royalties for both himself and the writer from the record companies, while ASCAP and BMI collect royalties due both publisher and writer for public performances and pay them separately. The Harry Fox Agency collects mechanical (record) royalties for some publishers, performing a service that many publishers may have difficulty doing on their own.

As far back as 1909 the mechanical rate from record sales was one penny for the publisher and one penny for the writer for each song on each record sold, and it is still the same today. No argument seems to justify the lack of inflation in these royalties, although soon they will move up to one-and-one-half pennies each for writer and publisher. Even the argument justifying royalty stagnation that today royalties are collected on millions of records, rather than on the few of 1909, carries little weight, because the record company makes up-to-date money.

Since records and performances are the two major sources of income, sometimes all the owner of the copyright (publisher and/or writer) has to do is sit back and watch or wait for it to roll in.

You hear amazing stories of people who put together small publishing companies and made a lot of money from the initial royalties, and then later on sold their catalog for six figures. There are stories of others — and these are few — who held on to their copyrights and are glad they did. A forty-year veteran of the music business said that a publishing company he owned was sold for $350,000, within just a few years after he and a couple of others began it. Other publishing companies in very short periods make millions on very slim catalogs. All of this explains why today's trade magazines are constantly reporting the purchase of small publishers' catalogs by large publishers and record companies. A small publisher could be a performer's (singer's, most likely) publishing company whether all the songs were written by him or her or not, or a writer himself who has kept his own publishing rights.

Often when unsigned songwriting talent drums up some interest from an experienced music business professional, the professional will say something like, "I like your stuff. I might be able to get your songs recorded. But I don't want to be your manager, or your agent. I just want all the publishing rights to your material." That means the writer, if he or she agrees, will be giving up 50 percent of royalty income. And, in many cases, to get one's foot in the burly gates of the music world, the publisher's efforts in getting a writer's work placed may be worth that 50 percent.

Setting up a Publishing Company

Many of the self-contained solo acts and groups, those who write and perform their own material, discovered that it would be a lot better to set up their own publishing companies, and so keep income close to home. And, in the Sixties, publishers weren't all that interested in the then contemporary music. Chappell & Co., Inc., for instance, has its basis in its standard catalog and is known as a publisher of shows. It didn't feel rock and roll was here to stay. It wanted to stick with what it knew, but, as it happened, after the incredible sale of *My Fair Lady* show album sales fell off drastically. Still highly interested in the Broadway musical, publishers will refer backers to producers of shows. Now Chappell is turning around somewhat to a more contemporary feel. However, it is still after songs it feels will become standards. A standard becomes a standard when more than one artist records it. Without a lot of covers a song that has been recorded on only one record will die. Because of the potential income "the song" has always been emphasized and is sought for by music-business people. Even rock and roll was imitated and/or covered by the major companies when rock and roll songs on small labels started to take over the charts. But in the Sixties and early Seventies groups developed a "sound" that couldn't be so easily adapted by just any person. People were not interested in *another* version of the hit.

However, publishers are now looking more for the self-contained group because, for one thing, they have learned that they won't have to plug the group's songs to get them recorded.

The business generally is overrespectful when speaking of an Elton John or a John Denver, because of their giant earning abilities, and also of the writers of standards like Rodgers and Hart, because of their continuous earning power. It is underrespectful of new writers, complaining that youth doesn't have the discipline, the background, the this-and-that that the old masters had. Publishers fail to see that vital material will always be coming from new people. All the writers they admire were new once (often not appreciated then too). If publishers truly realized this, they would be looking into the future and trying to be part of its formation.

From little ten-dollar copyrights big publishing companies grow. To set one up, it takes some cash; but it's fairly easy to do, as are most routines in the business world. 1. Early on, you have to check with the performing rights agencies (all three; see Chapter 15) to see that the name you've chosen for your publishing company hasn't already been taken. 2. Following the information in Chapter 15 under copyrights, you have a lead sheet done, fill out the government copyright form for *published* music (Form E), and send it in with your check. 3. Once you've got a copyright, you have to find some way of getting your song commercialized. Remember, you aren't a bona fide music publisher until you are accepted by BMI or ASCAP, who require one commercially recorded or *printed* song before they accept a publishing company as a member. 4. Publishing sheet music is a lot easier than selling it. You have to have a professional arrangement made of the song (say, for piano), which costs about $40. Then you take the arrangement to a music typographer, who is usually the printer. It costs about $30 per plate (page), with three to four plates for each typical song. Then the printer charges about $100 per thousand copies. So for around $250 to $300 you have a thousand copies of a copyrighted, printed, published song. 5. Then you find some record and/or music store to sell the sheet music.

Of course, there is a slight "scam" quality about step five, and BMI and ASCAP don't encourage that step. But there's nothing illegal about it, and it does make the publisher the operator of a commercial venture, when he sells some merchandise. And there are plenty of collectors who pay big sums for certain sheet music that was originally published on a small scale. The reality, of course, is that you can have a thousand songs listed in a catalog, but if none of them is covered, the whole catalog, from a commercial point of view, is meaningless. Small publishers often double as song pluggers. Eventually, when you get some songs recorded, you will feel more legitimate.

Having your own publishing company puts you in a professional position where people will listen. You can make deals with writers and sign them to your company. We just ran across an ad in our local paper saying that a music publisher and representative of record companies was looking for original material. We heard his phone never stopped ringing. The chances are excellent that the quality of the material that came his way through this ad would be good, because ours is a music-oriented town.

People who get a lot of exposure by performing and writing their own material either set up a publishing company or, when they come to record, are able to negotiate very favorable contracts with big publishers, who are looking for these acts themselves, because then they don't have to plug their songs initially to get them recorded. There are also many major acts that never actually write songs, but have royalty interests in much of the material they record, and own publishing companies that also earn royalties on that material. Songwriters will tell you that to get a major act to cover a song today, you have to be prepared to give that act some interest in your song. It used to be common for record companies to insist on the writer's signing over *all* his or her publishing rights to the record companies' own publishing branch before they would offer a recording contract. But powerful artists' management has altered this practice whenever possible.

Mitch Schoenbaum, now with Atlantic, was a professional manager at Chappell, the publishing giant. He told us that the songwriters under contract with Chappell for their writing only, but also active in producing, will either own a piece of a song if they produce someone, or try to get some of their own material into that session. "What it comes to is the green stuff. It's on the bottom line."

Sheet Music

Generally, only those pop-music tunes that make it to the top forty get printed as sheet music. The exceptions are specialty numbers that might have some appeal to high school bands, piano-bar entertainers, music teachers, and the like.

It works like this. The retail customer pays $1.50 (a price standardized throughout the industry) for each piece of sheet music. The retailer paid 75¢ each to the selling agent (distributor-wholesaler), who paid the publisher 60¢ each. The publisher pays about 5¢ each to the composer, and the printer charges, in runs of 10,000 copies, about 5¢ each. So the publisher makes as much as 50¢ each from the sale of sheet music. A tune that becomes a medium hit can warrant a printing of 100,000 copies, or a profit to the publisher of around $50,000. Often the publisher has to make a deal with the selling agent, which cuts into the publisher's pie. But then the success of the tune's distribution nationally depends on the effort of the selling agent. The major trade periodicals (*Cashbox, Record World,* and *Billboard*) carry charts of hit tunes; and you can always tell when a song has been considered hot enough to warrant publishing, because the selling agent is listed along with title, writer, singer, and record company.

A small publishing company, run by Chet Gerlack, was the publisher of a hit a few years back that not only was number one on the charts for weeks, but was translated into twenty-two languages and published in twice as many countries. A whole slew of arrangements was published and printed for every imaginable combination — high school orchestra, drum and bugle corps, chorus, a cappella choir, piano, organ — you name it. Chet's experience points up the fact that when there's a market, a capable person can pretty much put a whole complex publishing operation into motion on one hit. "When you get away from the strictly radio–pop music," Chet says, "there are all kinds of fields of music which are printed regularly, and national popularity does not dictate whether or not the piece of music will be printed. Hymns, brass-band tunes, ethnic music, classical compositions don't have to wait for popularity. The publisher of this kind of music depends on a good selling agent to create a market."

The Big Publishers

Mitch Schoenbaum presents very convincing arguments in favor of the writer's signing with a major house. His job at Chappell, as covered in Chapter 14, on the professional manager, was to move songs in Chappell's catalog, and to acquire new material and new writers. He points out that Chappell has offices all over the United States and the world, each staffed with professional managers whose primary efforts are toward placing Chappell's copyrights . . . broadly based efforts that no small publisher can match. When the staff of professional managers at a major house is "hot" on a tune, they can secure an array of covers, with ensuing royalties. A major publisher wields much clout when it comes to record companies, for the simple reason that no major label can exist without the license of copyrights from the major publishers. Chappell, with its catalog of almost 100,000 songs — including a lion's share of the best of hit show tunes — can negotiate a very favorable contract, obtaining clauses that will assure payment (of mechanical royalties) at the proper time and of the right amount. If the record company breaks the contract, these clauses will put that company on what's called "compulsory," meaning the publisher can have auditors (accountants and attorneys) right at the pressing plant adding up the records as they are pressed, and collecting immediate payment. This power gives big publishers a distinct advantage over a small writer-publisher.

Because record companies like RCA depend so much on big publishers like Chappell, Mitch says that the lines of communication between the two are more open; he had a relatively easy time getting A & R and producers at the major labels to listen to a cut he might have been pushing at the moment. A large publisher's relationships with the performing rights agencies are on a firm basis too: the big publishers are in the highest possible bonus position, an economic advantage that's passed on to the writer. And their international operations are able both to exploit foreign possibilities for their copyrights and to ensure the fair and accurate collection of royalties and fees due their copyrights.

All these advantages can work for some of the writers some of the time. But all writers aren't always satisfied; and many either switch to small publishers, or set up their own publishing companies.

Alan Abrahams used to be a professional manager for Chappell. Now, besides producing and managing, he is himself a small publisher. According to him, one of the best things about a small publisher is his accessibility: he's always there, answering his own phone. "They, the writers, know me personally," he says. "They can call me. All the writers that are in a huge company, everyone that's ever got a tune published by the big publisher, is at some point going to say to themselves, 'What is X doing with my tunes? I think I'll call them up and ask them.' Now, if they can get through, what they'll get is, 'What was your name again? OK, we'll look it up.' And then they may say, 'Well, nothing's been really happening.' But with the writers I have, I don't take them just to build bulk . . . I take writers with the idea of making money. Say I've got a catalog. Great! Who cares? I can tell you I have five hundred songs in my catalog. If they're not generating me any income, what's the point?" Alan, like other small publishers, says that often the small guy will do more and try harder. And there are literally thousands of small, one- to two-person publishing operations.

This is a business that has two mottos: you're only as good as your last hit; and, it's very hard to get a first hit and the essential follow-up — concepts that make it hard to get those all-important appointments. It's generally much more difficult for small publishers to have easy access to the many people who actually make the decisions to record a song — the artists and managers and agents and record company A & R people. So to increase the possibilities of placing material, as well as collecting mechanical royalties, many small publishers have signed agreements to let a large publisher "administer" the small one's catalog. The publisher is likely to want 20 percent, more or less, of the gross, depending on the desirability of the catalog, because it figures that its administering costs are 15 percent, and it likes to make 5 percent profit. These administration deals are made with single artists if the artist is highly desirable.

Publishing Deals and Contracts

Of the many ways a large publisher can secure copyrights for its catalog, the most traditional of them all, the salaried staff writer, is probably the least used today. Plenty of the most successful of today's writers — like Neil Sedaka and Carole King, to name a couple — were originally staff writers for publishers. But even though there are still staff writers around, there is a lot of feeling against the usefulness of the profession. Over at production-publishing CAM-USA, Inc., Joe Pellegrino says, "I basically do not believe in staff writers. It's too much pressure on the company, and a lot of pressure on the writer. I don't think that a staff writer is open to what is necessary, as far as growth is concerned. He tends to become stale: Friday comes around, and he gets his check." As we noted earlier, Joe advised Barry Manilow not to become a staff writer, feeling that the dry routine would harm his career, and the salary would be beneath his talent. "A staff writer will be turning out song after song," Joe says, "and wondering why the company isn't doing anything with them."

Mitch Schoenbaum says that at Chappell, where they have everything, "rarely, but on occasion" he might have wanted a particular writer on the staff of the company, filling in on the need, when someone at Chappell knew a particular artist was going into the studio and was looking for material. Mitch feels that staleness can be overcome if the publisher guarantees the writer not only a salary, but a bonus based on royalties earned from the writer's songs. Chappell has several staff writers who write for or work with artists like Helen Reddy, Carly Simon, and Melissa Manchester, and only when they are going into the studio.

Basically, new talent is added to the old catalogs by playing the odds. People watch the charts to see if they find any new names showing up there. When they do, that new name gets a call: "Hello, everyone at Giant Publishing loves your song.

We can do big things for you." Some publishers, when they discover a good writer, will give him or her a three-year contract in which the writer gets a guarantee, or an advance against future royalties. Or the publisher might agree just to "administer" a writer's catalog, which means that the publisher will handle all the paperwork of the songwriter — getting lead sheets, securing copyrights, and handling the collections of royalties due the writer's work — for which, as we've said, the publisher charges 15 to 20 percent of the amount collected.

Often today, as far as recording deals are concerned, it's the publishers who are in the key position. A record company might come to them and say, "Do you want the publishing rights for X advance?" Or the publisher can use a writer-performer's demo to convince a record company of the artist's validity, get a commitment from the record company, then make an offer to the artist, knowing it will recoup some (at times more) of the advance almost immediately. An exaggerated example: Bluestone Publisher gets a commitment from Laurel Records to give a $50,000 advance on mechanical royalties. Bluestone then talks to one of the performing rights agencies and says, "We might be doing a record with A producer, C artist, D musician, and Laurel has agreed to spend $200,000 *on promotion.*" The performing rights agency may then tell Bluestone that it will give $20,000 advance against the performance royalties. Bluestone, now knowing what it can expect, returns to the writer-artist and says, "We'll take you on and give you $25,000 advance against mechanical and performance royalties, in exchange for *all* your publishing rights." The artist agrees, but keeps his writer's share (one-half is publisher's, one-half is writer's) and gets the $25,000 when the contract is signed. Bluestone then collects $50,000 from Laurel and $20,000 from the performing rights agency. Bluestone pockets its publisher's rights share, one-half the total, or $35,000, the $25,000 advance to the writer, and pays the writer the remaining $10,000. Not all deals are that one-sided; but enough of them are to show you how publishers can make money without spending any. And often they will say, "Actually, we just recouped our advance until the next quarter" (royalty payments are made four times a year).

Mitch says that he tried to make the best deal he could for Chappell. He didn't show any overenthusiasm for a writer he liked, and he'd ask for *all* the publishing rights. But he believes the writer is "stupid" if he accepts that kind of arrangement, and goes on to say that "any publisher should be happy with fifty percent of the publishing rights." Sometimes, when a publisher is signing a writer with a good earning record, it will make a deal for only 10 percent of the publishing rights, plus, of course, 15 percent of the gross for administration costs.

When the publisher is an affiliate of the record company, publisher-recording deals can be mind-boggling. Most major record companies either have their own publishing company or the parent company owns one. April Blackwood is an affiliate of Columbia, Screen Gems for Arista, ABC Music for ABC Records. Chappell is a sister to Polydor (both owned by the Dutch Phillips conglomerate). Naturally, the attempt is made to keep all cash in the family. So, often the advances just circulate within related companies; and because of other advances coming from outside the family, from BMI or ASCAP, for instance, as stated above, the parent company makes a profit before it spends any money at all. It's all part of the "incestuous" world of music.

Frequently, the contract an artist signs with a record company provides that advances paid to the recording artist will be cross-collateralized against publishing receipts. If the record doesn't do well enough to repay the record company's advance to the performer, the songwriting royalties will be applied to that debt, a debt that Geoffrey Stokes in *Star-Making Machinery* says is often spurious.

Publishers and record companies are still separate entities. Songs have to be covered, and the right people to sing them might not be from the parent record company. The writer is almost always at a disadvantage when it comes to making deals with the power structure, which is one reason why over 3,000 writers and composers belong to the American Guild of Authors and Composers (AGAC), a unionlike association of songwriters, which has come up with a standard contract, setting minimum standards. One of these stipulates that a publisher has to get some action for a writer's work within a year, or all rights revert to the writer. This provision prevents publishers from acquiring bulk in their catalogs, hoping that one day something in that bulk will pay off without any effort on their part. Most publishers say this isn't enough time. Alan Abrahams says, "I'll just take a song, and if they [the writer] really hassle me about it, I'll do it on a term [meaning a year]. Like if they say, 'Look, if there's nothing happening in a year, can I get it back?' But I'll tell them out front that, for ex-ample, the things I've placed with Olivia Newton-John — those were written four years ago. And you can break your ass with a tune and not get anything, or you can just throw it out to someone in one week and get it recorded."

The AGAC contract stipulates a minimum of three cents a copy for sheet music on a sliding scale (depending on vol-ume) up to five cents for 500,000 copies and more. It insists on a 50-50 split for foreign royalties (half to writer and half to publisher), it gives the writer the right of approval to a deal the publisher might make, such as selling the copyright to another publisher, and it protects the writer against what is generally considered in the trade to be the poor practices of traditional writer-publisher contracts. Even though many publishers disagree with this or that clause, most will admit that AGAC has helped to create a more reputable standard contract.

14

Professional Manager

PROFESSIONAL MANAGER IS a new title for an old trade: song plugging. Song plugging is an attempt to get an act to record and/or perform a song the act hasn't written. Of course, almost everyone in the music business who is in any way connected with publishing rights and writer's rights does some song plugging. But the people who spend most of their days and nights trying to place material (and sign new writers) and who are connected with the publishing companies or with the publishing arm of record and production companies, are called professional managers.

In the early days of radio, the Thirties through the early Fifties, there was a romantic aura surrounding the song plugger. He was to be seen in lots of musical movies as a nice guy, a street-wise, cigar-chewing man, working out of one of those old Broadway offices with two desks and an upright piano. In Hollywood, song pluggers hung out on Vine Street, between Sunset and Hollywood Boulevards, drinking gallons of coffee from Coffee Dan's, which was located under the old Capitol Records office. Besides Coffee Dan's there were about thirteen Owl and Sontag drugstores in Hollywood at the time, whose soda counters served the song pluggers as offices. They intermingled with another group, guys in cowboy hats, Hollywood extras for westerns. Two different breeds they were, but both part of show biz, which was more colorful if less slick than it is today.

Even before then, during the time between Scott Joplin and the Gatsby era, when a music publisher had a certain song that he felt was hot, either he or a guy hired by him would make the rounds hustling that song to performers in vaudeville and nightclubs and to the few record companies. The Twenties were the hottest period for record sales until the Fifties. What killed them in between was radio. In the Thirties the emphasis was to get the big bands like Glen Miller's and singers like Crosby to cover a song on their radio shows, that being one of the choice plums a song plugger could win. Certain pluggers had reputations for coming up with under-the-table payments, payola, to get their songs played.

The Fifties and Sixties hit the song pluggers hard. Some were indicted on payola charges, and record companies organized in-house publishing and promotion departments, maintaining national promotion staffs whose job it was to get all releases some air exposure. At the same time publishers' catalogs grew, some backed up by huge international networks, and they installed sophisticated departments to handle the placement of their songs. Others, shrewd and lucky enough, owned the rights to so many standards that there wasn't much need for a plugger, since people needing material sought them out.

Eddy O'Laughlin is a professional manager at Midland International, a middle-sized record company. His job is to find songs from Midland's catalog and get them to the right artists. His methods of search and placement can go several ways: he hopes to find good material within the company's catalog for the artists signed with Midland who need it. He is also looking for outside acts to cover Midland's songs and he's on the lookout for promising writers (and performers). He attends studio sessions when Midland's acts are recording and makes sure, since Midland is active in disco music, that he knows what's happening in the discotheques. In short, his obligations are not restricted to just the placing of songs. He's all over the place and might find himself flying to Europe to see what kind of material and talent are available over there, keeping up the "International" part of "Midland." As mentioned in the chapter on publishing, most professional managers watch the charts for new names and give them a call, hoping to sign them.

Eddy went to the producer of Tony Orlando and Dawn with a song that had previously been turned down by other producers (which in itself isn't so unusual except that it points up the kind of thick-skinned perseverance required by the job), and they recorded it. When he believes in a song, a professional manager can't take no for an answer. Eddy's approach is to work with songs he thinks have hit potential, and keep trying until they're covered. He finds that he's spending more and more of his time taking songs to MOR performers because frequently they don't write their own material. MOR performers may spend chunks of time in Las Vegas and Florida, or in preparing for TV appearances, counting on their producers to guide them and to have the good judgment to select appropriate songs. Performers like Helen Reddy and Frank Sinatra have producers who are always in the song-buying market. The problem for the manager is how to get an appointment with stars and their producers.

Professional managers spend hours on the phone asking for time and seeking introductions, and even more hours on the street making contacts. Eddy, for example, was walking down Broadway when somebody casually mentioned that Al Martino was going to record in three weeks and needed some songs. This is the kind of good, fresh tip that gives Eddy the opportunity to search Midland's catalog for the right material and then get to work. As Eddy says, "It's a big business . . . but it's a small business."

The names of hot producers and performers are on everybody's lips simultaneously. A hot producer will get hundreds of submissions. If a professional manager places just one song on the next Melissa Manchester album, for example, the publishing income could easily be in the thousands! That's just from one cover, and the fact that a Melissa Manchester recorded the tune would automatically increase the possibility of additional covers from other performers. That's why it's a big business. But it's small, because everybody seems to know everybody who "counts" at any one given moment, and there are not really that many people out there actively selling, making a noise. If one's taste is right, pipelines will eventually be found to the decision makers.

Tip-sheet letters are obtainable through subscription, telling who needs what in the way of songs, with addresses where you can send tapes. They are fairly expensive, running around fifty dollars for fifty letters. They're long shots, better for the big publishers with songs to suit every need, and lots of professional managers don't subscribe to them.

Even though their catalogs might have thousands of songs, most professional managers only have about twenty or thirty in the front of their minds, songs they feel have hit potential. When they take material to a producer, for instance, seldom do they play more than two or three tunes out of the twenty. The professional manager wants to build and maintain trust with a producer, a working respect that he can trade on over the years, so material is chosen carefully, with the knowledge that with any given producer he might have four or five chances to score, but after that he's pretty much had it.

Mitch Schoenbaum was recently one of three professional managers of contemporary music at Chappell, the publishers. He took tapes around personally because then he knew they would be listened to personally. When he was in a producer's office, he was pretty quiet: "I let the record speak for itself. I'm not hype. It's not in me. If the person doesn't hear the song, I don't want to be there. If I get no enthusiasm, I say,

'See you later.' . . . I know when writers and performers come in my office and say Bla-bla-bla loves it and this and that, and So-and-so almost took it, none of it will make any difference to me." But he does say that it helps to point out the "something new" in the music to make sure it's noticed.

Eddy O'Laughlin doesn't always take a tape around. For about three dollars he has a single disc cut. He feels it's easier for a busy producer to put a single on the machine, thus saving him the trouble of threading and rewinding a tape recorder. He believes that a professional manager has to be on top of what is going on all the time. "You have to keep your ears open to improve yourself. There are no losers in the music business, just quitters." It's one of those jobs that requires a supernormal amount of optimism. So many songs have become famous because guys went around for the twenty-fifth time. Many of these songs became standards, songs that never die. "Let It Be Me" was turned down in the Fifties by everybody until the Everly Brothers took a chance on it, and the plugger who sold it felt that it wasn't right even for them. Mitch says that there's a lot of disappointment in song plugging when you know you have a good song and it's right for a singer and "you can't even get your parents interested!" (Mitch is among the many second-generation people in the business; his father, Jerry Schoenbaum, has done many things including being a record company president.) "It's really personal relationships, getting to know the people so that they will really take a *good* listen to what you have," Mitch says. "Of course, you have to come up with good material, you have to be consistent, and you have to be selective. You have to get to know the person, what they want to hear, and what's going to fit into the material they're about to record. You have to cast the material."

We drew a parallel for Mitch to the world of book publishing. There editors seldom think whether a manuscript is a sure shot, a possible "monster," or top of the best-seller list, before they take it on. In most cases they are simply concerned that the book will have a good chance of earning back its advance and costs; anything more is gravy. Mitch told us that a conviction that *every* song in his working catalog (twenty to thirty tunes) is going to be a hit has to exist in the mind of the professional manager, and on an intense level. When we asked him if he ever suggests to a writer to take her or his songs to another publisher, he said emphatically, "No. Never. Everyone's looking for a hit. No one's going to say, 'Go over to Famous Music because they are not looking for such big hits as we are.' " Of course this assumes everyone is going to make the same judgments as he does.

Both Mitch and Eddy agree that the demo they take around doesn't have to be extravagantly produced. A voice with just a guitar or piano can bring out the song adequately. This is called hearing a song "naked." But once again, as with everyone we talked to or read about, we weren't able to get the name of one writer without an established reputation whose songs were actually sold naked, although, no doubt, it does happen.

A & R people, personal managers, and producers eventually agree that the nearer to a master the material to be presented is, the better. Mitch, however, claims that if you present songs in a finished form, you are trying to show people what to do with a song, implying that they wouldn't have the imagination to bring out its best qualities themselves. "It's OK," he says, "to lay out a song, to give a feel of it, and give a sense of the direction one feels it should go, but to make it into a record is what the record company is there for." He feels the voice-and-piano demo must be well and cleanly made, otherwise the publisher will re-demo the tune, the cost for which will later be deducted from royalties and advances. Big publishers, however, are thinking of contracting in-house producers; that seems to verify what we feel, which is that as ears have gotten more accustomed to professionally slick productions, the pressures are on to have a song presented in a pretty sophisticated "demo" package. Chappell has just installed a 16-track studio in its uptown offices!

Just as the presentations of songs are more sophisticated

than ever so are the financial arrangements (see the chapter on publishing). Deals are complicated because people and/or companies are often interested in a song only to the extent that a *piece* of the song will be coming their way. Today everybody wants to be assured there's enough of the publishing pie for one more bite. Often the producer wants a share, and knowing that he will be getting one is a personal inducement to give the material special consideration; sometimes the arranger is in the same bag, and the record company wants some of the publishing rights as well. "What it comes down to," says Mitch, "is that everyone wants to get a piece. If you own part of a song that is played over and over again, songs that will still be earning twenty years from now because people still want to sing it, that's where the piece pays off." How lucrative this can be is exemplified by the story of a woman who years ago composed the verse on one of the first Hallmark greeting cards, when Hallmark was giving royalties regularly. Because her verse is still in print and still sells well she has practically lived off the royalties ever since. A rare story in the greeting-card field, but not so rare in the songwriting field, where part of the publisher's efforts are geared toward making songs part of the nation's standard repertoire. In companies like Chappell that have large catalogs, making standards and keeping them alive get special attention.

The trouble with success — everyone should have such troubles — is that "You're branded," says Eddy O'Laughlin. "Suddenly you get calls that say, 'We didn't know you were into *that kind* of music.'" Being branded is certainly OK as long as one has the material and as long as there is a demand for that material, but should either drop off, the brand can burn. And since the best catalogs are built up from a variety of material, a professional manager has to watch out that specialized taste doesn't get in the way of a career.

Mitch feels that there is frustration on every level in the music business, echoing what we have heard over and over, that those people who make the decisions have no musical taste, which is probably the greatest frustration of all if you're a song plugger. But the plugger's greatest attribute is probably not musical taste either; it's his bulldog tenacity when he's selling, and easy deferences when he's buying.

Professional managers make varying kinds of agreements with writers. Rarely, but on occasion, someone like Mitch will want a particular writer to be on staff, with a salary plus a percentage of royalties earned by that writer's songs. Sometimes a professional manager will just want to test the reaction to a writer's work and will ask for exclusive rights for a specific length of time, anywhere from a few months to a year, with perhaps no money involved, just good faith on the part of the plugger. There can be some up-front money involved, and from a major publisher an advance of a few hundred to a thousand is not much. Decisions like these, though, are not usually made by the professional manager but by other people in the company, based on the manager's recommendation.

As it is, many professional managers fill more than one chair, reaching out into other areas of musical influence. Today it seems that being a professional manager is one of those career stepping-stones on the way to a spot with more status, say a position as a major buyer of songs or as a controller of talent, something nearer the glamour of stardom.

The professional manager, the sales hustler of the music world, has a hard row to hoe, but once fertilized with a myriad of contacts, it becomes a foundation that can carry him for a lifetime in many other music-business roles. He's a long way from the pre–World War I image of the song plugger, he's less of the caricature we've come to think of from the movies, more like the young executive in advertising and other media-oriented corporations. It's a good way to get to know intimately the many levels of the music business.

15

ASCAP, BMI, and Copyright

Performance Rights Agencies

The American Society of Composers, Authors and Publishers (ASCAP) and Broadcast Music, Inc. (BMI) are performance rights licensing organizations. They license the public performance of music assigned to them by member writers and publishers. Radio and television account for the largest source of their income. Dramatic performance of music, as in stage shows and movies, is not licensed by BMI or ASCAP. These agencies negotiate the basis for fees to be paid for the public performance of the copyrighted music owned by their members. They collect the money and make payments due the writers and publishers.

These two agencies are giants. BMI collects for over 40,000 writers and publishers, and ASCAP for over 20,000. (A third agency, Sesac, is relatively small, and with a limited membership.) Writers may also be their own publishers, as stated in the chapter on publishing. Individual writers or publishers could, legally, license the performance of their own material. But since there are some 7,400 radio stations that might want to play their songs, the task of accurate monitoring would be virtually impossible. Direct licensing is done in the case of jingle music and pop concerts.

As is explained in the chapter on program and musical directors, some radio stations keep a log upon request; and since there is no way at present for every musical minute of all 7,400 stations to be accounted for, both BMI and ASCAP measure the programming through complicated formulas of their own. They come out with figures showing what songs were played over the air, how often, and to how many listeners. Theoretically, the writers and publishers get paid a fair amount. BMI goes over a sampling of some of the radio logs; ASCAP listens to (audits) some of the stations some of the time. ASCAP receives a very small percentage of what each station is paid by its advertisers. BMI's arrangement is similar, except that it charges less. This money is then divided up among the songwriters and publishers whose material, according to the formula, got the airplay.

But the results of any formulated system can, at best, only approximate how many times a song was played on every station. The current systems, with modifications, are the ones everyone is stuck with, until some computer is programmed to input every song played on every station. People we talked to in radio stated without reservation that both systems are unfair to writer and publisher. Sampling systems are very often arbitrary and that they are imperfect is the least one can say.

Flat fees are also paid to these agencies by nightclubs, resorts, concert halls, and so on, depending on the relative amount of music used, and the size of the performance place. Each jukebox now pays $8 a year, which isn't too significant a headway, considering how much jukeboxes are played and the administration–collection costs.

The tendency of ASCAP and BMI to become monopolistic powers has caused concern in the federal government. Both agencies operate under what are called "consent decrees," which means that the government is always looking over their shoulders. Government authorities modify their ways of operating, and check on how they both collect and dispense money. It's the government who has to some extent set the rules for membership in the agencies. Official thinking on membership goes something like this: since ASCAP and BMI operate practically without competition as collectors of fees for the nondramatic public performance of music, and since writers and publishers have nowhere else to go to obtain this service, the requirements for membership in the agencies should be pretty lenient. Basically, the reason the government has consented to let the agencies continue to function is that without them the individual writer or publisher would be helpless when it came to collecting money due for public performance. The services performed by the agencies are vital.

To be assured of getting a fair share of the profits, consequently, every professional writer must belong to one of these agencies. Many publishers are members of both. ASCAP accepts as a member any composer or lyricist who has a copyrighted piece of music that is *regularly* published. (At the end of this chapter we cover copyrighting; the chapter on publishing gives information on getting a song published, either by setting up your own publishing company, or by granting publishing rights to an established concern.) Being regularly published is the limiting stipulation; unless your published song is going to be printed or recorded commercially, you aren't regularly published. There is not, as a consequence, real reason to be a member, because there's no way for money to be collected for the public performance of your material. Your song would become dead weight in the catalogs.

Russel Sanjek at BMI describes the admissions procedure: "You come to the receptionist, and you say, 'I want to be affiliated with BMI as a writer, or as a publisher, or both.' Then someone comes out and sits down with you. There's the thing to fill out [an application form] . . . and if you qualify, you're in. If not, not."

216

Which agency is most desirable? Which of the two should you join? What's the difference between them? To some extent, these questions can be answered.

Both agencies have histories you might want to look into. Such an examination might persuade you to join one or the other. But, essentially, people tend to join the licensing agency that either gives them the larger advance or seems to pay the larger royalties. The advance is money paid against potential performance rights earnings. If the music doesn't earn back the advance, the agency loses. The other reasons would be inherent in the policies of collection and the way the money is distributed.

Advances have importance for the newcomer, as well as for established writers and publishers. Once a record contract exists, the agency considers the recording artist, recording company, producer, track record of the writer, plus any other assets, and determines what the probable exposure of the material will be from airplay or TV or other. Using this estimate as a base, the agency makes its advance. BMI has the reputation of making the heavier advances. Both organizations at different times, for one reason or another, might be in a position to give out bigger advances, because, perhaps, they might be trying to build up their catalogs, or be getting ready to negotiate new contracts with the broadcasters. Both agencies try to attract the big names through big advances. Perhaps they have found that spreading small amounts of advances to new writers in order to sign them up doesn't pay off because few ever really make the superwriter category.

A newcomer composer approaching either agency with a recently won recording deal will find the agency's advance is as little as possible to win him or her over. Paul Adler at ASCAP says, "For a brand-new person without a track record but who has a record deal, we will make some small advance. Rock bottom is one hundred dollars. We take into consideration the producer, et cetera." Russ Sanjek at BMI says, "If somebody comes in and shows some reason for an advance against his earnings, then yeah. But you don't give advances without some potential of return."

Sanjek constantly referred to "BMI grubstaking." "We've grubstaked the publishers, we've grubstaked the writers," he explained. "We recognized the unwashed in this country, which is something that ASCAP refused to do for a long time." BMI "grubstaked" Berry Gordy of Motown Records fame, once for $500. But when it comes to helping a writer without a track record, who hasn't that record contract in hand, both agencies are emphatic about wanting little or no involvement.

Although each agency has a small writers' department for its members, when Leeds Levy was in that department at ASCAP he told us his hands were tied by the membership. "There are 7,000 publishers," he pointed out, "and we know there are several who want new material. We can't discriminate between our publisher members, so we can't sit here and recommend everybody we hear over to Warner Brothers — just to pick a name. It's awkward, anyway, because what if we send someone to a publisher and he comes back and blames us for the bad deal that the publisher gave him? We like to give writers a choice." By that Leeds meant that he would send an ASCAP writer to several different publishers.

The two agencies compete with each other for members, and occasionally members change over from one to the other. Sanjek said publishers and writers migrate. "If the next fifteen hits are written by BMI writers," he said, "X is going to be a big BMI firm. And if the next fifteen hits are written by ASCAP writers, X is going to be an ASCAP firm. And that's true of —" and he gave us a list of the major publishers.

Apart from their divergent policies on advances, the advantages of one agency over the other are difficult to figure out. Nevertheless, they are there, especially for writers with earning ability. One agency has a bonus system, by which the writer-publisher is paid an additional percentage above his normal share if performances go above a specified number.

Such a possibility for increased profits can induce a publisher to put all or most of its copyrights under one agency. The publishers tell us that one of the many reasons it is more advantageous for writers to work through established publishers, rather than to create their own publishing companies, is that their percentage from the performing rights agency will be greater (BMI).

Paul Adler says of ASCAP, "We treat everybody the same way. No one gets a better deal than anyone else. A small publisher doesn't get a lesser rate than Warner Brothers Publisher, and Irving Berlin doesn't get a better deal than the newest guy that walks in the door." Since the two organizations are so complex, to know the whole story would be a full-time job.

In the long run, when it comes to comparing the two agencies, the bottom line about their differences will probably be a personal one or a technical one. They are competitive. ASCAP's Adler believes that because BMI is owned by radio stations, there is a conflict of interest. ASCAP, however — run by writers and publishers — has historically been charged with being controlled too much by its publishers, thus implying that writers were being slighted.

Both agencies handle collections for foreign performances. There was a time (up to 1965) when the foreign equivalents of ASCAP and BMI collected so little that many American publishers and writers left it all up to them to police their cousin agencies in other countries. But since The Beatles and the internationalization of rock and roll, many writers and publishers, rather than having an American agency handle their collections abroad, have set up foreign publishing companies, or have worked out arrangements with foreign publishers through which they have a more direct means of receiving payment for the foreign performance of their copyrights.

If a writer or publisher is dissatisfied with the agency's accounting of his or her material, there exists no right to audit the accounts as is standard for writers in the book publishing field. Complaints can be taken to an internal board of review at ASCAP. Adler could think of only four cases between 1967 and 1975 that went that far. At BMI, according to Sanjek, the doors are open to dissatisfied members or their representatives. To us that may reflect the inflexibility of an arrangement in which writers and publishers have hardly any alternative. However, if no performing rights agency existed, writers and publishers would have to create one.

Copyright and Common Law

Effective January 1, 1978, copyright will subsist from the time that a work is created, or to use the legalese, "fixed in a tangible medium of expression." The new copyright law is still being unraveled and interpreted but it is pretty clear that when the writing of a piece of music (or lyric) is done, a copyright in the material exists. Nevertheless, it is wise formally to register any creation with the copyright office and affix a proper copyright line. Any queries regarding the niceties of the new law and the proper copyright application forms and procedures should be directed to the U.S. Copyright Office, Library of Congress, Washington, D.C.

16

Forming the Group and Keeping It Together

SINCE THE GROUP has been and still is the most effective way for musicians to get a start in the music world, their unity means survival and strength. Every group, no matter how much it's denied, does have a leader. Starting out, it can be the best musician. When it comes to a major group, the leader is most always the lead singer, and/or the writer of the group's original material, because the talent is where you find the economic power that propels a group into turning out hit singles, getting those good bookings necessary to an intensive tour, and selling out those sixty-thousand-seat stadiums.

For those bands for whom huge amounts of income are still dreams, it might be well to agree on a leader who has some natural leadership abilities, rather than letting purely aesthetic talents be the determining criteria. Probably the best requirement is to have a head for business. Select the kind of person who finds it most natural to look after all the group's affairs, from persevering on the phone in getting gigs to caring that the equipment is upgraded; the person who is willing to accept responsibilities; the one who sees to it that ideas get acted upon. Don Brewer of Grand Funk is the business leader of that group. His simple explanation says it all: "If I don't do it, nobody else will."

That's the way most leaders evolve. There seems to be a mutual understanding in many groups that a certain person is the leader because he or she has put the most effort into the group, and there doesn't seem to be much sense for that person not to run the outfit. But it should be an out-in-the-open arrangement, so that the leader knows that he or she is making decisions with the explicit support of the entire group. For really major decisions, verbal approval should be sought.

Lately, there has been a trend among musicians just starting out for the leader to be the virtual "owner" of the group. Here the leader has or raises the money, gets backing to hire the musicians and to rent or purchase both a sound system and transportation. He or she may do the booking for the act and will then collect the subsequent profits if any. This kind of group operates just like any other kind of business, and by guaranteeing the musicians a salary, the leader's decisions are under a minimum of dispute. Many of the big names have been doing this for a long time, of course, but it's happening now on the minor circuits as well. Martha Velez, rock and reggae singer (one of the original stars of *Hair*), says that now that she employs her group, her life is much smoother and she's in total control of what she wants to do.

In an interview in *Crawdaddy* Ronnie Hawkins, leader of the old Hawks, the group that gave birth to the immensely successful The Band (without Hawkins as a member), relates that he believes in educating his band members to make them aware of the world's hard realities. "I try to teach all the guys," he says, "it's a dog-eat-dog world out there." Being realistic and tough is one thing. But if a leader becomes bitter, there is a chance the whole group will sour on the world.

The leader may accept the responsibility for the welfare of the whole group, but that doesn't mean that he or she has to *do* everything. Keeping the group supplied and functioning can just as easily be accomplished by delegating chores to all the members according to their interests and abilities. And each group member should accept such responsibility. The person most into gadgetry, for instance, could take care of the equipment. If someone has a super phone personality, that person should be the one to handle bookings rather than the leader. The clothes freak can keep the stage clothes in order and keep everyone conscious of his or her appearance. People will accept responsibility and eventually like it, even if at first they don't appear to want it. It's a democratic approach, perhaps an idealistic one; but when it works, the smooth machinery will enable the group to project upbeat well-being, an image that never hurt anybody!

Aesthetic Direction

Choosing a musical direction is one of the most important decisions a group can make, because it will influence the group's immediate future. Later on the music you emphasize will become your background, your foundation, so to speak.

A great many bands get together out of a group of friends who share a common appreciation of a certain sound. Since this kind of jamming tends to always sound like *jamming,* it doesn't really help the group to get down a tight, innovative concept. It may offer the quickest creative gratification and important musical education, but jamming offers the least advantage when it comes to commercial possibilities. Even club owners have learned to shy away from most groups that jam.

No group can be all things to all people, though many musicians think their particular sound will be appealing to just about everybody. There are a lot of stylistic crossovers, such as mixing country and western with any number of rock styles, with everything seeping more into MOR than it used to. Consciously thinking about these details, such as knowing for whom the group's music will have the greatest appeal, what age group, even what sex, will help give focus to your work. Although these kinds of decisions may seem premature, ultimately success depends on making them wisely; success depends on acceptance by certain markets. Making sure you know the target you're aiming at will help you hit the mark.

For a group that wants to perform its own material, the primary sound can stem from any major style (blues or rock or whatever) and develop into some unique aspect of that style by experimentation or other means (if the development or assimilation hasn't already come about naturally). So right away the group, if it wants to go out on dates, should decide on a direction. If its choice is to have a repertoire of original material, then it has to work out a specific emphasis and/or identifiable sound. Whatever the final decision is, it should be the agreed goal of the entire group, coming from their natural inclination.

Across the country, though, except for the groups who are into playing their own original material, the majority have adapted to a modified top-forty playlist, adding new tunes as they become hits. Most club owners and patrons have the easiest time appreciating the top forty. The group that moves away from top forty into C & W, progressive jazz, and so on, will find that their gigs are limited to those clubs or areas open to their sound. Those groups that are drawn to rock as their medium will probably choose among distinctive styles, such as hard rock, soft rock, progressive rock, funk rock, punk rock, country rock, plus a dozen other merging combinations. It's possible to show an influence from a generation of music and still be unique. It is not always easy to come to agreement, but the element of compromise can work like a good glue. A little give and take, a tolerance of another point of view, a willingness to try a tune out even if you don't initially like it, all done in the spirit of mutual respect, will help.

Often a group's choice isn't motivated totally by purely musical concerns. A person might be "in love" with a particular image, glitter rock, say, of the Seventies, which was more of a look than a sound. Or perhaps the lead singer might have real abilities in the Streisand tradition. Maybe the guitarist is really more comfortable with folk, yet has a conflicting compulsion to identify with the cowboy image of the Nashville music scene. One either has to make these splits work, or work them out of the act. For a group to progress it has to know where it's at and where it wants to go, and the thing that counts is the ability to fuse the two into a force.

Sometimes there's no way for a group to stay together other than to alter its sound, recognizing that a mistake was made originally: there is no work for the group, or general artistic dissatisfaction is felt by all the members. More positively, maybe the change is called for because the members have found a new sound they all like, which is more exciting and opens up wider possibilities. Unless everything is working out well for the group, it shouldn't stay fixed. Change when you feel you're all getting stale and your audience is getting bored . . . change if you sense a new direction is where the action is, and you like both the direction and the action. Evolving from playing top forty to composing your own tunes is a surer way to a record contract, as we stressed in the first chapter.

Economics

Right off, no matter how poor or prosperous, the group should set up a mutually acceptable, clear economic structure to handle its finances. Any CPA should be able to put you on a straight path and won't charge much for advice. The first thing a CPA will want is one person to assume the responsibilities of bookkeeping, signing checks, collecting income, and following the budget. There isn't a business alive and well that doesn't keep accounts in some clear way, so that everybody concerned can know where it's at. A lot of musicians will say, "I'm not into business; it's not my thing." But music *is* a business; and when musicians turn away from business, they inevitably get ripped off — and worse, become unbearably suspicious out of ignorance of all the business that's going on around them. The group that's lucky enough to have someone good at it should encourage that member to take over the business end.

Regular meetings should be held in which the group doesn't discuss material, doesn't rehearse, but only goes over business matters. Not that everyone will ever totally agree; but at least it's a time when every issue can be brought up, and no one can claim ignorance later on. If there's one thing that destroys the communal spirit fast, it's shocking surprises, the kind where somebody decided to do something, and all the others can do is yell in protest after the deed is done.

If the group is going to function on the democratic principle of majority rule, then every major economic decision should be arrived at through a vote. It might sound paranoid to keep a record of the decisions and of the subjects discussed at the meetings, but there's nothing like a written record to fall back on where there's a dispute over what went down in the past. One tends to exaggerate income and minimize expenditure. When it's all written down, it's easy to see where the cash is flowing.

It's also important to have written records for tax purposes. Most gigging musicians receive a significant portion of their income in cash, and tend to ignore federal and state taxes for as long as they can. But many such musicians are probably spending more toward furthering their careers than they realize, and so, for tax purposes, are operating at or near a loss. So there is a good chance the taxes can be negligible. In any case, you should be able to prove all expenses, and that's where the written record comes in.

For most groups the biggest item of expense is equipment. When they first get together, many groups use equipment that is privately owned by one or more of the members, and have some vague arrangement about it. Everyone tends to be most generous then. Indeed, personal equipment can actually be used by the owner as bait, in drawing musicians into a group in the first place. Mostly, though, the group pools whatever equipment the individuals have to make up the best possible sound system, and it's hardly ever true that each member makes an equal contribution. All equipment (used or new) can be a business deduction.

Eventually there's trouble: the speaker gets worn from many trips in and out of the van, a mike gets lifted, the amp blows, and it's usually the owner who unhappily suffers the loss. It's great, though, if from the beginning the band is making enough to put a regular percentage into an equipment fund with two ideas in mind: (1) compensating the original owner for a loss, and (2) eventually purchasing or renting equipment. This equipment slush fund can also be used to buy out a member's share, when he or she is either forced out of the group or voluntarily leaves. Since most groups exist on a survival basis, it's always tough to take something off the top from every gig, but it could be done more than it is.

We can all spend more than we make, individuals as well as corporations, which is the reason for the existence of a budget. A budget lays out a good idea of the prospective income and the prospective expenses, such as equipment, stage clothes, transportation, and so on. It's a way to check on the tendency to overspend in one department.

Rehearsals

If you can land a place where your equipment can be left set up, where neighbors won't object to amplified sound, and where there isn't going to be a burden on one of the group, you're supremely lucky.

The healthier the group economically, the more space it needs: for individual privacy, for equipment storage, and for rehearsal space. In 1975 The Rolling Stones were summering out at the tip of Long Island at Montauk Point, and rehearsing in a jetport hangar at Newburgh, New York, up the Hudson — a distance of about 160 miles. Newburgh was the nearest place where they could rent the kind of space they needed to simulate their show. Unused hangars there rent for about $1,000 a month — cheap for that kind of space.

Most acts don't need a jetport for rehearsal. Some rehearsal studios we've seen were heated and enclosed barns, others old lofts in the industrial sections of towns and cities, truck garages, moving-van and storage warehouses, daytime restaurants that were empty at night, church halls, unused space anywhere — preferably in nonresidential areas. Often the rent is minimal, or the space is available on a work-trade basis. The important thing is to get that space, so that rehearsals can be something the group looks forward to.

Another thing a group should think about right from the start: people are going to grow unhappy if reheasals aren't run with enthusiasm, a positive attitude, and on schedule. Setting an immediate goal will inspire people. The tendency to treat schedules offhandedly by being late screws up everybody's time, and creates lots of discontent. Being too casual, informal, cool, and above-it-all sets up immediate resentment that isn't conducive to cooperative effort.

Hanging Out

One of the reasons a career in music has such universal appeal is that it defies the nine-to-five routine. Roger Daltry calls the rock musician a "working-class eccentric." But *indulging* in eccentricity can lead the musician down some dead-end paths. Hanging out is one of them.

There are hundreds of legendary stories of how hanging out brought about someone's first big break, whether it was shuffling around outside the studio, lounging wherever the biggies lounge, or patrolling Broadway or Sunset. That's one kind of hanging out. If it's backed up by product and expertise, it is a way of being professional.

The kind of hanging out that's anathema to a group's welfare is the kind The Eagles experienced when they were hanging around in England, sort of *waiting* for an album to get itself together, but not really working at it. The "lethargy of the group got stifling," so they decided to pack it in and return to the States, where they went to work in Hollywood. From that point everything started happening for them. The so-called Puritan work ethic has positive side effects, in that it can keep one from depression and perhaps even alcoholism, probably the greatest killer of musical talent there is.

Frank Zappa of The Mothers Of Invention talks about a singer he once hired who lasted three days with the group: "The first day he was fantastic, the second day he started going down, and the third day he was in trouble. . . . One day he ran up a bar tab of ninety dollars for himself. I didn't know he was an alcoholic."

What we're really talking about is many people's natural tendency to sit around wasting time, which can include everything from smoking dope to watching TV to drinking in bars. Again, in moderation, and if for the right reasons, hanging out can be socially and professionally redeeming, and even therapeutic. Roger Daltry says, "I don't like clubs, but I love the company, so I hang out sometimes." Sometimes.

Group Therapy

Every group has its own ready-made following composed of people who are related to the group through direct associations with its members. Wives, friends, hangers-on — all psychologically involved with the group, all adding their two cents' worth.

Wives have received the most blame, rightly or wrongly, for the demise of groups. A wife, siding with her husband out of loyalty and lending a sympathetic ear to all of his complaints and insecurities, might feed the fire by pointing out negative things her husband never noticed. Before long the members are no longer friends but enemies. Sometimes, too, wives are scapegoats for the real discontent.

One of the best and most realistic ways of handling discontent can be through some sort of straightforward exchange. *Creem* magazine reported Bobby Lam, the group Chicago's composer, as saying, "Define Chicago? Well, I think it's probably the most successful experiment ever in group therapy." He continues to attribute Chicago's nine-year "experiment" to its group meetings, where all personal gripes and grudges are brought out and *apologies* are made.

Jealousy can destroy the equilibrium of any group. The rhythm guitarist is jealous of the lead singer, the bass and the drummer can't stand the keyboardist's new car. The drummer attracts more girls, the conga player has charisma, and on and on.

Many times you read about a group breaking up, and the answer often given is, "We just weren't communicating anymore." Behind this polite statement could be a thundering rage, but the essence of it is always that the group members didn't fully respect one another as individuals, and probably hadn't made the effort to bring problems out in the open and hash it all out. You can call it anything you want, gripe session, group therapy, whatever, but if it's conducted on a regular basis, the group will have a chance to clear the air. Acquiring experience in learning how to settle differences maturely for the good of the whole is a skill that will serve one well in marriage, friendship, business, any partnership at all.

17

Getting Gigs

YOU'VE GOT TO PUT some thought to the business aspect of your music — especially if you're just starting out. One of the real fundamentals (besides musical competence) is booking your act. You've got to get and keep on getting gigs, and one of the chief ways to do this is by having a good and varied repertoire. If you're able to perform three to four hours without repetition, you're doing all right. Sooner or later someone will want to book the act. You'll come to some agreement with the club owner about the fee, you'll sign a contract, and that's about all there is to it.

If you're responsible for booking either yourself as a solo or as part of a group act, or if you are trying to get started as a booking agent, the options, the general direction, the necessary stance are the same, whether you're a Dick Fox at the William Morris Agency booking Barry Manilow in the Hollywood Bowl, or an agent-wife booking her husband, a singer-guitarist, in a campus coffee house. The main variable is the quantity of money involved.

A young group we know that plays for $25 to $150 a gig recently had a chance to move up to a $350 club gig, but found some weak excuses to turn the offer down. Some of their $75-a-night bar gigs are tough, requiring four sets, lasting from nine to three in the morning, and involving less favorable working conditions than the one they turned down. What was really behind their refusal, when it all came out in conversation, was a fear of committing themselves to the big time.

Hirth Martinez worked in Los Angeles clubs for years, on a relatively small-time circuit, until along came Robbie Robertson (leader of The Band), who took Hirth under his wing, got his songs worked out, and produced an album of Hirth's songs. Hirth later said of Robbie that he was the first one to make him think big. There are lots of stories like this in the music world.

A late pianist friend, Tom A., a suicide, had songwriting and musical abilities far beyond his wildest dream — which was to play piano bar in a mill town. He, too, always felt this conflict between small time and big time, being naturally cut out for the latter, yet drawn and adapted to the former.

You've got to jump in order to get anywhere. In working one's way up the musical ladder, there is a tendency to stay too long on one rung. Big-time pop musicians are always talking about paying one's dues, as though hardship were an absolute part of the learning process, as though having your teeth kicked in a few times were a prerequisite for success. People generally resent easy ascents, and one has to be on the watch in the music world against making life unnecessarily tough on oneself to escape that resentment. Yet all those really young groups of the mid-Sixties like The Beach Boys, The Blues Magoos, Young Rascals, and so on, somehow spared themselves part of that-awful-rut school of musical education; when the big chances came around, they didn't respond with a "we're not ready yet" attitude.

Booking Unknown Acts in Small Clubs
(and Stars at the Waldorf)

When we were gathering material for this book, knocking around the streets of New York, seeing executives and creative people, everyone was puzzling about the fact that Ike and Tina Turner and the Ikettes and their band were appearing at the Empire Room in the Waldorf (a not very energized nightclub). It couldn't possibly have been exclusively for the income — the act was expensive even for the Waldorf — and they had so much equipment up on the small stage that it looked like Manny's music store on Forty-eighth Street. We later found out that the probable reason for that booking — and even booking agents we were talking to at the time hadn't figured this out — was that they were showcasing in the Empire Room for people who book the hotels on the Vegas Strip. Vegas hotel-nightclub contracts have the biggest jackpots for the longest runs. Wayne Newton, for example, reportedly picked up $35 million recently for a five-year contract to appear at the Nevada chain of Howard Hughes Hotels. So Ike and Tina must have been showing at the Waldorf primarily to try out for a Vegas-type crowd.

At the same time that Ike and Tina were getting polite applause at the Waldorf, downtown in a scuzzy neighborhood on East Fifteenth Street Bobby Tullipan had booked his wife, Cathy Chamberlain, at Tramps, a bar with about fifty tables and a postage-stamp stage. They were losing money on their two-week gig. Cathy and Bobby figured that with the band really good now and Cathy at a peak, this would be a shot at getting some coverage from the press, building up the press kit, getting Cathy's name around the New York café scene as a fresh, new entertainer. So Cathy and Bobby were willing to pay the band members (five of them) full scale and put up extra money for advertising in *The Village Voice* and other not so key publications, all to get a chance at better gigs and more important bookings, maybe at one of the uptown clubs.

Booking Clubs

Compile a list of all the clubs around that book live entertainment. Make time to go out and meet the club owners, tell them of your services, maybe play them a tape with a couple of tunes you think would be best for their particular space and audience.

It's a good idea to have a press kit; it's a sign of professionalism. It's a kind of concrete presentation that will help to sell the act. Cathy Chamberlain has, as part of her press kit, a live videotape of her act. On a lesser, more realistic scale for most performers, a press kit should consist of a short biography, emphasizing the professional history of the talent, some good photos the club can use for reproduction in small ads and posters, good reviews and notices the talent has received, a list of the best clubs and concerts at which the talent has appeared, plus whatever else feels right. All this, of course, is used as a backup for the cassette, which should be as clean as you can manage and should feature the act's best numbers.

Before you talk contract with a club owner, you'll want to have a pitch. The pitch is what you tell him to convince him you're professional. The cassette will speak for itself, but he might want to know things like how long the act's been together, the kind of repertoire, whom you know around, and what kind of crowd the act can draw.

One last thing: a contract isn't always necessary. One group we know, a sort of soft-rock, top-forty group, who do $150 gigs, always used to get a contract signed, which simply stated date(s), dollars, location, and so on. But for a couple of weekends in a row the club owners broke the agreement. Since no lawyer would take a case involving such relatively little money, and since it might have taken a couple of Friday nights in small-claims court — nights they could have been working — they dropped the whole thing and gave up getting signed contracts. Our point is not that we advise against contracts, but rather that it's the spirit behind a contract that counts.

Booking Colleges

College booking is a beast all its own, particularly when you're acting as a middle person between major booking agencies and the colleges. Harris Goldberg began doing this in the late Sixties. He saw that there was a need in the New Hampshire–Maine area for someone to bring in the most popular acts for the colleges and said, "Why not me?" He now books big acts for a string of college campuses, manages singer-songwriter Tim Moore, and has his own music publishing company.

This is one field that a woman can enter without facing the traditional obstacles, especially because the people one is dealing with at the colleges, the heads of student social activities, are also likely to be women.

There is a trend in college booking today that's almost impossible to buck, and it makes working the colleges especially tough — that's the drive to book only the biggest name performers in order to fill the house and make a profit. College social directors, seeking to fill a gym, would rather spend the entire budget on one or two surefire acts a semester than take a chance on ten acts with small reputations. So the chance of an unknown group getting booked at a major college concert today is somewhat slim; even opening acts have to have some kind of reputation for the most part.

One hope for the unknown to get campus exposure is to try for bookings on weekend nights in the student lounge or in the campus pub or at dances off campus. The rates are minimal, but the exposure can mount up and will count when the first album comes out. There are plenty of gigs available if the material of the entertainment suits the campus population. But one of the pitfalls to watch out for is the small-time booking agent's tendency to favor his own musical taste, when in fact it might not be appropriate to an audience. A bluegrass country band might not go over well at a University of Miami dance. In fact, most state campus populations are pretty middle of the road.

235

Harris got started — and anyone, agent or musician, can take a lesson from him — by realizing right away that if he could cut the fees to the colleges and at the same time arrange it so that the acts would gross more money, he would have it made. So he instituted block booking for an area. By enlisting the verbal agreement of about twenty campuses, he could book an act that had the time to perform on three or four campuses over a weekend, or maybe a week, each campus paying 25 percent less than usual, but the act grossing quite a lot from all the combined fees. It worked out very well, and it's a method still used today.

Many acts, of course, will ask for a guarantee against percentages. A Peter Frampton, for instance, may want $20,000 for one night against 70 percent of the gate. If the school sells 3,000 tickets at $10 a clip, then Frampton would get $21,000; if the school were able to sell only 1,000, Frampton would still get his $20,000 guarantee. Most big acts will go for this, since they can pretty well determine ahead of time the amount of tickets they can sell at any given location, and they figure that anything more is gravy.

One of the biggest headaches a booking agent has is whether an act will show up or not. It's written in most contracts that a musician can call in sick if it's absolutely necessary. It's called an "act of God" clause, and it applies to sickness, accidents, storms that prevent travel, earthquakes, and other types of uncontrollable circumstances. Some musicians take unfair advantage of the clause. Or a performer might show, but be so high or down or whatever that he won't be able to go on.

One of the first acts Harris booked was Tim Hardin, whose jazz–C-&-W–rock balladeering was popular on campuses then. Tim not only showed up late by two and a half hours, his clothing was torn, and the set was so terrible that the audience was really angry about it. But as only Tim can do, he returned for a second set that was dynamite, and the kids went home loving him. Harris, however, was having premonitions of a bleeding ulcer long before bedtime.

The business side of booking schools also has its differences. An independent agent is usually paid directly by the school the night of the concert. The going fee is 5 to 15 percent. If the act is signed with an agency such as William Morris, the agency gets its commission (10 percent) from the performer's fee.

Usually an agency representing a big act will want the school to pay from half to all the fee up front, even if the act is booked a year ahead of time. Such up-front money is insurance against the school fund's going bankrupt or the committee's changing its mind.

Some regional agents will try to get half the commission from the school and half from the act. There is one problem with this: all the people involved might think the agent is getting full commission from both ends, whether he is or not. And when people start thinking overtime, it tends to destroy the trust that makes for good business relations. In some states there are laws specifically regulating fees and prohibiting crossovers. For instance, you can't be both a booking agent and personal manager for the same person in New York. Commissions are best paid and received on an above-board basis, where all parties involved know the exact arrangement. As Harris Goldberg says, "Your reputation follows you around like a day-and-night shadow."

College gigs, being removed from the superprofessionalism of the music centers, can be really amateurish when it comes to stage equipment such as lights and sound systems. That's why most groups maintain their whole system, from speakers to smoke. But there are elements they can't provide themselves, such as plenty of the right kind of electrical outlets. A couple of years ago we went to a college concert featuring Ten Years After. They went on two hours late, because the equipment demanded a sophisticated electrical supply, and neither the group nor the local booking agent nor the college had anticipated the need. The error blew the concert for most of the audience; we left early.

The college social committee comes to a decision on an act

by majority vote. Since usually each member wants a different act, the whole process can be laborious; then, after all of that, the committee may find out that the act they've chosen is booked solid or the fee has gone out of their reach. This is where a local agent can come in handy. By working with the committee from the beginning of the fall — or even earlier, from the previous spring semester — and by thinking the whole program through with them months in advance, the agent can make some money and the college can have a chance at major acts.

For the act that's not a headliner, working with a regional booking agent, maybe even getting him or her as manager, can be a bonus. Agents are always the first to know when there's a cancellation, or when a social committee will agree to have unknowns fill in to help satisfy the crowd. Sometimes there may be enough advance notice that a major act is going to be late to be able to put on a warm-up band or act. This can be a good opportunity for an unknown to get exposure and experience. Many major acts want to have an opening act, and they'll accept the advice of the local booking agent.

Some schools can be poor at promoting and advertising a concert. Often there's no one on the administration who oversees the operation, and the members of the social committee change every year; thus learning the concert process becomes an annual thing. This is where an act and a booking agent can fill in with more than just verbal advice. Posters, display ads, radio announcements, and other forms of advertising and promotion have to be supplied or suggested.

The barometer for success is the volume of ticket sales and whether the student body wants the act back. Sometimes it's surprising what the kids will respond to. When Orleans was just a bar band, Harris would get them gigs in colleges like Vassar as the opening act for a major like the New Riders. Orleans was asked back, the New Riders weren't.

Booking High Schools

The booking of known professional talent into high school auditoriums and gyms is a relative latecomer to the scene, because high school administrators are basically afraid of crowds; and, furthermore, the music world has traditionally undervalued the exposure. But the pressure is there in some schools to open up the facilities, often the biggest and best in an area, to concerts and dances featuring everything from local talent to superstars. And as the stars' record companies will testify, high school kids buy the records. Many new artists do free high school concerts to build a following — because that's where there is the most potential. In some enlightened high schools the decisions might be made by a student committee operating pretty much like its college counterpart. But you can be sure that almost always the agent or act will be more in touch with the administration, so a conservative approach is called for.

If an act is not grossing $1,000 or more per performance, it may be difficult to find an independent agent to handle it. So it may have to do its own booking. Since there is a scarcity of small-price booking agents, therefore, here is the perfect opportunity for a performer-agent to start out.

Starting a Regional Booking Agency

Probably the best thing that can be said about someone starting a small booking agency is that it can lead to bigger and better things. Irv Asmoff, still under twenty-five yet one of the biggest successes in the business, started booking and managing his friends in the Midwest. As Lorraine Traum, who has done a lot of booking, says, you have to be "enthusiastically ready to book your people into everything from a wedding reception at a nearby Ramada Inn to a bar mitzvah party." You can't start off at the Astrodome. And even though weddings may be the least attractive to some groups, they mean experience, exposure, and income.

Most people, before they go into business for the first time, are accustomed to using the phone only for a few errands and for socializing; but when you are booking outside of your own toll-free area, the phone bill can easily and quickly shoot up to a hundred dollars and more, and one should be prepared to pay it without grudges. It saves a lot of running around. And it's the nature of the business. More important, good booking agents develop a confidence, even a smoothness over the phone. Some are quite charming, with an ability to make you feel close without ever having met you, joking easily, naturally, bringing up little personal concerns of theirs and yours. A good phone personality, one that can combine charm with an alertness for the right deal, is the talent of a booking agent, one easily adopted once you experience that it works.

It's a relatively simple thing to get going. Let's say you're going to start out by booking four or five groups who are living in the area. The most important criterion in selecting the groups to represent is their dependability. Do they say what they mean and mean what they say? Will they cancel at the last minute? Will they regularly show up an hour late?

Odd Gigs

The Benefit

When an act needs exposure, it can look for benefit gigs. Sometimes it can create a benefit concert. Every town and city has hundreds of organizations that exist on philanthropic money, and they will be open to a fund-raising concert.

Most benefits are poorly organized, and the resultant chaos detracts from the music, agitates the audience, and makes the whole thing seem like a waste of time. Also, if there are several acts on the same show, there tends to be a lot of jockeying to see who comes on at the best time. And if there is money involved in a multiple-act benefit, it's unlikely that the allocating of the money is going to be very democratic.

The positive side is that benefits can be a lot of fun. One benefit we went to was for bluegrass artist Johnny Herald, who had watched his guitar burn up along with all his possessions in his cabin. About thirty friends of Johnny's wanted to play at that benefit. There was much ego-shifting, as well as getting together and partying, so that a few of the major reputations couldn't get it together to go on. It turned out that some new acts who *were* together stole the show.

Showcase

Today, talent can get inspired at the mere mention of a showcase. It promises so much — like being discovered, instant recognition, and possibly a super record contract. That's what happened to the currently touring singer-songwriter, former pizza-parlor counterman Tom Waits, who got his first important break after appearing on several amateur night performances in a San Diego club. And later, on showcase night at the Troubadour in Los Angeles, he caught the attention of a producer, who brought his talent to the attention of Elektra-Asylum president David Geffen, who signed Waits to a recording contract.

Amateur night, audition, talent search, showcase — they are often interchangeable terms in today's music vocabulary. Showcase is used the most and has the most prestige. Showcase really means to audition. If you're a performer, you can showcase with or without a public audience, in clubs, rehearsal halls, theaters, just about anywhere, the one requirement being that hopefully an interested, influential party who can do you some professional good will be present. Business people have turned away from the more traditional private audition in favor of seeing the entertainer live, observing the audience's reactions. This arrangement also gives the business person the freedom to disappear after the show without being confronted by the performer or the performer's representatives. And, too, there are good reasons for the artist to shy away from the old-fashioned, private auditions. We attended an audition recently where the performer put on a unique and highly creative show, and the four music business executives present didn't even display the common courtesy of clapping. We've heard old pros advise against private auditions. They are often deadly experiences; the business people present tend to withhold judgment until the most powerful person present expresses an opinion, which, whether positive or negative, tends to have a domino effect on the others.

Some of the showcase clubs take pride in being part of the musical underground. In 1976 a New York club, CBGB, featured a week-long showcase called, "A Festival of New York's Top 40 Unrecorded Rock and Roll Bands!" By 1977 many of the groups who showcased there had landed record contracts. Often in showcasing the club owner books entertainment free, or almost free. Recently, the concept has received a status input with the appearance of clubs like the Bottom Line in New York, perhaps the premier of showcase clubs. Exposure at the Bottom Line can mean good reviews, which bring the act to the attention of the major booking agents and promoters. If the act doesn't have a recording contract, it may bring them to the attention of A & R in record companies. But to get booking at the Bottom Line is a *struggle* for any act without a major name, or the backing of a recording company. Big name is the bottom line at the Bottom Line. Clubs like Catch A Rising Star, also in New York, operate pretty much exclusively as showcases for unknown performers. The two Improvisations — one in New York and the other in Los Angeles — are almost exclusively showcases for standup comics; there's hardly a comic, male or female, who hasn't performed often at one or both of the Improvisations.

Some of the music business companies have instituted forms of showcases of their own. BMI funds a songwriter's showcase in Los Angeles. We feel that it could be the coming thing, and that the smart money in the music industry will eventually set up a kind of national network of showcases. Such an arrangement would bring to the industry's attention performing and songwriting talent in the early stages, much as farm clubs, spies, and scouts have brought new talent to the attention of both college and professional ball teams for a long time. A more regular, active, and widespread network, set up to locate and build talent, would be an inspiration to all the playing and singing and writing youth. It could provide a steady stream of new energy into a business that repeatedly puts out amazingly expensive campaigns to hype the same old thing.

18

Booking Agent

IN THE MUSIC BUSINESS an agent gets work for an act or an artist much like an employment agency gets people jobs. In exchange, it's agreed that the agent will take a commission (usually 10 percent) from the total amount paid the artist.

There is a special booking agent for every kind of show-biz talent. There are agents who handle only tours, and of those, some who handle only rock tours. Others will concentrate on musical attractions at fairs, some will only listen to auditions with hotel nightclubs in mind, while others will be experts in placing talent on steamship cruises. Every medium has its specialist, and for every kind of entertainer there is also a specialist, so it would be impossible to cover them all here. Since the national nightclub scene has pretty much been destroyed by the resort hotels (they pay more) in Las Vegas, Miami, Puerto Rico, and a few other places, such as the Catskills, we will be talking mostly about agents for concerts and tours, for that's where today's excitement is.

Agents come in all shapes and sizes, the smallest being the regional, one-person kind of operation we talked about in the last chapter. The largest ones operate out of the key centers of

244

the music business, New York, Chicago, Nashville, and to a lesser extent, San Francisco, Atlanta, Miami, Boston, and Dallas. It should be understood that the large agency's concerns are the same as those held by all good agents, large or small.

There are giants in the field, such as the William Morris Agency, International Creative Management, Premier Talent Associates, and a few others, that have such clout, influence, and control over all facets of the entertainment world it's said they have the power to make an artist an overnight success.

The efforts that a William Morris agent can exercise on behalf of its clients can be so thorough that the agency takes on much of the function of the personal manager. This is one reason why people new to the business tend to confuse managers with agents. The manager is there with the artist on a day-in, day-out basis, overseeing every aspect of the artist's career, and a management company usually has only a few artists in its stable. A really big agency might have thousands of clients in almost every aspect of entertainment.

Some maintain several different departments covering many specific fields: books, film scripts, acting talent, film and TV directors, singer-performers, and so on. A singer-performer, for instance, will be able to make use of many other subdivisions to further his or her career: TV variety shows, concerts, tours, film scores. Or the agency might have special departments (or persons) to handle different types of acts: rock to MOR. There might be a one-nighter department, whose staff have various specialties, such as an agent who knows just what promoters to deal with in the Boston area and one who can tell you the best halls for each kind of act.

Agencies represent their clients by making them available to all media. But seeing a chance to keep that income in-house, the big agencies have, over the last ten to fifteen years, developed the skill of putting together packages. A movie, a TV show or series, many kinds of tours, are all productions for which an agency, if it has the resources, can provide all the creative talent: directors, writers, actors, singers, and so on. The big agencies have meetings all the time in which department heads keep other department heads posted as to what's going on and what's needed. Maybe the film department has just interested a producer in a book it represents and now wants to come up with stars, director, theme song. Television shows are often put together in the same way, especially variety shows. This is the unique service that a multiple-talent agency can provide for its clients and at the same time making more money for itself.

There are also likely to be agents within the house who concentrate solely on particular artists who practically become the private property of that agent as far as in-house activities are concerned. At the time we interviewed Dick Fox at the William Morris Agency, he was handling Neil Sedaka, Barry Manilow, and Melissa Manchester, among others, and it seemed as if almost everyone we were seeing in New York at the time had these three names on the tip of their tongues.

There's a saying that any artist is only as strong as his or her agent, but it works the other way too. An agent's professional reputation is based on the success of the artists he or she represents. Besides salary, agents usually get a bonus, which is determined by the gross business income the agent's clients bring in, and many agents make over $100,000 a year.

Even when an agency showers heaps of attention on a client, there is still the need for a personal manager. In fact, most agencies want all their clients to have one. It's the manager's function to make sure that the agency keeps the client in mind for all appropriate jobs. He or she serves as a constant reminder to the agency that the performer is alive and well — and available. The manager also acts occasionally as a buffer between client and agency to divert quarrels, relay bad news, and simply maintain good relations. Management wants to do everything possible to see that its client is being represented fairly, a task that requires some skill when you remember that agencies have a large roster of talent, all more or less competing for the same plums.

246

True Market Worth

The booking agent, perhaps more than any other person in the music business, knows the true market worth of a talent. It's determined by what the agent can get for the act from more than one promoter; in a way it's like an auction.

Agents know how to keep that "property" (a word sometimes used instead of client or artist) hot. Agents don't like clients to take prolonged vacations. The public forgets very easily, they say, and quickly. The merchandising department at Coca-Cola bases its ongoing promotion campaign on the premise that there's a whole new generation of Coke consumers coming of soda-pop age every six months. Not wanting the public to forget their clients, agents encourage them to keep on working, keeping that calendar filled with dates as far into the future as possible. Presley was a phenomenon, even for show business; he could be away for years, gain a lot of extra pounds, be overexposed on TV (the kiss of death for many artists) with reruns of his Fifties films, and still not one agent or promoter would hesitate to book him just about anywhere short of the Congo. Presley was on top, but there's room for few up there.

It takes only a few attempts to get advance bookings before the agent can really know how the world of concert promoters values the client. The artist might have a top-ten hit, which nets him/her significant bookings into the *near* future. But because the promoter knows that the public can cool on that artist and not be willing to pay eight dollars a seat to see that act without a hit on the charts, it's not always easy to obtain bookings six months to a year in advance. Fox calls those artists with past hits but not a steady stream "middle acts," and he says most promoters hesitate to take a chance with one. A superstar is something else. "Promoters will take the chance any time they can" — if you can call that taking a chance!

Agents can sometimes talk a promoter into booking a particular artist, but if the artist fails to draw a crowd, the promoter loses money and will have deaf ears to the agent's future suggestions. This is one of those built-in control mechanisms, because unlike some other kinds of selling, the agency business is not a one-shot deal; although agents are not above making a quick few thousands on occasion.

Booking at its best is a long-term strategy. Good management tends to be wary of agents who concentrate on making the most commission but have little concern for the artists' career plans. Dick Fox reflects the attitude of those agents who are looking for a long-term relationship when he says, "The biggest problem with new artists is that they want to go too fast too soon." He would like to see more performers with that first hit or two agree to bookings as opening acts for headliners, thereby getting good exposure and an association with established stars without having to take on the responsibility for filling the house. These kinds of appearances will often require the financial sponsorship of the record company, because many acts even with records out cannot afford to rehearse and otherwise prepare for a concert, much less a series of them, where there isn't considerable income involved to cover expenses.

After a while, when the act has built up a following and, one hopes, a second hit, its name will have gotten around. Then maybe the agent will book a two-thousand-seat venue (the place where the performance will occur) and if that works, move on up to a five- or seven-thousand seater. There is a limited number of large venues in the country. According to *Billboard,* during the winter of 1976 there were fewer than fifty venues with a ten-thousand-seat capacity or more. That's not very many when you think of how large the country is.

The knack for choosing the right exposure is part of a good agent's expertise. Oddly, many stars have images of themselves that don't harmonize with what their fans see and hear. Neil Sedaka at one time wanted to be associated with rock and roll music as performed by his friend Elton John, so one of Sedaka's dreams was to play at Hollywood's Troubadour. His agent had to convince him to go in another, more natural direction, one where he'd find audiences that were right for his style.

Agency Mechanics

When an agent books an act, he/she wants to get as much of the guarantee as possible up front. With the big agents it's usually half the guarantee on signing. Agents listen to promoters' hype with one ear, knowing that promoters of concerts go bankrupt every five minutes; there's a risk of not being paid the rest of the guarantee.

Management wants the agency to make sure that the artist is not going to lose out by working for a promoter who can't or won't promote. So the fee most agents charge a promoter is a guarantee against a percentage of the gate, whichever is larger. The amount an artist can demand varies hugely, from the token fee asked by a new act that is willing to perform for the exposure value alone to what a Bruce Springsteen, say, could get, when he found himself on the covers of both *Time* and *Newsweek* simultaneously.

Agents like to tell you they won't bargain. To illustrate, Dick Fox repeated one of his typical telephone conversations: "Look, I don't want to negotiate with you. I need five thousand. Don't hit me with thirty-five hundred. I'm not going to hit you with seventy-five hundred. I want five. If you can do it, fine. If not, I'll go somewhere else." In most real-life business situations, however, where an artist is not surefire nor an agent cocksure, deals are made only after some attempts at bargaining. If a client needs the work and if the promoter claims the fee is too high, the wise agent is going to give a little with some face-saving excuse like, "Remember, only once."

When the agent himself does all the booking for an artist who is about to go out on the road, he or she will outline an itinerary, working out all the arrangements with specialists within the agency, with the artist's management and road manager, and with venue management. Agents have to be up on what's happening with the venues because what's good for one kind of artist might not be good for another. For example, with David Bowie's arrest, the Long Island venue where he had performed got a reputation for having local police who would hassle any act whose fans might be associated with dope. Word got around the booking world, and agents refrained from booking some rock acts there.

Most agencies collect all the money for the artists they represent. All performing artists are members of one or more of the various entertainment trade unions. These unions dictate commissions and give agencies a franchise, which is authorization for them to deal with union members and collect and dispense monies, among other functions.

Agency-artist agreements are relatively standard. Besides the commission rate, typical contracts stipulate who within the agency is to handle the career of the artist, and usually the artist gives the agency the exclusive rights to represent him or her nationally, and even internationally if the agency is set up for it with overseas offices. The length of the contract is often for three years.

From a struggling artist's point of view, landing a contract with a major agency can be tough if the artist isn't already filling the venues. Major agents simply don't sign talents who aren't already receiving significant bookings or who don't have a contract from a major record company or don't have prestigious management with the clout to put the whole career together. The dilemma begins to take shape for the newcomer when even prospective managers say that they never take on a new talent unless the talent already has an important booking agent. Record companies will tell an artist to come back and see them when he or she gets a good agent. For the new artist the big juggle is to bring all three together simultaneously in a package of his or her own.

Getting into the Agency Business

Lots of agents work into the spot from a background in other aspects of the music business. Some people ride along with an act they've been working with ever since the first $50-a-night roadhouse gigs. As the act gains in importance and record companies start listening to tapes, some combination of the ingredients of success may start to click, and the act gets meaningful attention in the trade. Being loyal to the person who stayed with it throughout the hard times, the act may go with an established agency only if the company also agrees to take that person on. And that's how a very few become agents.

Then there's the well-publicized William Morris Way. First you get a college degree, then you apply for a job in the William Morris mailroom. From the mailroom you get promoted as a secretary to one of the agents, so all along you'll have to have been going to night school to learn typing and some form of shorthand to prepare for your advancement. Then when you're a secretary, you eavesdrop over the phone to hear what your boss or anyone in the company is saying to clients, managers, promoters, and colleagues. You look at all the contracts, letters, and interoffice mail until you understand the mechanics of the job from firsthand observation. And when there's an opening, you move up to agent. David Geffen, still under thirty-five yet now president of Warner Brothers, was a William Morris secretary.

Not particularly impressed with the college degree, Dick Fox feels that the main requirements for a good agent are having the kind of personality that can deal well with both business and creative people, a knack for spotting talent, a good sense of what is commercial, and an instinct for coming trends even before the public picks up on them. Since he also feels that the William Morris ladder can be very slow these days, he says that agenting an act on your own is an immediate, firsthand way to learn what it is all about.

After a few years as a general booking agent you might want to change. And because of your central position in the total entertainment scene, you'll have a good idea of all aspects of the whole music business picture.

19

Promoter

"WE BOTH CAN'T be God on the same day." These words, spoken by the country's most celebrated promoter, Bill Graham, to Michael Lang of Woodstock Festival fame, point out the intensity and excitement of creation and power that are experienced by major concert promoters, and one could easily imagine a motion picture based on the life of a concert promoter in today's music scene. Besides Graham in California, there are Scher in New Jersey, Bauer in Seattle, Kapp in Chicago, Zuckerman in St. Louis, some of those who comprise the power structure in the concert world as reported in *Billboard*.

Concert promoting is far removed from a routine kind of business life. It's a do-or-die profession, calling on the promoter's abilities to fuse so many kinds of elements into a whole that it sometimes does seem like a miracle when the actual event comes off. Not only Woodstock but many other festivals have become instantly famous, such as the one at Altamont where The Stones played on as a Hell's Angel killed a man; Watkins Glen, known as the largest of all (over 500,000) for paid admissions; Newport for its innovations;

and perhaps the artistic apex of festivals, Monterey. Some smaller indoor concerts have achieved real status, such as the legendary Concert for Bangladesh at the New York Academy of Music, the famous Beatles concert at Shea Stadium, and the 1976 farewell concert of The Band in San Francisco.

Promoter-producers of concerts, festivals, and tours often receive more attention than the acts they sign up. They are interviewed, photographed, and quoted, and if they last they become famous and powerful. The power is real. People say that there is a kind of concert clique around the country that definitely controls who plays where, referred to as the "concert Mafia."

Power leads to big bucks or vice versa: they go hand in hand. The income from concerts can be enormous, and as we write this, concert records are being broken all the time. In the spring of 1976 several groups made short (less than ten appearances) concert tours that together grossed over a million dollars each. The promoter doesn't pocket the whole nut, of course. The act gets the giant share, the facility gets its share, and publicists and media are paid for promotion and advertising, but what's left belongs to the promoter and backers, if any. Amazingly, some of the most famous concerts and festivals have brought little or no profit to the promoter, because disaster in various forms eliminated the income. Being paid in cash evolved as standard procedure because the acts found out early on that promoters' checks were often rubberized. So they insisted on payment in bundles, and it became common for managers and acts to carry around tote bags full of money (Mike Lang recalls the use of his Frye boots). With the gate receipts getting bigger, look for bigger tote bags.

According to Los Angeles–based promoter David Forest, the receipts are more promising than ever, and he should know, since he produces concerts with acts of top drawing power like ZZ Top, Kiss, Bachman-Turner Overdrive, David Bowie, and Aerosmith. When it comes to that kind of concert promoting, where the profit is practically (and often actually) in the pocket before the concert takes place, we're talking about the powerhouse dozen, the guys who run the nation's top grossing concerts. Ron Delsener, one of the dozen, said in *Gig* magazine about his position as top rock promoter in the New York area, "I like it that way, and I wanna stay right here. I believe everyone should make his own living in his own little area. The business gets ugly if we start to get greedy." *Gig* reported that he produced about 180 rock shows a year. But this is the top of the iceberg, with profit almost guaranteed. The rest, the bulk of concert producing, is very iffy.

In fact, generally it's a high-risk business. Dick Fox at the Morris agency, who spends most of his life on phones talking to promoters, says, "Every five minutes a promoter drops from sight." What he means is that the promoter went bankrupt.

Speaking of the risks and nerve-wracking aspects of the trade, Bobby Tullipan said, "You can get wiped out . . . and also like I got ulcers at twenty, you know . . . from doing that stuff. When Cathy [his wife, singer Cathy Chamberlain] found me, I was completely burned out. I was living in the South and the whole thing . . . my office was in my living room, and all these guys were hanging out there, and I couldn't get away from them, only in a car driving to dates. I burnt myself out doing that."

The appeal to become a promoter is so great, though, that for some, the prospect of success is worth the risk. Some people find concert life so fantastically glamorous that there's nothing like it. In a *Time* magazine cover story on The Band, the author commented on all the beautiful young women that were backstage at every Band concert. For years we've been seeing feature stories about the big English groups and their elegant entourages. Many high-society people have become associated with pop music over the years, while writers like Truman Capote and Tom Wolfe have actually gone along on tour, hanging around backstage, picking up material for their articles.

According to a *Billboard* survey, out of the top six concert promoters in the country during the very late Sixties only Bill Graham is left in the field. All the rest have folded for one reason or another.

Close to home we know of a couple of examples of beginners' mistakes. The first is about a twenty-four-year-old woman who had been working regularly at a clerical job for about six years. All along the one thing she really wanted to do was promote a concert. So she borrowed and raised about $10,000 with which she rented a large old movie theater, booked Odetta and Deliverance, paid them all the necessary deposits, and began her advertising campaign. On concert night, about three hundred people showed up. Her career as a concert promoter ended when she figured out she was about $8,000 in debt. Her determination and commitment are admirable. But her error was a simple one. She had paid too much and booked the wrong act for the area. At the time Odetta could probably have made money for a promoter working a theater in a metropolitan area that had a soul-blues following. But in a fairly small, predominantly middle-class town of 40,000 the audience just wasn't there. Also, both Odetta and Deliverance had been appearing in local clubs, on occasion, so they were neither new nor different enough to fill the theater.

Another acquaintance, who for eight years had operated an art cinema in a college town, was always looking for a wedge into the business of presenting live performances. Practically on impulse he sold his business for a song, bought a theater in a larger city, and began the expensive process of remodeling. Enthusiastically, he booked acts for a whole season, acts that ran the gamut from the comedy team of Proctor and Goodman to ballet and chamber ensembles, including rock acts. Needless to say, he had to commit plenty of money to the tradesmen, to advertising, to the agencies for the acts, and to the banks that held the mortgage and notes. Midway through the first season he went totally bankrupt. He just disappeared. Even his friends couldn't find him, although people put big ads in the papers to try to communicate. His mistakes? He said afterward that the remodeling ate his bankroll up, but he felt his concept would work given another year's financing. From our point of view he made even more mistakes. Why do anything on so grand a scale without first testing the market? Why try to be culturally all things to all people, unless you're in a city of 500,000 and up? Why book a whole season? Or even part of one until an idea has been pre-tested? He was probably flirting with a fantasy. Things like that have been known to work out, but they work much bet-ter when the fantasy is backed up by reality and experience in the field of concert promoting.

Newcomers do succeed, though, and while we were in New York doing research, we kept hearing bits and pieces about some first-time producers' concert upstate that had been a sellout. By accident we ran into the promoters in an agency office, and they were excited. A lawyer and a real es-tate broker, they had put up the money on a hunch that Neil Sedaka could fill up their local theater, which he did, so they were in the agency office finding out about the concert-promoting business. Though it was unusual for an MOR act to have a sell-out concert in a rural community, these novice promoters took a fling on a hunch, weighing the size of the theater (number of seats) against the combined costs of the act and theater rental, and figured that it couldn't be too awful if they shared the loss should there be one.

Sid Bernstein, New York–based promoter and manager, says that hedging against loss by sharing or selling pieces of the action is standard procedure in the concert business. Throughout his career Sid has had an angel with a fat purse, a jeweler who has always been there for him, a financial sup-port when Sid needed it. Bobby Tullipan told us that he was asked to bid on a whole package tour for Stevie Wonder and said that if his bid was accepted, he'd be able to raise the money in ten minutes. To bankroll a Stevie Wonder tour of six weeks would take millions, according to Bobby. First, Stevie would have to be paid, then the venues, then anywhere from 10 to 15 percent of the expected gross would be spent on advertising and publicity, plus there would be staff salaries for half a dozen people.

Evidently there is a regular, if not very large, supply of people who are interested in putting up money if the chance for success looks good. Raising money is a rat race; you never know who's going to come up with a supporting bankroll. Mike Lang tried unsuccessfully for half a year to raise money for the Woodstock Festival, only to find it by following a hunch and answering an ad in *The Wall Street Journal*, placed there by two young men with practically unlimited resources. Their very funny (if nightmarish) experiences as festival promoters are in the book *Young Men With Unlimited Capital*. Other people getting started have put the touch on relatives, put themselves in debt, talked it up among friends, taken in the Mafia . . .

The main problem actually is not the money. "Having the money is the least of importance," says Sid Bernstein. "It's having access to the big acts." The acts can generally be hired only through booking agencies and personal managers. If an agency is doing a lot of business in a city with one particular promoter and along comes a newcomer and wants to book one of the agency's prime properties, it's not about to give the property away and jeopardize its working relationship with the first promoter. "Booking agents have the relationships," observes Tullipan. "That's all the publicists have, that's all certain producers have, and that's what this business basically is. I've seen so much all based on relationship and not experience."

People in the business say that the big promoters rarely lose. They don't lose because they have access to the big names which are sure to draw the people needed. It's the promoters of the so-called middle acts, who have hits but are not superstars, who take the chances. It's also said that it's not the booking agents or the promoters who dictate which per-

formers concertgoers will be allowed to hear. Record companies who "guarantee" a tour or a concert to introduce or promote a band do so by purchasing enough tickets (papering
the walls) to make good possible losses.

For learning concert promoting the best college is the booking agency. After his first concert, Miami Pop, Mike Lang,
whom the legendary beat poet and leader of the Hog Farm,
Wavy Gravy, calls in his book *Hog Farm* "a capitalist with a
heart," went to New York and, as he says, "hung around the
Morris Agency with my friend Hector Morales to see how it's
done."

Since a newcomer typically meets with a heavy runaround,
one way to compete with the biggies is to find an area either
musical or geographical that isn't under their dominance. San
Franciscans Linda Friedman and Joy Johnston, with their
backgrounds as music-world publicists, saw an opportunity
for a future in concert promotion by establishing a secondary
circuit of concerts. So they booked people like Bonnie Raitt,
Tom Waits, and Taj Mahal, names the public will pay to see,
if not in large numbers, into secondary cities like San Diego,
Sacramento, and Bakersfield. Even then they must have had
a hard time competing with Bill Graham (unless they made
an arrangement with him). *Billboard* reported in late 1975
that Graham had in the last year "presented" 250 concerts in
Northern California alone, plus another 50 outside, for which
"3 million people paid a gross of $20 million to see those
shows."

Besides competition with other promoters, the problems are
never-ending. Acts don't show up, or they cancel at the last
minute (in spite of contracts). There can be trouble with the
crowd. The PA systems fail. Storms ground flights. Nothing
seems to happen on time. At Saratoga Performing Arts Center, once the biggest problem at the pop concerts was how to
beat the sneaks, whom even a ten-foot-high fence didn't stop.
It seems that throughout the season word went out that it
was an easy fence to scale, and by the middle of the season at

concert time it looked as though an army was going over it. Except for the Sing Sing auditorium, very few venues are sneakproof. And likewise very few theater managers, from the promoters' point of view, can count very well, which is one reason why Bobby Tullipan says a promoter should always have a person there from his own staff with a head clicker.

One way of bringing the whole show off is to copromote the concert with the local power. Sometimes they control the advance-ticket outlets, without which there is no advance sale outside of the theater box office. Rumor has it that there is one guy in an eastern city who literally *runs* the putting up of posters; if he doesn't get paid, the posters get ripped down, period.

It's a kind of dog-eat-dog business, where power comes from realizing that profit is everything. It's tough, it can take everything you've got, and it often puts its professionals out on the limb. Moreover, promoters often come under biting criticism from the press. They make "too much" money, are always keeping the press at respectful distances from the acts, are usually very outspoken — all elements that bother journalists. After the smashingly successful Dylan tour, Graham held a press conference where reporters kept pecking away at him. "Hey, gang," he said, "you're right. I would have been a better waiter."

20

Publicist

JANE FRIEDMAN IS A VETERAN publicist at New York's Wartoke, a public relations firm that has handled such famous accounts over the years as the Woodstock Festival and The Chicago Seven (when they were young and idealistic, they say), Don McLean, Stevie Wonder, Rod Stewart, David Bowie, and Patti Smith (whom Jane also manages). She describes her function: "We try to make them famous. Let people think that a lot of things are happening with them and that they're very young, *au courant,* riding the tide, whatever the current thing is. We help form an image. We take on an artist and help the public discover the artist in a favorable way. We deal with newspapers, magazines, radio, television, and any kind of communication media . . . constantly looking for new media, new ways to get to the public, new ways to open up new markets for an artist or product or company."

Other than simply getting favorable media coverage for a client (getting the *name* in the public consciousness) the publicist is sometimes asked to either create an image, alter the image, or fit the client to an image. Managers have great faith in the power of images.

Stevie Wonder came to Wartoke sometime around 1971, just after leaving the management branch of Motown Records, wanting a new image and a big white audience. He was selling plenty of records, had a huge black following, worked the predominantly black Apollo circuit of theaters. The main thing Wartoke did to get him that white audience was to land him on a Rolling Stones tour, and since then, his white audience has grown to what it is today. Something similar happened to Miles Davis, who was brought to the pop-conscious public by playing at the Fillmore way back when it was happening. Association is an important element in changing images or in helping elevate an artist's status.

Rod Jacobson, who is Friedman's partner at Wartoke, told us he feels that managers really don't understand what image-making is simply because they don't understand publicity. "Some artists are born theatrical, and no matter what they do, they have showmanship, but," he pointed out, "most don't, and that's why they come to us."

Lynn Goldsmith, who helped form Grand Funk's image, told us that professional image-making depends on what the artists want. "Some of them want to be what they are. Some want to make money and be stars, and those are willing to let other people come in and direct them. It's not that they have a less personal thing to say, they're just more concerned with getting recognition and getting their songs played. Bruce Hall King doesn't want his music or his image or anything messed with. He wants it simple country. I can respect that. And so basically I'll do the ads like that, in that kind of truth. He sees himself in the line of The Band or Dylan."

Publicists make good, not great money. It's the kind of work for a live-wire type, an outgoing person who is not shaken by rejections. Publicists work under a great deal of pressure both because of the urgency of publicizing news when a story is hot and because clients tend to blame them when a publicity campaign fails to boost record or ticket sales, even though no publicist is foolish enough ever actually to guarantee results. Cathy Chamberlain, who is working hard to break out, gain a following, get attention and the backing of a record company, says, "You like to think that if you're good, there is going to be some kind of spontaneous happening — but it doesn't because so much is happening in New York, for instance, why should anyone come and see you? How many people call the press up or people in the business and say, 'This is a great act, you must come and see it'?"

A publicist will help in putting together the press kit (see the chapter on getting gigs for a description) necessary for establishing some kind of credibility for a new artist, helping them to get dates, an agent, or whatever. Cathy has tried to get that spontaneous press coverage to build up her press kit, but it's difficult. She feels she has to start making noise, so recently she hired a publicist, Myrna Post (who also handled Carole King), to get press attention. "You can't really call for your own press, it's bad form, so you have to hire these people, and that's three hundred bucks a week. You only hire them when you're working, so they can bring attention to you. It's got to be when you're ready. What frustrates me the most about the business is that there are certain things that bring success and that depend solely on dollars and cents, and that seems to me so wrong."

Some publicists may charge a modest few hundred dollars a month as retainer, while the big ones sometimes command several thousand or more. When a record company feels that one of the artists on its roster is really going to take off, it customarily picks up the tab, knowing that an all-out campaign can really establish that star or album.

Reviews are a kind of publicity. Conflicts of interest are sometimes behind favorable reviews (not just in music but in any art field).

Hype

Hype is one of the most used words in the music business, which is one clue to how widespread the practice of it is.

SUCCEEDING IN THE BIG WORLD OF MUSIC

When you want to sell something, you're usually going to have to underscore its good points, but hype is any statement from enthusiastic exaggeration to gross lying. It can be so extreme that at times it can stretch a reasonable person's credulity. Oddly enough, hype works. It's an integral part of showbiz promotion; no one has ever heard of a movie being billed as "the worst film ever."

David Bowie isn't a publicist — except maybe at heart — but he does accept the attitude of the business toward what can be seen as "imaginative exaggeration," which has become acceptable within the business's ethical-moral structure. In the April 1976 issue of *Circus* magazine he is quoted as saying: "I love it [rock and roll] because it's so full of liars . . . I've never been in anything in my life where I could tell as many fibs."

Publicists will tell you that hype can destroy an artist psychologically, however. They say that all performers love getting the hype treatment, and most begin to believe everything — good and bad — that's said about them. An act can also suffer after the campaign is over and they're on their own again. Suddenly there may be no more attention from the press or there may be criticism; then it's showdown time. A current example is the Bay City Rollers, whose members, it's reported, are suffering from low morale. They were hyped for almost a year as the "New Beatles," which is a hard image to live up to. Since in truth they never were on a par with the early Beatles, the press has come down pretty hard on them now.

The general public more or less understands that exaggerations are in the nature of the game. It accepts hype, feeds off false enthusiasm, and rarely considers the question of ethics. But outright distortion is something else again, and the public as well as the critics may react negatively. When the act is said to have certain attributes in order that the public will be sold on it and these turn out to be more than the act can deliver, there is sometimes a slowdown in the act's career that can destroy it forever. Some publicists, in fact, would rather not take on an account about which they have constantly to say things that aren't true. It's a matter of integrity and also of just plain self-preservation. Rod Jacobson says: "See, we've done a lot of hype things too, which we don't enjoy doing. I don't want to mention the names of the accounts — where we've been pressured to do hypes — which make something out of somebody or attribute qualities to someone or talents that they really don't have. You can get great press on it, but if the client can't live up to his own image or his own hype, he's dead."

Publicists pay dearly for their willingness to produce a steady stream of hype because eventually they themselves will lose credibility with the media. The more established publicists are smart enough to not risk losing the relationships with all those contacts they've built up over the years, and they've learned to temper their enthusiasm with honesty. Jane told us that once in a while she'll need some help getting a client's name around and she'll trade on that honesty by calling up a contact and saying, " 'Look, this account is lousy or this record's lousy, but we need it, we need a push with it, we need some help or we need a break, and here's the reason why' — but you can't ask for too many favors either."

Hype is another way of saying that you don't have to be involved with an artist on an aesthetic level in order to sell him or her; you don't even have to like the art. Jane told us: "We're expensive and we're good. Most of the time the acts we turn down, it's either somebody who wants the kind of hype we were talking about, acts that can't live up to it, or acts that can't pay our price. Sometimes we take an account and I'll never listen to an album, and I can do the best job not knowing what the group does, just by my own hype. When you start believing your own hype, you do a better job."

Believing one's own hype can backfire somewhat. Jane and Rod told us that when they were planning a post-concert press party for Bowie, they found that many people had to be eliminated from the guest list, and they thought they were going to require heavy security to keep all these people from crashing. Suddenly they realized that they had become paranoid as a result of believing their own hype, which suggested that people would literally *die* to get into a Bowie party!

Methods of Getting Publicity

Among the less humdrum publicity-making procedures is the press party. It is an event based on the premise that most people love a party, free booze and eats, and a chance to meet celebrities. Sometimes, when the budget allows, the party is blown up into a high-level affair, with a live band and dancing. When they become big deals replete with beautiful people, you usually get good press, because of the chance it affords to take photos. Ostensibly, the reasons for the party are typically the announcement of something special, like the release of a new album or the beginning of a tour. More specifically, press parties are concocted for the publicity. Most parties, however, in contrast to the more glamorous ones, are small-scale celebrations in a crowded hotel room, where hopes are high that contacts will be made and things will click, and coverage gained.

You don't have to know personally the people you are asking. Important people from magazines, radio, or TV who are total strangers will show up at these parties. The secret of success is the guest list. A few guaranteed celebrities will be a useful calling card, even if they're only local ones.

Since the campus population comprises one of the biggest markets of concert tickets and album sales, the person who writes a column on records and concerts for the campus paper is in the enviable position of being solicited by both the publicist and the record company with all kinds of music-biz freebees. Such press people can be counted on to love going backstage after a concert to toast the star and are frequently among the invited at press parties.

Taking people out to lunch or dinner is expensive and uses a lot of time. But in the business world it can get results, because people like personal attention and the chance to waste a couple of hours. In return they tend to do favors, which in a nutshell is the whole idea. One enterprising literary agent likes to do business using the typical protocol of business over lunch, but he gets three times as much done as most people because he has drinks with one client, lunch with another, and finally dessert and coffee with the third client.

"If you're really good at your job," Jane Friedman told us, "you don't need to spend an hour or two away from your office." She related the claim of a very famous press agent that some of his greatest accomplishments happened because he was by the phone at the right time. But show-biz favors sometimes are easier to get when they've been preceded by the token lunch or dinner.

There are some publicists whose specialty it is to know what the various TV producers want and how to arrange a tour of TV appearances that can, because of the number of stations involved, go on practically forever. The trade generally considers television the best exposure there is for a client and will pull all the strings possible to land appearances on the choice national network shows. Guests usually appear on talk shows without pay, for the value of the publicity alone. It is often just a chance for a star to build his or her image and to project it to the public. What they are selling is themselves. So they are paid anything from nothing to minimum union scale. When publicists feel their client has some current topic or gimmick, they try to bring their clients to the attention of the producers of the shows.

Radio is slightly different because what everyone wants most out of radio is the artist's performance via record play. Publicists arrange personal meetings between a recording artist and radio personnel, such as deejays and program directors, from which taped or live interviews may result.

The absolutely essential day-to-day tool of the publicity person is the standard release. In fact, it's so heavily used that it sometimes has minimum effect. Nevertheless it's the only way of reaching a lot of newspapers quickly; in fact, many editors, when called personally, will ask to have a covering release sent to them. If you're working a regional area, the release can be written to zero in on local concerns, and many of the smaller papers, always pressed for time, will print the release word for word, glad to be saved the effort of writing the story. Whether you're working on a large campaign or a small one, the writing of a release follows pretty much the same pattern, the who-what-where-when-and-why of journalism, all questions answered in the first paragraph, all written with few adjectives, seldom longer than half a page, 150 to 200 words. The best way to learn is to study the releases in the paper. Rod Jacobson's definition of the publicist's journalistic style is: "You leave out all your adjectives, and you slip in something while nobody's looking."

The best releases hinge on a twist if you can come up with one. When Wartoke was publizing Don McLean, their press releases featured news of his involvement with the sailing sloop *Clearwater,* which was dedicated to cleaning up the Hudson. This was at a time when every paper in the country was looking for positive stories that touched on the environment. Wartoke's real purpose, of course, was to spread the word about McLean the recording artist.

The main wire service in the United States is United Press International (UPI), with offices in all the major cities, where a staff of journalists write stories on the news as it breaks in their respective areas and then teletype them to their thousands of subscribers, the country's newspaper editors. These editors, in turn, make the final decision whether or not to use a story. To the publicist the wire service is a way of taking away the stigma of the press release and giving it more credibility as a story originating from the powerful wire service. Publicists try to arrange interviews between clients and wire-service staff reporters when there is something interesting happening with the client, in the hope that a feature story will develop.

Getting national magazine space is particularly tough. Securing coverage in magazines is highly competitive because of the limited and valuable space. Every publicist tries to figure out a magazine "angle" for his/her clients. Today, more and more magazines are featuring the music-world stars. Recording stars are even more popular than movie stars, and all the magazines are beginning to realize that the public is interested in what they are doing. Consequently, *People* magazine is beginning to feature a music figure or two regularly each week. *Rolling Stone* is increasing its gossip about the biggies, and Lisa Robinson, ever-present reporter in the fan magazines, is the Rona Barrett of the pop stars.

Geoffrey Stokes writes in *Star-Making Machinery* about record company procedure in getting magazine coverage for their artists. Since magazines typically pay very little for articles, the record companies make it very attractive by paying for plane fares for the writer (and perhaps the writer's friend, and perhaps the hotel bills, too) to attend an out-of-town concert halfway across the country. Some magazines say that some record companies get so heavy-handed that it's not worth the price of a ticket and won't accept it. Record companies also expect reviews when they place heavy ads. Stokes writes that some fan magazines used to publish articles written *by* record company personnel as though they were independent authors.

In-house publicity departments have to know what reviewers tend to like, what kind of performer, or what kind of music. They will send a record to a big staff writer or editor and let them get a crack at reviewing that record first. Publicists have to know the policies and tendencies of the magazines. Country and western is seldom covered in fashion magazines like *Vogue* and *Glamour*. *Seventeen* might feature a rock act, but *Rolling Stone* will seldom look kindly on MOR stars like Engelbert Humperdinck and Lemongello. The braintrust mags like *The New Yorker* and *Harper's* are less likely outlets for rock or pop stories, and when these magazines do print musical items, they tend to give negative coverage, although they may speak highly of a Broadway musical. Generally, the nation's daily newspapers have only recently given coverage to rock and roll on a more or less regular basis. *The Village Voice,* which used to feature literature, now features pop music. Advertising from record companies, music-equipment companies, and so on, is heavy in such papers and magazines. *Playboy, Gallery,* and other popular magazines like them publish stories that deal in depth with pop music and the pop artist because of the age and sex of their readers, who are still buying lots of records. For some more off-the-wall groups, the fan magazines are the places to push feature stories with a new angle. Alas, it's still typically the case that no major national magazine offers much hope of publicity for unknown talent.

Understanding the press is essential. It will help you manipulate them and accomplish what you want. Lynn Goldsmith, who works in many capacities in the music world, including selling photographs of artists to the magazines, handling publicity and promotion, and functioning as career manager for Grand Funk, started out in 1973 with "American Band." She told us: "I would find a producer to go with the act — to create some excitement. I knew because of my association with the press as a photographer that they were very much in favor of Todd Rundgren and trying to help him, and the idea of writing about him stimulated them, but their editors couldn't give them the space to write about Todd because he wasn't selling enough albums, and yet they didn't want to write about Grand Funk, but Grand Funk *was* selling a lot of albums. So to me it seemed a good press thing to put Todd and Grand Funk together, because it meant that the press would have a more positive attitude toward Grand Funk, they would have something to write about, it would make news in the music industry, and I honestly felt, outside of the press value, that Todd as an engineer-producer could do what Grand Funk needed to have done."

Women in Publicity

According to Meridee Mercer in *Gallery* magazine, only 2 percent of the women in the music industry have jobs above the secretary level. That 2 percent is mostly in publicity. Eddy O'Laughlin at Midland International said that he was shocked to meet women who were heads of some of the European record companies, not because he was prejudiced, he was just not used to it in the States. But publicity is one of the few branches of the music industry where no one is shocked or has to "adapt" to women. They are in the publicity departments of record companies and publishing companies and are the principals of many major publicity firms. Jane Friedman's casually friendly and open manner transmits her own individuality as a person rather than as the kind of ploy she describes as working for women in publicity. "Women can be soft and charming and bat their eyes, and that's why in all areas of the entertainment business there have been mostly woman publicists but very few women in any other capacity. They always think of publicity as 'soft,' as somebody who goes out to a lot of lunches and dinners; and a man would just as soon go out with a woman a hundred times more than with a man. You're supposed to be wily and use all your womanly ways. . . . Also, a woman is a good typist, a woman is a good mailer, a woman has a sexy voice over the phone if she knows how to develop it."

Lynn Goldsmith, on the other hand, is less ready to take you in, and to her the business is tough. She fought and worked hard to get where she is. She is unusually open, however, about revealing the simplicity of jobs in the music business. She told us that if everyone knew how easy it was, how "all you have to do is dial someone's phone," they wouldn't believe it. She has told a few people how to do jobs and how to get them and found that those people became competitors and underpriced her bids, so she stopped passing information.

As a kid, Lynn wanted to be a studio engineer at a time when a woman engineer was absolutely unheard of. When she told her uncle, who was then head of Decca Records, about her wish, "He thought it was very funny, that it was charming. He dissuaded me from having anything to do with the music business as a woman unless I was going to be a secretary." So Lynn went on majoring in television in college and went to NBC as a writer and production assistant.

It's interesting how she eventually landed a job in publicity: "A friend of mine was working for Elektra Records, and at that point the national director of publicity was leaving and there was going to be an opening. My friend made an appointment for me with the vice president. I had learned during my job-hunting in New York that I was either overqualified for everything or I didn't have working experience and they couldn't believe that I could do anything and that I wasn't for real. So I'd come to a point where I was disillusioned, so I figured I'd take a chance and I'd lie. I lied completely about all the things I've ever done. I dropped names, and I did everything I could to get the job. He hired me on the spot. Within a week he came in the office and he said, 'I checked up on some of those things you told me,' and I said, 'Yeah, but you hired me to be head of publicity and I fooled you, didn't I?' So I stayed there." There would be meetings every Monday, and the album releases would be gone over. Lynn would wear the highest-heeled boots she could find to these meetings. It helped not to have to look up at everybody.

Anyone who has read *On Power*, a book about how people get and maintain power, by Michael Korda, can appreciate Lynn's initiative. In fact, she took advantage of everything.

While in publicity she got into producing radio spots and promoting artists. She got into photography because publicity needed photos — and she was there. From that she went to work with Joshua White (of the former Joshua Light Show); Lynn provided video magnification at the Garden and other huge places and Joshua did the taping. She also photographed the acts when she had access to the stage and sold them to magazines. Later she teamed up with Andy Cavaliere as part of a management team. She did album covers (Alice Cooper and five Grand Funk covers).

Lynn's advice to women is: "Don't become a secretary. If you let everyone use you as a secretary, you will stay a secretary. You shouldn't take that position. The only way I ever saw a secretary move up is when they were so motivated that they found things to work on that they developed alone *outside* of the secretarial job."

You might want to read the novel *Number One with a Bullet* by Elaine Jesmer, which centers around the life of a female publicist. Both Bernard Purdie and James Tyrell, two people we have written about in this book and who have been on many floors of the music business for many years, felt that it was pretty accurate.

The basic fact for anyone to know who is seeking work in press publicity is that it's all a matter of coming up with a story that has appeal and then finding the right market for it. As Jane Friedman says: "There are all kinds of little tricks of the trade that you have to learn for when you're desperate, for when you can't get something by ordinary legitimate coverage. You have to figure out a way to get it in the media in a roundabout way."

Of the publicist's role, Rod Jacobson says, "What we're trying to do for somebody is to open up their career in a methodical and rhythmical way. You don't rush an artist or an artist's image, you help build it. It's like opening it up and making it bigger and bigger, until you get to where it's believable, where it's believed, where you can see the artist and believe the hype because they both work together. That's what you try and do."

21

Personal Manager

"MY FAVORITE COMPOSER in those days was Sibelius but in these changing times, he is now placed alongside my affection next to Paul McCartney and John Lennon." This quote from the late Brian Epstein's *Cellarful of Noise* expresses the intense conviction that most good managers have toward their artists' work.

The personal manager can work alone or with the help of a staff, depending on the commercial importance of his/her acts. The manager's function is to care for all aspects of the artist's career, negotiating record contracts, working with booking agents, arranging for publicity when a publicity agent isn't being retained, working with the producer in the selection of material and production of a record, overseeing the work of clothes and set designers; in short, the manager is both guiding light and kind of career valet. Often the management company cares for all the personal affairs of its artists and the artist's family — including sometimes his/her friends — making sure that the artist stays healthy and that personal finances are in good shape. In the case of a songwriter and/or performer the manager will work out advances

275

with the licensing agencies and sometimes handles the publishing company that administers the artist's songs. Short of performing himself, the conscientious manager is there all the way, all the time.

There's always a demand for good management, the kind that has the reputation for honesty and accepts the responsibilities of its position. Of course, there are a lot of the other kind, managers who are there only for the fees and commissions. It's interesting to note that in England the lawmakers have evidently felt that the personal manager's role should be so time-consuming, if done right, that they have limited the number of clients a manager can take on to just three. In the United States there are as yet no such restrictions, although before both the California and New York legislatures there are laws proposed that would restrict and control various aspects of personal management. Some would restrict the commissions managers receive and prohibit income from sources that might involve a potential conflict of interest.

When a manager represents a healthy stable of artists, it is possible that the various acts will have access to each other. For example, when Bobby Darin and Tim Hardin shared the same management, Darin made several hits out of Hardin's songs. Such negotiations in other instances could reveal a conflict of interest; the advantages include being able to get the artists' work on one another's albums and booking them on the same bill on a concert or tour. Good management will use its clout, clout earned from managing successful acts, to further the careers of all the "new" talent in its stable, talent that manager Dave Krebs calls his "baby bands." Says Krebs in *Gallery* magazine, in reference to the never-ending work load, "You could equate managing an act with fighting a war. . . . Every little thing is a battle. . . . The manager's job is to surround the act with what's best for it." It calls for a lot of energy, which possibly explains why many managers are under thirty-five, and plenty in their twenties.

For their services today's managers make from 10 to 50

percent of an artist's gross income (after management expenses are deducted) on a sliding scale. That is one reason that the big earning superstars are beginning to manage themselves by setting up management companies and paying the employees a salary. A good manager, however, can save money for an act and can make money for it by being there at contract signing time.

"The big money in the music business is in management." This statement is commonly made by people in the business. Big money is there if you're lucky, have the right kind of personality, and can make a few right decisions along the way. Manager Sid Bernstein (Bay City Rollers and Laura Nyro are both in his stable as this is written; he also had a seven-year association with the Young Rascals) says of his own career: "Success in this business? It's your status. I've found from my long experience — and I've been up there a couple of times and have been knocked down a couple of times and am now trying to fight my way up again for the third time — success in this business is measured by how big an act you have. It's not really your experience. It's measured by how fat your purse is right now. That's the barometer right across the land. Now, no one really *knows* how fat your purse is, only, unless you've got a guy that's up there with *hit records*. If you're managing someone who's got hit records, then you're a genius, you're wealthy, you've got clout. And for ninety-five percent of this business clout is the important yardstick. Not integrity, not talent, clout!"

Bobby Tullipan, co-managing his wife with herself, agrees that, "It's all run by accountants and lawyers with managers who aren't open that much to creativity." However, knowing that it's a frustrating business, knowing that artists are tough to deal with, knowing that in the world of music one's personal worth is typically measured by one's success, both Bobby and Sid love it, and continue to work in management capacities.

Albert Grossman, perhaps the most culturally significant

personal manager of the last ten years, contributed to the careers of a whole group of history-making artists, such as Janis Joplin, The Band, Dylan, Peter, Paul and Mary, and Todd Rundgren, to name a few. In Pennybaker's documentary movie, which depicted Dylan's mid-Sixties tour in England, the viewer sensed that Albert was there for a single purpose: to protect above every other concern the interests of his client. Anyone who has felt strongly protective toward another person will appreciate the dexterity and timing of Albert's ability in the final scene when they are driving away from the concert at Albert Hall. Dylan is pained, perplexed, and unsettled, thinking about what it was that seemed so special about the concert. Albert turns him onto the challenging present: he tells him the newspapers called him an anarchist! Dylan's attention switches, his face brightens. Albert helps Dylan fulfill the title of the film: *Don't Look Back.*

Mike Lang, who is both a manager and a production company president, told us that he had been turning down plenty of management opportunities with name acts, because he didn't want to do the baby-sitting number. Lang told us that he wasn't cut out to completely annihilate his ego. In the trade, managers are often called baby-sitters. Sid Bernstein says that he has found that taking care of all the little personal problems for an act takes more time than handling the act's business affairs. When a manager has to do this for a performer, he or she has to subject his or her own ego to a near-total eclipse. It can be perhaps the most wearing aspect of management. It leads to another professional hazard, one for both managers and artists, that management will get overinvolved in the total life of its acts. From the manager's angle, there's the danger in living out all his or her personal fantasies and dreams through the artist. And the artist feels this as the suffocating sensation of being overprotected.

Loretta Lynn, who is managed by her husband, complained in a *Village Voice* interview that her management was smothering her. "I've got sixty or seventy people working for me and they have all got their orders not to say anything to me about anything. My husband feels that I would be better off, that I would worry too much . . . I worry because I don't know." This goes for reggae singer Martha Velez too. She has spent her entire career managing herself, functioning in almost every capacity for her act, including roadie. Now that Martha is becoming more recognized, everyone around her wants her to concentrate only on her music. She sees the business aspects slipping away from her control. But she seems to have a well-rounded capacity for accepting responsibilities; she puts it succinctly: "I don't like surprises. I like to know what's happening before it happens." As a songwriter, she feels that it's not a good idea for artists to become removed from the nitty-gritty details of life. "How could I have written 'Mr. Money Man' if I didn't know what it was like having someone else's hand in my pocket?" Keeping exposed to life's root happenings is good for her music because, she says, "If you don't, your songs are not going to relate to the public for long."

In reading and hearing the tales about Colonel Tom Parker, Elvis's longtime, flamboyant manager, it sometimes seems that Parker's essentially carnival-oriented approach, for all the success it's had in sensationalizing his client's career, may also have kept Presley from a more natural growth and expansion, with which his wealth and talent might have provided him. (But then, criticizing managers seems to be one of the favorite sports of writers and editors in the trade.) There are all kinds of managers, from the character, Colonel Parker, to Albert Grossman, perhaps the dean of cool, entering management from a variety of backgrounds.

Cathy Chamberlain, when asked what it was like working so closely with her husband (a common occurrence), said, "It's real hard . . . you can never leave work at the office. *You can never shut the door on any aspect of your life for a breather, you know.*" It seems that a lot of writers get offers to manage acts, particularly publicity writers. Lawyers and ac-

countants become managers of artists they originally represented. And promoters, so closely in contact with artists, inevitably find management opportunities surfacing.

It's good to remember that many of the people new to big-
time management come into it through the management of
an unknown act that suddenly makes it. They then increase
the size of their stable the same way established managers do.
The most common technique is to "pirate" talent, that is, to
steal it away from other management. Sometimes the method
of wooing talent is surprisingly simple, often just the casual,
positive expression about an artist's career. Music-business
lawyers can be another source of information on talent avail-
ability, since they know the expiration dates on contracts
they've negotiated. Some managers go to other countries looking to be the American representative for foreign acts. One of
the messages in Robert Altman's film *Nashville* is that talent
is most available in a music center, which is where most
managers concentrate their talent-searching activities. But
the history of talent discovery in pop music reveals that talent
is not restricted to a geographic limitation. Manager Steve
Paul went to Texas after he heard that some incredible blues
was coming out of the area. "Steve called every day," says
Johnny Winter in *Raves* magazine. "It was obnoxious, but he
made sure that everybody who mattered was there when I
played New York for the first time, and I got some nice offers." Right now people in the business are making trips to
Louisiana on tips that unsigned talent can be found in the
bayou country.

Getting into the management profession on a beginning
level is a lot easier than one would suppose. Every act in the
country needs management, and many acts are either dissatisfied with their present management or haven't got any at
all. Joe Pellegrino at CAM-USA, Inc., involved in both publishing and management there, feels that it's all very simple:
"You go to an act you like and tell them that you respect their
talent and you would like to help further their career." Dick

Fox at the Morris Agency says, "Through any number of caprices a person finds himself with a hit act, not through management design but through luck, and one hit attracts another hit, and that's the way it often goes. Suddenly he's got a stable."

It can happen so fast and with such intensity that people will inevitably suspect the ethical fiber of the manager who's making a lot of money. Alan Abrahams, a general all-around music-business head, says, "You always hear the stories about the artist getting ripped off by the manager and the producer and the publisher . . . but there's just as many stories of the talent ripping off the producer, publisher, manager."

In the middle Seventies, Sid Bernstein was working with a new singer, handling all kinds of professional and personal affairs for her. Sid and his client were close enough that they went to a Weight Watchers meeting together. The idea was that this singer was going to come into Sid's stable; and she was a good property to have, her album selling well, ticket sales good, and there was a lot of attention from the press. Sid thought all was going well and they had apparently reached, according to what Sid told us, a basic artist-management agreement. Suddenly, the negotiations terminated. As Sid says, "I had been serving her best interest for over ten months, without a contract, which was a serious error on my part and yet in good faith." In these cases, what often happens, in Alan Abrahams' words, is, " 'Oh, by the way, you're out. I've just made this deal with Screen Gems for a million dollars.' That happens all the time!"

Managers often maintain a stable of acts as a hedge against going bankrupt from the unforeseen loss of one's main income-producing act. Many acts don't last all that long (three to six years); groups break up, or the star burns out.

Some artists have reputations for being wild or spoiled or are so devious that one wonders why a manager puts up with them. But as Jerry Schoenbaum told us, you have to understand that "this is a get-rich-quick business," and that "lightning strikes in very few places." So even if you know that someone is emotionally disturbed or impressionable or self-defeating, and "likely to do anything at any given time," you take the risk. "Business people know perfectly well that an artist may prove extremely difficult," Jerry says, "but they look at the volume that that artist can contribute, and they take their chances."

But the person who is really super-paranoid about being ripped off is almost always the creative person, and every star seems to be suing his or her ex-manager. Recently, an acquaintance who believed in the commercial comeback of songwriter Bobby Charles was trying to get him a contract. Charles wasn't too enthused, claiming that managers rip off millions of dollars from their talent, apparently reflecting his experience. Our friend, street-wise, felt anyone should feel lucky if a manager could put him into the position where his earning capacity was in that category!

Being ripped off, both real and imaginary, is an acknowledged part of the game. The thing that can eliminate some of the doubts and temptations is a good management-artist contract. Some contracts are so biased in favor of management that they are referred to as contract slavery, in that the artist is owned by the management for unreal lengths of time and on bad terms. Many of these contracts have proved indefensible in court, which is one reason why in the music business contracts are broken regularly and why people usually settle out of court.

There are two areas that can be abused. Managers can exaggerate the expenses that come off the top of the artist's gross income. It's possible to receive more money for expenses than the artist and manager receive as a percentage. Expenses can mean just about everything — office overhead, lunches, phone bills, plane fares, etc., etc., etc. The other area that can be abused is in having power of attorney. Ostensibly, managers need this power to sign for acts while they are away on tour, and so forth. As a manager you want to manage someone, not have them manage you. Therefore, you want to guarantee yourself that you can make the decisions. It seems natural. Brian Epstein had power of attorney for The Beatles, individually and as a group. An artist puts all his or her trust in the manager when signing over general power of attorney. This authorizes the manager actually to sign any and all documents as though he or she *were* that artist, without seeking previous approval. The manager, then, can take care of the artist's entire life, personal and business affairs, all money and bank accounts. The manager signs if the artist wants to buy a house. Managers can sign everything for someone except a marriage certificate.

It does seem ironic to think that rock stars, at the peak of their functioning ability, sign over general power of attorney, just like old people do when they can't, or don't want to, handle their affairs and business responsibilities. For old people, when they find they can't drive their cars any longer or have to sign over power of attorney (usually to their children or their lawyers), feel it is the end of life for them! Power of attorney is a fiduciary responsibility, one of the heaviest of legal acts. It means living up to the trust someone has invested in you, and the courts are very severe if they find a misuse of this power. Michael Sukin advises managers to leave it out of the contracts they want him to draw up. If they insist, he tells them never to use it. If the artist believes the manager is misusing this trust, he can "have him hung from the rafters!" says Sukin.

It's not always easy to leave a management company when the management feels it has invested time and money to build up an act. The people at Wartoke reflect on this subject: "XYZ Record Company? You don't leave a company like that and expect to get away scot-free. They don't like that. They don't like you walking away."

Enlightened management, which is not as rare as some would have you believe, will express an interest in their artists' well-being. Out on the West Coast manager David Robinson claims that he never touches his acts' money; he wants to remove himself from his artists' cash by encouraging them to have professional business managers and tax accountants to handle the actual cash flow (for which they usually receive a fee of 2 to 5 percent of the money they handle). Sometimes, however, even in this case the manager controls the money through the business manager.

Rod Jacobson at Wartoke feels that most successful managers have a good grip on everything, but the best have a special flair for showmanship, instinctively knowing what will catch the public's imagination gearing acts toward keeping the image, the name, in front of the public. Sid Bernstein, who came into management in his college days as a pop-concert promoter, notably proud of his fabulous first Beatles' sellout in Shea Stadium, talks about the career planning for a new act in his stable, a male duo: "I'm going to use every means that I can. Right now I'm embarking on a game plan to break this group. I call them the goyish Simon and Garfunkel, because they are two good-looking Gentile boys who play a lot in the Simon and Garfunkel style. The difference here is not so much the ethnic thing, but that both boys play a lot of instruments, and both boys are very good-looking and have tremendous sex appeal. That's really important now . . . and I think the marketplace is ready for this act. The audience will be from seventeen to forty-five, that's how wide they are."

In Sid's mind the talent is there, pretty much taken for granted; it's those show-biz extras that count: looks, versatility, and sex appeal. Sid's name does open doors and for good reasons — many of his acts have become standard names. "I am aware of my good reputation," he says. "I've fought for it. I continue to protect it and keep it intact." But that's one reason that Sid doesn't want to take on someone who doesn't already have a built-in desirability. He doesn't want to go through the sadness of rejections, or to have his name associated with them. "I'm not an opportunist, I do things only that I think are proper in my judgment," he says, "but I'm appalled at how little of that exists. I don't say it's nonexistent. But I'm appalled at the amount of bullshit that gets you further." Sometimes it does seem that bullshit is indeed the great fertilizer of the entertainment world, but what is bullshit today often becomes tomorrow's truth, sometimes a happy one, sometimes sad.

Referring to Ian Mitchell, a recent replacement in the Bay City Rollers, Tom Paton, their full-time manager, said in a *Rolling Stone* interview, "I don't know if by making him a Roller, I've given him a blessing or a curse." Most of the article reflected Paton's worries about the problems of success. He said of the Rollers, "I think they're all very unhappy. They're happy being Rollers, but I think they're disillusioned with the constant attack on them, that people say they're rubbish. It can't help but affect you. It's not like you can sit back."

There is the whole moral question of star-making, really one of the main things management is hired to do. They're expected to forge full speed. Yet without really knowing whether or not the performer can handle it all, and without holding back and properly pacing the artist, avoiding breakdowns, they are responsible for a lot of the problems as well as for the successes.

Unfortunately, breakdowns do occur when the artist is at the end of his or her durability. A *People* magazine article about Karen and Richard Carpenter pointed out they weren't immune to the effects of being on the road: "Karen dropped worrisomely to a gaunt 90 pounds. Quickly, they canceled a tour to Europe and Japan and a command performance for Queen Elizabeth — their first blown gigs in six years. Karen was suffering from 'physical and nervous exhaustion,' and it took two months of bed rest at home to recuperate." Maria Muldaur likes to tour only three weeks when a record comes out. She has done tours of five to six weeks and found that she is totally depleted. Possibly exaggerating, she told us that

285

she doesn't know any musicians who do extensive tours and keep up the rigors unless they take drugs.

One of the reasons why the music branch of show business is particularly treacherous for those who aspire to stardom is that its changes are as a rule abrupt and extreme. One three-minute song can make a vocalist a star for a month, only to become a distant memory the next month.

Bernstein says, "The forty-five, the LP, is probably the most powerful instrument the world has ever known, in entertainment, for making an artist, regardless of his talent. If he has a hit record, he makes a lot of money. The second hit record, he makes even more money. If he has three, he becomes a superstar no matter what the quality of his talent. The record has eliminated what used to be heavy thinking, planning and programming and staging and lighting and directing, and building. It cuts that short. It used to take ten years to make a star, via nightclubs, big hotels, RKO chain, Loew's chain. Now there are fewer clubs in America . . . coffeehouses are still helping spawn new talent, but artists still never get beyond one-fifty-a-night starters unless they have a hit record."

Smokey Robinson tells in a *Crawdaddy* interview that Motown Records (which at one time had its own management branch) used to maintain a school for its performers called Artist's Development, where artists had to take lessons before they recorded for the first time or went out on a date and where they learned stage presence, choreography, hygiene, and so on. The old Hollywood star system was a way of building a personality into an image the public wanted. Dick Fox notes, "Some claim that Fabian and that whole class of singers in the Fifties who were pretty slick and gooey were manufactured by their management and record companies, that they had relatively little natural talents."

But all this doesn't mean that there isn't some kind of career planning going on today. To a lesser extent the star system of molding manners, elocution, and deportment is still with us, and management, when it's good, tries to do whatever it can to make its acts successful. There are career managers like Lynn Goldsmith, emphasizing the career guidance aspect in a management team. She'll take notes at reheasals, maybe change the placement of the musicians, make videotapes of the act to show them when and where they can improve. Some stars take on this type of responsibility themselves, while their managers just make the deals. Lynn says that Albert Grossman and Todd Rundgren are perfect examples: "Todd runs his own show. Look at his album covers. Todd takes care of all that stuff for himself. He does his advertising lines, he does all of it."

Many managers take the responsibility for the act's total career strategy. Sid first booked the Rollers into small halls for test runs. When a small town, Bay City, called him asking for the Rollers, Sid immediately reflected on the exploitive nature of the Bay City Rollers performing in Bay City, and agreed. For Fred Neil's first concert after a five-year absence Mike Lang booked him into Montreux, Switzerland, as an out-of-country tryout.

Managers who want to help build a talent and direct it, as Wartoke's Jane Friedman did for Patti Smith, have got to have patience. It took five years for Wartoke to see Patti to the point of being a headline act. Patti would read her poetry in front of rock audiences before the rock act came on. "She never sang until about two years ago," Jane told us. "She started doing real good, and we developed it little by little after that. That's why it took five years. We never took any money. She was kind of self-supporting to a point . . . but we really worked for years and didn't make a cent." It might have been more difficult for Wartoke to develop an act that needed a lot of money for equipment and band members; fortunately, Patti didn't need this for quite a while. However, management that doesn't just come in at the peak of stars' careers has a reason to be proud of the success their acts, such as Patti's, finally attain. As Brian Epstein said in a nutshell, "It isn't the money that worries me, it's the failure." For any career is really measured by accomplishment, and managers in talking about the high points of their careers refer to the events and associations they are most proud of.

22

Touring—Roadies and Road Manager

Roadies

Making fortunes in music by going on the road is a fairly recent phenomenon. Although big bands like Dorsey's went on the road, the style, effectiveness, size of audience, and number of acts on tour changed with the Sixties, when many of the problems of intensive touring were worked out. The rock groups proved tours to be a profitable and economical way for a performer or a group to get a lot of exposure quickly and so promote record sales.

Today, touring has become increasingly more complex. The sound and light equipment is more complicated, there is more of it, stage sets are more elaborate, and everything is much more specialized. So, today, roadies, the guys on tour who handle the equipment and staging, like to be thought of as technicians, and many like to refer to themselves as tecs, rather than roadies.

Two very verbal roadies, Rob Davis and Tom Edmonds, both working for Todd Rundgren, felt that "roadie" was an unfair term, connoting a tough, "ass-kicking guy, one who is going to kick a guy's head in if he says the wrong word." Yet there was a certain truth in this concept. Rob says that at one time he himself used to be in that bag — like being a Road Angel, rather than a Hell's Angel. "I was like the mean man, no shit, no shit from anybody. One foot on the stage and that was it!"

Tom, whose first job was working for the Full-Tilt Boogie band because his sister was going with the drummer, likes to think of roadies as being like cowboys without horses. He picked up that image from a stranger who could tell he was a roadie just by looking at him and told him why. He digs it, because going on the road has a quality of opening up new territory. The adventures of the Wild West compare with the adventures of being on the road.

A roadie's duties vary, depending on the kind of gig the artist has. If the act he's working for plays mostly bars, he may do everything including booking the act. Most roadies have worked on club gigs, and say they put everyone in a much more vulnerable situation. Even though most of the stories of violence that reach print have to do with big acts in big crowds, playing bars is really the toughest level of the roadie's life. You get punched by drunks, treated badly by management, and after a night of this you might get ten bucks. But that can be the beginning for a professional roadie. If there is any breakdown in a big show there is always a backup for every instrument, or at least one that could substitute. But if you're doing club gigs, you have to know how to jury rig and make do. You really learn how to be inventive; you're never sure what can happen, because so much depends on the club, rather than on your own setup. Sometimes, too, there are battles over whether the bar picks up the beer tab for the band and the roadie. Usually the club will give everyone some free drinks. This is a long way from what happens on the big tours today, where it's written into the contract that the management provides all kinds of things, dinners, and other extras.

The roadie must not only cope with technical problems and troubleshoot, he must also be able to handle people and the tense and pressured situations they can create. Early in his experience Tom noticed that he was always uptight about things that were happening on tour. He decided that if he'd cool down and just handle the job as a job, he'd be much happier. The kind of personality who doesn't make it as a roadie is the complainer. You always have to have that smile on your face, no matter how many times someone asks you to do something, even if they're being totally unrealistic. You have to be able to suppress your own ideas and feelings all the time, whether you like it or not. This is especially true if you work for several groups, which may each work in different ways and with different styles. You have to remember that you are working for those people and are there to serve them no matter how crazy they get. Everyone has his own little idiosyncrasies, but the roadie has to have the least of all. Roadies must be constantly showing approval. They must not intrude their own personal attitudes; being suppressed is part of the job. If people can't do that, as one roadie told us, "they don't hold their jobs."

The performer-artist has the same needs as most of us. There is one difference: their needs can be abnormally indulged. Roadies that are fairly close to the stars find out they have to be both mother and father to the star, and as one roadie told us, "sometimes a sister, too." Managers play the "older brother" role, but the roadie never gets away with it — an older brother is too much of an equal. There is more distance in the mother-father relationship. There your job is to worry constantly about his or her food, clothes, comfort, if she or he is happy, disappointed, sick, or going too far out. And then too, the pride mothers and fathers naturally have in anything their offspring do is something the roadie has to simulate and deliver to the star he's working for. The performer has got to feel it. That's why some people say there are two kinds of roadies: the groupie and the technical type. One roadie we know is paid to be the constant companion to a star in his dormant period. He calls it the worst "baby-sitting job" he's ever had!

Some roadies and road managers are treated like servants, while others are respected enough to become managers, such as Grand Funk's Andy Cavaliere and Jefferson Starship's Bill Thompson. Often, however, in monster groups the relationship between the roadie and the performer-artist is a cold one. Rock and roll groups are harder to work for than, say, Tony Orlando. Most roadies are simply employees with a function, and it stops there. At the end of the tour it can be, "Thanks a lot, good-bye, get lost" — until the next tour.

Roadies may never really hang out with band members, because performers in their groups meet so many people all the time that it doesn't make any sense for them to get involved; but still the feeling of respect and goodwill will come across. Other performers just "don't give a shit," don't care or know if you're "bustin' your ass" to do the job. When the relationship is a cold one, the roadie might just as well accept conditions as they are. A sound roadie, who, because of the nature of his duties, is most removed from the performer, can be the most estranged person on the gig.

Usually, roadies work with partners but some bands, rather than hire extra help when they need it, work the roadies singly and hard. The roadie should be as unobtrusive as possible. He should also be self-censored, noncritical, yet a cautious but honest critic when that seems appropriate. And he should protect the performer he works for, whether from wasting himself or by warding off all kinds of undesirable situations. The degree of protection depends on the nature of the relationship with the performer, of course.

There is much more division of responsibility working for a big act. Everyone is a specialist in what he does. It's not that easy to just jump over and do lights after doing sound. Some groups have light units that are totally separate from sound system, and roadies who work them are separate from everyone else. Besides the specialists who work lights and sound, there may be all kinds of other special roadies. Peter Rudge, manager of The Rolling Stones, The Who, and so on, says, "Keith Richard even has his own personal guitar tuner — well, he plays thirteen guitars during the set." Tom Edmonds, who is in charge of band gear for Utopia, has to be there with lots of strings and extra guitars because, he says, "Todd is a stringbuster." Some people go through several guitars in a night. Stephin Stills takes seventeen guitars to a concert. Then there are the electrical-device roadies in charge of all the uncommon equipment, such as the sparks you see emanating from a performer's body, or smoke, or whatever.

Lynyrd Skynyrd travels with six people on sound, lights, and trucks, and three personal road managers. The Rolling Stones' road gang consists of about fifty people. It takes twenty-six people to handle sound and light equipment for Emerson, Lake and Palmer. Sound towers are erected on both sides of the ELP stage. There are specialists who handle the sound mix and also supervise the electrical technicians from the company hired by ELP to produce the sound system for their shows. There are three roadies in charge of Keith Emerson's keyboards alone!

Utopia's crew start setting up the stage around twelve noon and are there until the show ends at eleven, when they load it all on the semi, finishing about one in the morning. When they arrive at the next venue, the boxes just come right out of the truck by number, they're unpacked, and set up the stage. Tom's equipment is usually set up on stage by about 3:00 P.M., waiting for power, which gets to him about 3:30. Then he has an hour to himself. About 4:30 the band comes in to do a sound check, and he has to be there through the whole thing because it's "Tom, I need this, and Tom, I need that."

There has to be a system to all the packing and unpacking and there is. Everything is numbered and goes in sequence in a certain place into the semi. Tom has his pack the way he wants it, and he's written it all down. It goes in and out like that every time the same way. Last year they used a forty-two foot semi, which was completely loaded all the way to the back doors with thousands of dollars' worth of equipment. This year there are more trucks and more equipment. (Emerson, Lake and Palmer use three forty-foot trailers, with heavy-duty forklift trucks used to bring out the equipment and put it down on the back of the stage.)

Everything is on casters, in special Anvil cases. When you're loading and you have eight guys who know what they're doing, they can bring the cases out faster than you can pack them. The heaviest box in Rundgren's equipment weighs 800 pounds. Sometimes there are union crews who know what they're doing; but you'll ask someone to move a box and he'll say, "I can't move this box. I'm this kind of stage-hand," so you have to get someone else. In big towns like Los Angeles or Chicago or New York, the stage crew is specialized, and sometimes because of union laws they are the only ones allowed to do the patching (wiring into the equipment), so the roadie has to stand there and tell them what to plug. There can be thousands of complex wires, and even though the roadie knows he can do it five times faster, he's not allowed.

This crew works a straight twelve hours, more or less. When the show is over at eleven, the house lights come up, and sometimes classical music is played through the PA in an attempt to cool people out. All the stuff is usually down, out, and packed by 12:30 to 1:00 A.M. That's only one hour and forty-five minutes to pack and load. Then there is always the possibility of having to drive five hundred miles right after the gig. The band usually flies to the next date, while the roadies travel straight through the night with the equipment.

Most roadies are incredibly alert to their environment. Once in the Sixties we were talking to John, a teenage roadie for The Who, on the street. He spotted a car with old license plates half a block away. He went up to the car's owner and told him what he should do and what kind of a fine to expect in New York state if he didn't get new plates. This amazing ability for alert observation and practical knowledge is one of the key things to admire in a roadie, and all seem to have it to a certain degree. It can be a real relief to be around a roadie, especially if you've been with a lot of introspective people for too long. Roadies' ingenuity and capability for quick action are also tremendously admirable qualities.

Things are all worked out ahead of time today, especially for the big acts. "You've got to be totally self-sufficient," says Peter Rudge. "Don't ever rely on anybody else." But there are always things happening that need quick reactions and improvisations. One time a gust of wind toppled an eight-foot bank of synthesizers during an Emerson, Lake and Palmer performance, then the rain started. The synthesizers were soaked, but the three roadies rushed them to a nearby warehouse and blew the circuit boards dry with air hoses. *Rolling Stone* reported a concert in Providence, Rhode Island, during which Leslie West felt something hit the side of his face, and immediately his hair started smoking and flaming. Backstage one of the roadies dashed out with a towel and smothered the flames. Someone in the audience had thrown a smoke bomb at him. Tom told us about an event that required a double take when Rundgren's amp started smoking one night on stage. Tom ran to get the fail-safe amp. But he had to stop in his tracks when he saw that Todd was theatrically exploiting the smoking amp. "You just have to watch every move. And you have to be able to see things break before they do break."

One of the bummers of being on the road is the ever-present possibility of theft. It can happen at any time, and in as many ways as you can imagine. Right after the show, the crew usually grabs the guitars. They are the number-*one* item most likely to be stolen. There's the story of a fan who ran up on the stage, and before anyone could stop him, he handed an amp out the window. Stories about theft are told so often that some of the exploits have become almost legendary. It's as if the roadies were the Texas Rangers of rock and roll, and were constantly matching wits with the badmen of the concert halls. When a band is playing two or more nights in the same hall, the chance of theft increases with each night. It's with exposure that theft can be plotted, in the same way that the big Brink's heists are figured out by watching the routine of security. It's possibly very often an inside job, by someone on the hall's staff — and often the evidence shows that someone has broken out of the hall, not into it.

During the 1972 Stones' tour in Canada one of their trucks was stolen, and blown up. In some towns there are mean elements with big resentments against rock bands, although certainly not as explosive today as in the days of *Easy Rider*.

Rolling Stone, in 1976, reported Ike and Tina Turner's trouble on the road in Asia. When they arrived in Djakarta, Indonesia, they found that the sound system waiting for them consisted of two guitar amps. They refused to perform, feeling that a good system was crucial to the act, until a policeman showed up with a gun, and Ike decided to go on. Later, when they were ready to make a quick getaway to Hong Kong, the police wheeled off $22,000 worth of their equipment before waving their plane off. The agent, Dennis Rubenstein, said, "I guess we will have to sue the government if we want to get it back."

One real occupational hazard in being a roadie is that the constant barrage of high decibels is actually physically dangerous to hearing. There is almost always a roadie positioned right up close to the amp. Our eye, ear, nose, and throat specialist recommends the use of cotton lined with Vaseline packed loosely in the ear; others feel it doesn't help. (No one should put objects like earplugs in his ears.) When ears ring, you know you've been overexposed. A hearing test should be taken periodically to determine the extent of the damage.

Most roadies are totally committed to guarding the principal performer, and this too can be a hazard. They can never take their eyes off the person they're working for, particularly at the bigger concerts, where fans often try to rip the star's clothes off. Today is not quite as extreme as the era of Beatle-mania, when fans were so hysterical that they once ripped the door off The Beatles' car. Bill Corbett, The Beatles' driver, de-veloped the ability to drive fast enough to keep fans away and off the car and yet get safely, without fan fatality, to and from the destination. Still, anyone on stage can tell you how it feels to sense the threat of hysteria, that emotion bordering on vio-lence, that is just under the surface with some audiences.

Two different attitudes prevail: one is that the roadie is there to take the punishment meant for the performer; the other is that the roadie is there to administer the punishment before it's necessary to take it, to reverse the situation. One roadie, simply doing his job, who interfered between Bill Gra-ham and a cop, trying to stop them from arguing, ended up in jail himself.

The audience knows that the roadie is there to protect, always alert not only to the performer but to the audience it-self. Rob, who has had a long history as a roadie, first with the Cat Mothers, said, "We are all bouncers, and it's all how you take care of a problem. You feel security would just automati-cally kill someone, beat them to a pulp or something, but we like to grab someone first and talk to them like, 'Say, man, lis-ten, I work for Todd, I'm with you, cool out.' "

The presence of uniformed police can contribute to setting up bad vibes at a concert. Michael Lang attributes the sanity at his Woodstock Festival to the fact that although the secu-rity he used were regular policemen, they were carefully screened by well-considered tests, with questions such as: "What would you do if someone blew smoke in your face?" And they worked on that occasion *out* of uniform.

Another constant occupational hazard is electrical shock. Tom always wears rubber-soled shoes when he works. You can get an electrical shock from your own equipment; this happened to Keith Richard from The Stones and also to Uriah Heep's Gary Thain. One English lead guitar player was actually electrocuted on stage.

The most dangerous period is when the power gets divided during the setup. The sound crew and the light crew both start hooking into the main power sources, and that's when serious problems can develop. You have to know how to keep all your leads separate and not to ground a hot lead. If you lose a ground somewhere, you're in trouble.

It's a hard job, and one that seems to demand exuberance, muscle, alertness, and youth. When we asked Rob and Tom what age they were referring to when they spoke of "old" roadies, they said twenty-nine or thirty. When The Blues Magoos were making their hit records and traveling in the late Sixties, their road manager, Al Vita, went on to accounting school in Detroit after the band broke up. But he got so bored with it that he decided to get back into going out on the road with a band. By this time, however, Al was around twenty-seven, and found that he was really too old to relate to the younger roadies, so he went back and got his degree in accounting!

Tom and Rob love working so much they're really happy to be on the road all the time. After a six- or eight-week tour, they can't wait to be home; yet once they *are* home, they find themselves going "out of their minds" after about a week. They get restless and can't find anything to occupy themselves.

A performer has his or her own trip and load. Most performers generally don't like the road; most roadies do. Perhaps for the roadies it is a commitment to a life-style, while for the performers it is only a small part of the total mission, just a means to being up there on stage. Their only obligation may be to be at a specific place at a specific time — still, it gets to be really exhausting for the performers, and a lot of emotions are involved. Just working to get the sound they want to come off from the stage is a worry, and then they also have to think about whether they are coming across to the audience. Musicians worry on their way to a gig; they worry about whether they will be good or get a reaction, they worry about the money they will make, and they worry about the next gig. Tom and Rob are very sympathetic to the pressures and strain the performer is under. The roadies know that it's the artist's performance that not only keeps the artist himself working, but also the band and a whole staff of people working too.

A roadie helps mitigate the artist's emotional strain by continuing to put out as much positive energy as possible to keep it all happening. It helps to say things like, "Hey you played your ass off tonight," if you're sincere.

The touring scene has changed. Just as there is a tradition of storytelling about the obstacles and problems that happen while on the road, there are hundreds of stories about the rebellious, independent, and reckless behavior of the early groups and their roadies, especially the British groups. We're talking about the period between 1965 and 1970, which was when the current touring format was evolving. Groups did some pretty wild things in those days. Once The Blues Magoos' plane couldn't lift off the runway, because they had such a heavy load. So they threw their equipment out, letting it smash on the runway, so that the plane would be light enough to take off. The Magoos used to throw smoke bombs in mailboxes as they drove down country routes, and they may have inspired The Who to even more crazy behavior when they traveled together on The Who's first American tour. In those days, groups were banned forever from hotel chains and airlines, to the extent that one British group never had any place to stay when they were in the States.

Today, people say, it's not a big party all the time. It's a job. Business is business . . . where before groups were getting $60,000 a gig, things have tightened up, and they now get $20,000. Only the biggest acts that can guarantee a sellout play to large crowds anymore. It's competitive, and the whole scene has changed. Everyone who had anything to do with the late Sixties laments that business is no fun anymore . . . it's just business. Groupies aren't groupies anymore either;

"they're wives or like wives," as one person told us. Relationships are more serious, where a few years back they were loose. There is more "respect" for the establishment, now that the big, once-rebellious groups have *become* the establishment. Some groups, though, keep up the image of rebellion, even though they may be approaching or in their forties. And some roadies, though generally younger, still carry on with flair.

Traveling is hard on your whole system. You eat at varying and odd hours and drink different qualities of water all the time. Down South it's chicken and ribs. Health foods are sometimes portable, and lots of roadies try to stick to them, but they're not always as available as the proverbial burger.

The kind of pay a roadie can expect varies. If a band is just starting out, a volunteer roadie will do bar gigs for nothing. Pay ranges from there up to $500 a week as a member of the road crew, which is about tops. Road managers can make a lot more. But this is only for time on the road. When you're off the road, enlightened bands keep you on part salary of half to a third of road time. You may get no salary at all when you're not actually working. Remember, road salary is not for a typical, routine eight-hour-a-day job. Sometimes you work as much as eighteen hours a day from gig to gig. A typical equipment roadie will earn $200 to $250 a week, plus a fifteen- to twenty-dollar per diem for personal expenses. Or one could receive as little as $75 for a week's work. The band usually picks up the tab for hotels and travel.

Management used to pick up all tabs for the crew, but with room service sometimes costing $30 a meal, and hotels $50 or more a night, a full per diem is used, which means the roadie is given typically $30 to $50 a day to cover road expenses. If the roadie can live for less than that amount, he keeps the difference. It's a good way for some roadies to save money; they bank their per diem, which may sometimes be larger than their salary. However, it's easy to overspend on the road. You figure you can always make up what you just overspent by finding a cheaper hotel at the next gig and eating yogurt and carrot juice instead of eating out, but it usually doesn't work out.

Sometimes crews try to save money by renting a motor home, such as a Winnebago, and traveling in it as much as possible. But they say life gets pretty hairy after a few days or weeks in such close quarters, so they find relief by taking turns in a hotel room where they can take showers, watch TV, or what have you.

When everyone is happy and it's been a good show and one of the musicians thanks the roadies for a good job, it's a great reward for all the effort.

Road Manager

If there is one key word that sums up what it takes to be a road manager, it is *responsibility*. When an act is on the road, it is the road manager who has the job of being on top of everything from beginning to end. He or she is a coordinator who attends to anything it takes to get a band from one gig to another. And if you carry it a little further, you'll see that a lot of wheels have to turn before an act shows up at a gig, and they're all vital: allowing for sufficient rehearsal time, transportation, lodging and meals, preparing wardrobe and set, keeping track of all personnel and all equipment, maintaining security at the gig, often managing the publicity and scheduling personal appearances with the media, seeing that everyone gets paid, making sure that the place of performance is ready for the particular demands of the show — all this and more the expert road manager oversees. It's a job that calls for great flexibility, more so than almost any other, and the kind of duties that may be required depend on the kind of act or group you're working for and can vary from gig to gig.

Another major job of the road manager is managing the economics of the tour and cutting down on overhead costs.

The more skillful you are at making the best arrangements at the least expense, the more valuable you will be to the group or management company you're working for. One Los Angeles company has become successful just by leasing jets to acts less expensively than they can be gotten through the airlines. There is also the *Official Airline Guide* (OAG), which you'll find very useful. It comes out every two weeks, and a year's subscription costs about $20. It lists all the flights and prices, plus all the options available, and the smart manager makes use of these. For instance, there's a way to fly from Los Angeles to New York, or vice versa, and for $25 more to make a stop in Miami along the way. Could be the perfect answer. There are night flights and other ways to save money.

In fact, everything spent while on the road must be accounted for to the road manager, and by the road manager to the management company. Prior to a tour it is his responsibility to make out "leaders," which are outlines allocating sums for the many needs of an act. When all the bills and vouchers are in, he'll go over them to see where the money has gone, and then make reimbursements. The money comes initially from the act's management offices, and some road managers are so highly trusted that they are able to walk in and out of there carrying huge amounts of cash without even being bonded.

There are various ways of getting the job of road manager, but one of the most common is through connections. Barry Schultz became a road manager for Tim Buckley because he was a friend. When Tim's manager was looking for a road manager for him, Barry just happened to hear about it, and then just happened to think that maybe he'd like the job when Tim asked. Paradoxically, it was specifically because Barry is *not* outgoing that he felt he *ought* to take the job. He knew it would be good for him to learn to assert himself, and he also knew that he'd have to do just that.

Maybe the life-style of the road manager isn't so disconsonant with Barry's former self after all, because Barry tells us that road managers lead rather isolated lives. Driving all night or waiting at airports, staying at motels, eating in diners or out of a paper bag, experiencing other people's loneliness, and being the one who sees to it that everyone does things that at times they really don't want to do — this isn't the most intimate kind of existence. In fact, the road manager may just have the loneliest spot of all — in the middle, with management on one side, the artist on the other.

The road manager often takes on the function of being a buffer. Since he's with the act every minute (and is therefore answerable for them), his number-one responsibility is to see that it shows up for a date. But breakdowns, freakouts, or whatever can occur while on the road, to which the businessmen back in their offices in the city, not having lived them, may not be particularly sympathetic. On one tour, for instance, Barry booked Buckley's whole band into one hotel, giving them no per diem (and therefore no leeway to manage their own accommodations) because he wanted to keep them all in one place. "The bass player used to pull a vanishing act that you wouldn't believe. He'd be there one minute and the next, gone. When we were in the Midwest, he'd leave his bass with us so we had a little bit of security that he'd show up."

So, like a shock absorber the road manager gets it from both sides, finding himself relaying complaints and apologies, shepherding his charges from place to place, soothing their wounds at the same time that he eggs them on.

If the hassles with management get serious, however, the road manager usually sides with the act. This is probably why road managers don't usually migrate up into management (though some do). In many cases, the road manager becomes best friend to the star, who is typically isolated, too, from the rest of the entourage. Barry told us that because he was Tim Buckley's best friend, it made it easier for him to be tough. He'd wake him up with a "Hurry up, get your clothes on, we have to be outta here, and that's it, no screwing around, no bullshit." Buckley understood that that was Barry's job. "I had to be the bottom line to get something done. You're stuck in an awkward position."

Road managers don't typically handle equipment, though they may help from time to time. If it's a small act just starting out the road manager may actually do everything, but as the responsibilities increase and the commitments grow more numerous, technicians (roadies) will be there to do all the handling, and the road manager will merely supervise.

This last fact, that there is little need for physical exertion, plus the fact that the road manager's talents come mostly from the realm of his own psychological maturity and sensitivity to others' needs, means that women are not excluded from the profession, and in fact there are quite a few female road managers.

One requirement for being a good road manager that is not usually nurtured in women is self-confidence. For that matter, not so many men have it either. But it's definitely a trait to cultivate in a hurry when you're on the road, because a road manager has got to be able to handle shocks and surprises of all kinds, to eliminate emergencies as they arise, and to have the kind of attitude and energy that say you're in charge, to the extent that you could walk through a contingent of security guards in such a manner that they wouldn't even question you.

A road manager doesn't necessarily have the kind of bodyguard duties associated with Beatlemania; you can always rent a cop when you get to town if there's a need, real or imagined, by calling the police department. Working *with* police is often one of the road manager's duties — actually sometimes working *against* the police. Most road managers seasoned in security problems will tell you that in some kinds of crowds the worst enemy to peace is armed and uniformed police. Keeping fans off the stage in Altamont fashion (using Hell's Angels as police) can turn a crowd against an act, and often the road manager is called upon to redirect the best intentions of the police by keeping them *from* doing their duty.

Touring has become the prime way to make a lot of money fast. Club dates may be favored, for that way new or underground artists can earn a living and build a reputation through showcasing to the critics and the press. But when it comes to selling records, it's the tour that really does it. Record companies like to hit hard and fast to promote a record release. And, obviously, tour dates have to be as concentrated as possible to keep down the expense of supporting so many people while out on the road. Combine these things and you get tours that are so intense as to be close to inhuman, where stars and crew alike work and live under conditions of unremittingly high stress.

This is the single biggest occupational hazard for everyone who goes out on the road. In fact, it's so predictably cruel that it's standard knowledge in the industry that a group can look forward to the possibility of only three years of touring before it burns itself out and breaks up. To point out how hard it can be, one road manager told us that after a tour he goes to a place where no one knows him and where the TV reception is good, rents a motel room, and watches color television for a month, keeping himself in a semicatatonic state. Barry himself said that after his first tour, he just flew down to Miami to his parents' house and didn't get out of bed for over a week. "My whole nervous system was shot."

By the time Barry's second tour came around, however, he had learned how to take care of himself. Whenever he had any free time at all, he made sure to use it to get into himself and remove himself from the scene. He added $50 for vitamins to his expense sheet for the group and for him, and he handed them out to everyone each day. He took care to eat certain things and avoid others. But all of this didn't mean that things lightened up all the time. On the last tour Barry made with Tim they spent the final two weeks recording in Los Angeles in the afternoons and performing in Long Beach at night, with over an hour's drive in between. Toward the end the whole thing accelerated, and they would record from eight in the morning until six at night, then play the Troubadour from eight at night until three in the morning. For one solid week Barry didn't even have time to take a shower, because in whatever time he did have he slept.

You might think that road managers are in love with the music of the acts they work for, but in reality some care for the music that pays their way, some don't. What matters is that you be efficient at your job; if you also happen to like the music, so much the better. Some performers are going to be loyal and even good friends, and some, people say, "would sell their mother for a nickel." The pay is good — when you're working — at least $300 a week (and we've heard of some who make over $1,000). It has to be good, because few road managers work year-round.

Anyone who has successfully managed a tour will have come away with an experience he or she will never forget. Almost everyone we've ever talked to who's spent time on the road wants to write a book about it, and a few are.